State, Security, and Cyberwar

This book examines the complex interactions amongst states and security apparatuses in the contemporary global order, and the prospect of peace with the emergence of cyberwarfare. Analysing why states consider cyberspace as a matter of security and strategic concerns, it looks forward to a possible foundation of "cyber peace" in the international system. It examines the idea of cyber territory, population, governance, and sovereignty, along with that of nation-states referring to great, middle, and small powers.

The book explores the strategic and security aspects of cyberspace along with the rational behaviours of states in the domain. It explains the militarisation and weaponisation of cyber technologies for strategic purpose and traces the progression of cyberwar and its impact on global stability. The last section of the book examines the possibility of building peace in the cyber domain with the endeavours of the international community to safeguard cyber sovereignty and promote stability in the digital sphere.

It also discusses India's position on digital security, cyberwarfare, and the pursuit of cyber peace. The book offers valuable insights for students, researchers, practitioners, stakeholders working in and on military and strategic affairs, peace and conflict studies, and global politics, as well as interested general readers.

Thangjam K. Singh, with over two decades of experience in defence and strategic affairs, is Associate Professor at the Department of Strategic Technologies, School of National Security Studies, Central University of Gujarat. He previously taught at the Central University of Jammu and served as an Officer on Special Duty at National Technical Research Organisation. He was a researcher at the Manohar Parrikar Institute for Defence Studies and Analyses (MP-IDSA), contributing to the Centre for Net Assessment, and the Centre for Terrorism and Internal Security. His expertise includes cyberwarfare, national security, strategic thoughts, terrorism, and military affairs.

Sanjay K. Jha is Professor and Dean at the School of National Security Studies, Central University of Gujarat. With over 20 years of experience in security and strategic affairs, he has served in research institutions like the Institute for Conflict Management, MP-IDSA, and the Government of India. His research focuses on international relations, national security, South Asian politics, internal security, terrorism, insurgency, and border management.

State, Security, and Cyberwar
The Quest for Digital Peace

Thangjam K. Singh and Sanjay K. Jha

LONDON AND NEW YORK

Designed cover image: @ Getty

First published 2026
by Routledge
4 Park Square, Milton Park, Abingdon, Oxon OX14 4RN

and by Routledge
605 Third Avenue, New York, NY 10158

Routledge is an imprint of the Taylor & Francis Group, an informa business

© 2026 Thangjam K. Singh and Sanjay K. Jha

The right of Thangjam K. Singh and Sanjay K. Jha to be identified as authors of this work has been asserted in accordance with sections 77 and 78 of the Copyright, Designs and Patents Act 1988.

All rights reserved. No part of this book may be reprinted or reproduced or utilised in any form or by any electronic, mechanical, or other means, now known or hereafter invented, including photocopying and recording, or in any information storage or retrieval system, without permission in writing from the publishers.

Trademark notice: Product or corporate names may be trademarks or registered trademarks, and are used only for identification and explanation without intent to infringe.

British Library Cataloguing-in-Publication Data
A catalogue record for this book is available from the British Library

ISBN: 978-1-041-03309-7 (hbk)
ISBN: 978-1-041-04861-9 (pbk)
ISBN: 978-1-003-63031-9 (ebk)

DOI: 10.4324/9781003630319

Typeset in Sabon
by Deanta Global Publishing Services, Chennai, India

Contents

List of Figures		*vi*
List of Tables		*vii*
Preface		*viii*
Acknowledgements		*xvi*
List of Abbreviations		*xviii*
1	Cyber Affairs in the International System	1
2	Characteristics of States and Cyberspace	16
3	State Security and Cyber Defence Frameworks	50
4	Interstate War and Cyberwarfare	110
5	Towards Cyber-Peace Initiatives	165
	Index	*207*

Figures

1.1 Concept of Cyberspace (security/threat and Peace)	4
2.1 Schematic Diagram of a General Communication System	26
3.1 Concept of Security Agenda	51
3.2 Cybersecurity Structure of India	85

Tables

2.1	Comparison: Elements of States and Cyberspace	20
2.2	Components of Cyberspace	29
3.1	Security Dimension	57
3.2	Non-Traditionalists	60
3.3	Cybersecurity Framework (Level of Analysis)	68
4.1	Typologies of Cyberwar	112
4.2	Cyber Espionage in Physical and Logical Layers	116
4.3	Physical and Virtual Dimension of Cyber Power	134
5.1	Impact of Violence and Peace on Network Facilities and Humans	172
5.2	India's Approach to Cyber Peace	191

Preface

The book, *State, Security, and Cyberwar: The Quest for Digital Peace*, aims to explore the "triological aspect" or "three-level analysis" of the state, security, and cyberwar in the contemporary world order. Cyberwar is a component of national security, which in turn is an integral part of the state system. By examining the intricate relationships between the trio of state, security, and warfare, this book will analyse how states view cyberwarfare as a critical component of security within the contemporary international system, and how this may require peacebuilding efforts.[1] This is how the title of the book, *State, Security, and Cyberwar: The Quest for Digital Peace*, was aptly devised. This book primarily focuses on post-Cold War era narratives, a period when cyber networks expanded globally in the 1990s. No specific country is mentioned in the title of this book as a case study. However, since the research is conducted in India, the country serves as a referent object of the study. Consequently, the Indian perspective is integrated at the end of each chapter rather than being presented as a separate chapter.

This study theoretically compares the origins and key elements, such as population, territory, governance, and sovereignty, of both states and cyberspace. It explores the behaviour and strategies of great, middle, and small powers within the realm of cyberspace, referencing the general norms and policies implemented by various states, regional associations, and international organisations. The book examines the securitisation of cyberspace, highlighting how it has become a top priority in national and international security agendas. It also discusses the evolution of cyberspace into a theatre of war, focusing on its militarisation and use as a tool to achieve strategic objectives and enhance national power. As the fifth domain of warfare, following land, sea, air, and space, cyberspace not only functions as an independent battlefield but also serves as a crucial support system for ground forces. The book analyses efforts made by the international community, including the United Nations (UN) and its member states, to uphold cyber sovereignty and maintain peace within this domain. Additionally, it highlights India's approach to digital security, cyberwarfare, and the concept of "cyber peace" wherever relevant.

After reviewing materials related to the topic of this research, it has been observed that a descriptive analysis of states, security, and cyberwarfare in relation to the current international system is either lacking or minimally addressed in the existing academic literature. While few scholars have touched upon these three sectors (state, security, and cyberwar) in their academic research, a comprehensive combined work on the subject is yet to be undertaken or seen published. To fill this gap, this study seeks to work on the three levels of "state, security, and cyberwar" and their interactions in the 21st century.

Regarding states and their approach to cyberwarfare, the majority of potential nations have developed their cybersecurity strategies, doctrines, plans and command structures to counter the threat of external aggressions. However, due to the lack of international standards on cyberwarfare, states act in their own ways using legal or illegal means, leading to maximising digital conflict with the possibility of triggering kinetic combat. Therefore, a comprehensive study on states' behaviour in regard to a cyberwar approach with a rightful method accepted by the international system is pertinent. On the aspect of security, a proper theory on the securitisation of cyberspace was not available when the literature review was undergoing for this book. A comprehensive securitisation process of cyberspace is discussed in this book to fill the missing gap. This section highlights the concept of security studies (cybersecurity), including militarisation of the domain, an arms race, deterrence, balance of cyber-power, strategies, and others relevant to the national cybersecurity programme. Although numerous scholars have written on the concept of cyberwar, there are conflicting perspectives. Some argue that cyberwar is real, asserting that digital attacks can cause significant damage to national assets, while others contend that it is not real, as it does not result in bloodshed or loss of human lives. This book will attempt to clarify if it is real or imaginary based on how the states perceive cyberwar and how they respond to it. An inclusive discussion on the *jus ad bello* (conduct of war) and *jus ad bellum* (reason for war) concepts of cyberwarfare is missing or minimal in the existing literature, which this book would like to fill. The absence of such proper international guidelines for cyberwarfare in the globalised world makes it difficult to achieve peace in this domain. Thus, this study also aims to theorise the concept of "cyber peace" and seeks to establish harmony within the domain.

The book explores India's perspective on states interests in cyberspace, cybersecurity, and cyberwar. As a member of the UN Group of Government Experts on cybersecurity initiatives, India plays a significant diplomatic role in interstate digital affairs, advocating for norms that promote responsible state behaviour in cyberspace. Its cybersecurity strategy, as part of its foreign policy on global cyber affairs is state-, regional-, and interstate-centric, grounded in high moral values. Meanwhile, India's cyber command was strengthened by the introduction of a dedicated cyberwar doctrine (2024) to regulate the ethical conduct of digital conflict. Even before this, existing military doctrines and tactical guidelines had already integrated cyberwarfare strategies, emphasising the armed forces' preparedness in this evolving

x *Preface*

domain. Furthermore, India plays a significant role in global efforts to promote cyber peace, actively contributing through both public and private organisations.

This book also aims to examine fundamental questions concerning theories, state behaviour, security, war, and peace in the realm of cyberspace. For a better understanding these questions are divided into five groups as follows.

A) *Theories and approaches*: What are the potential theories and approaches that define cyberspace? How does cyberspace operate within the international system both in times of peace and conflict?
B) *State (cyberspace)*: What elements constitute the intersection of virtual cyberspace and the physical world? How do states, whether great, middle, or small powers, conduct themselves in international cyber affairs? How does India, as an emerging power, perceive the role of cyberspace in the global system?
C) *Security (cybersecurity)*: How can cybersecurity theories be conceptualised? How has cyberspace developed into a crucial domain for both international and national security? What measures have states implemented to safeguard the cyber ecosystem in the modern world order? What are India's cybersecurity policies and approaches?
D) *War (cyberwarfare)*: How do traditional war theories apply to cyberwarfare? Why do states engage in cyberwar? What components, strategies, and tactics do various nations employ in their cyber warfare? How are countries preparing for cyberwar, and what is India's stance on these issues?
E) *Peace and development*: How can traditional peace theories contribute to the development of a modern theory of "cyber peace"? Is it possible to achieve peace and prosperity in cyberspace? What role does the international community play in fostering cyber peace? What are the current and future mechanisms to prevent war in cyberspace? How does India approach both domestic and international cyber-peace initiatives?

With these questions in focus, this book aims to offer relevant answers to how states perceive cyber affairs, the complexities of cyber threats, the ambiguities surrounding cyberwarfare and digital peace initiatives. It seeks to explore why cyberspace is viewed as a critical issue for national and international security, examining how states behave within this domain and navigate its challenges, opportunities, and dilemmas. The ambitions of great powers to become "cyber power nations" will be a focal point of discussion. The security aspects of cyberspace will be thoroughly analysed using the Copenhagen School's theories and frameworks, considering cybersecurity as a crucial element of both national and international, military, and civil affairs. The book will investigate how cyberwarfare is integrated into the contemporary understanding of war, conflict, and security, examining the militarisation and weaponisation of cyberspace, along with the relevant doctrines and tactics.

Additionally, it will assess the role of stakeholders and explore which policies, both national and international, could help prevent conflicts in cyberspace. The discussion on cyber peace will cover both state security (negative peace, as states mostly focus on the absence of hostilities) and social security (positive peace, as civil societies chiefly work for inclusive digital rights and development). Meanwhile, India's position in the global cyber landscape will also be explored, with relevant recommendations provided for Indian stakeholders, including policymakers. Overall, this book will serve as a valuable resource for students, academics, analysts, technocrats, strategists, and politicians engaged in cybersecurity studies.

The research methodology for this study involves a comprehensive approach that includes the use of primary sources, secondary sources, interviews, and participation in symposiums and fieldwork. The study refers to government reports, policy documents, military papers, and strategic doctrines published by various states, international bodies, and both public and private sectors. Additionally, reports from multilateral institutions such as the UN, the European Union (EU), and the Shanghai Cooperation Organisation (SCO) were thoroughly analysed. To develop a comprehensive understanding of the subject, the study has surveyed a wide range of secondary sources, including research articles, monographs, books, periodicals, and e-materials published both in India and abroad. This not only assisted in covering the literature review but also allowed for an analysis of expert writings and identification of gaps in the existing literature. Furthermore, interviews with technocrats, military personnel, political figures, and law enforcement officials, both retired and serving, who have experience or expertise in the field were conducted. Finally, the research incorporates insights gained from participation in seminars, roundtables, conferences, and related events, with fieldwork being undertaken. This multifaceted approach ensures a thorough and well-rounded exploration of the subject matter.

The purpose of this research is to provide valuable insights that can assist state and administrative bodies in policymaking and contribute to knowledge enrichment. This study could be classified as "descriptive research", as it systematically examines the emerging threats and vulnerabilities in cyberspace that have developed since the end of the Cold War and the onset of globalisation. The research will methodically explore how states respond to cybersecurity challenges and digital warfare, while also addressing the formation of peace within this domain. As a qualitative study, it adopts an unstructured and flexible approach aiming to enhance understanding of interstate cybersecurity and cyberwarfare dynamics, and to support the development of policies by government officials and other relevant organisations. This work may also be seen as a form of "applied research", which, while not strictly systematic, seeks to find specific solutions to particular problems or concerns. By gathering and analysing pertinent information on cyber issues, this study aims to produce reliable findings that will be beneficial to students, stakeholders, and policymakers alike. While the study would highlight

xii *Preface*

suitable approaches of International Relations (IR) or Security Studies, this study explicitly follows the theory of realism since it is imperative for any state (for survival) to be protected against emerging cyber threats and insecurities in the contemporary world order. The theory of realism is ideal for this research work (book) as it focuses mainly on state and power, security and threat, and war and military in the context of cyberspace in the anarchic international system.

The entire study is discussed in five main chapters as outlined. The introduction and conclusion chapters of the book are also written with distinct titles to highlight a meaningful theme of the chapters. Abstracts of each chapter are provided below to feature the theme and content of the book. As mentioned in the beginning, there shall be no specific chapter on India though it will be referred to in each chapter as and whenever it is relevant.

Chapter 1: Cyber Affairs in the International System

The first chapter, "Cyber Affairs in the International System", will provide a brief overview on the significance of the book, which will cover the background, history, origin, concept, and meaning of cyberspace as well as its connections to the international system. The chapter will adopt the theoretical approach of security studies (or International Relations) mainly on realism and how states behave in anarchic affairs of cyberspace. While providing a basic overview of the cyber-world order, it will briefly mention the relationship between the great, middle, and small powers (countries) in cyberspace, though it will be covered in more detail in Chapter 2. This will be followed by a comparison between the state and cyberspace with the characteristics of their existence. If humans live in the real world, cyberspace is populated by data, and the principles of their survivalism shall be briefly reviewed. Meanwhile, the process of securitising cyberspace, which was never a national threat earlier, shall be briefly emphasised, though discussed in depth in Chapter 3. States' motivations for engaging in cyberwarfare, their rising interest in the idea of cyberwar, and their methods for preparing for the conflict are all briefly examined in the chapter, though they will be covered in more detail in Chapter 4. Although the possibility of developing "cyber peace" in the international system is briefly addressed in the first chapter, it will be elaborated in the fifth chapter, which is the conclusion of the study. Overall, this first chapter lays the groundwork for the ideas explored in the subsequent four chapters.

Chapter 2: Characteristics of States and Cyberspace

The second chapter, "Characteristics of States and Cyberspace," discusses the comparison between the features of the state and cyberspace in the geopolitical system. It will examine the theory of the origin of state and cyberspace. While the former is created by nature and human norms, the latter is created by human brains and technology. The elements of states will be analysed in comparison with those of cyberspace, such as population (as data), territory (as cyber network limits and jurisdiction), government (software algorithms), sovereignty (cyber power or decision-making capability of AI, etc.). Accordingly, the population of the states and cyber components; the territory of states and cyber jurisdiction; states' governance and cyber administration, and state sovereignty and cyber power are thoroughly analysed in the chapter. Meanwhile, by selecting nine nations (three each from great, middle, and small powers), this study examines their digital behaviours, which are considered to have significant potential in cyber affairs. The US, China, and Russia are selected as the great powers; the UK, Canada, and Japan, chosen from different continents(not all from Europe), are the middle powers for the study. As they are considered as states of concern and potential in the cybersecurity domain, Iran, North Korea, and Israel are also chosen as the small powers for the research. Their cyber potential, governance, jurisdiction, and cyber power are analysed in a systematic order. In addition, a separate section on India and cyberspace has also been discussed focusing on its cyber geography (coverage area), governing structure, jurisdictional framework, and cyber sovereignty.

Chapter 3: State Security and Cyber Defence Frameworks

The third chapter thoroughly analyses the theory of security in the international system by referring to various hypotheses propounded by notable theorists. This will be combined with the aspects of cybersecurity including cyber threats and its defensive framework. The chapter explains that security is an ambiguous, non-static symbol that changes through time and space. While thoroughly understanding the agenda of international security, it will question whether contemporary security is a product of the Cold War. Security has evolved from traditional to non-traditional dimensions and it has been widened and deepened by theorists such as Jaap de Wilde and Ken Booth respectively. This will be followed by a definition of elements of cyber threats by examining the perils of cyberwar, cyberterrorism, and cybercrimes. Meanwhile, the level of cybersecurity frameworks adopted at the international, multinational, national, subnational, agency, and individual levels are examined by taking standard examples from various countries and institutions. Consequently, the cybersecurity framework of the EU, SCO, South Asian Association for Regional Cooperation (SAARC), and great power (US, China, Russia), middle power (UK, Japan, and Canada), and small power or state of cyber concerns (Iran, North Korea, and Israel) are examined with their cyber agencies and policies. A separate section on India's cybersecurity structure is analysed along with the threats posed by internal and external elements. This includes the collective cybersecurity initiatives taken by various Indian security and non-security institutions, or law enforcement and non-enforcement agencies. Hence, the role of various cybersecurity divisions

xiv *Preface*

established under different ministries of defence, home affairs, electronics and information technology, telecommunication, finance, science and technology, information and broadcast, along with the security council are discussed for a proper understanding of India's digital security structures.

Chapter 4: Interstate War and Cyberwarfare

The fourth chapter, "Interstate war and cyberwarfare," explains the concept of international armed conflict (war) and its application to or comparison with cyberspace. It will explain the theory and origin of regular and irregular warfare, referring to classical theorist Kautilya and modern scholar Liddell Hart. Meanwhile, the theory of "new war" will also be analysed with the idea from Mary Kaldor. Cyberwarfare will be examined as a form of new war where its actors, economy, soldiers, and objective are different from the old form of warfare. The chapter will discuss the domain powers (land, sea, air, and space) in connection with cyber power, referring to theorists such as Mackinder, A.T. Mahan, Douhet, Colin Gray, Joseph Nye, and more. It will analyse the concept of conventional war in connection with cyberwarfare dealing with the revolution in the military affairs of cyberspace (or military cyber affairs), international laws (*Jus ad Bello* and *Jus ad Bellum*), cyber-security dilemma, cyber arms race, cyber deterrence, and cyber doctrines. Meanwhile, a descriptive analysis of cyber weapons and strategic command systems will be explored referring to the militarisation and weaponisation of cyberspace, cyberweapon capabilities (mass disruption), and states' desire for cyber weapons. In the last section of the chapter, considering the threats India perceives from external opponents, it will elaborate on India's approach to cyberwarfare, focusing on national threat scenarios, its cyberwar doctrine, and its command structure.

Chapter 5: Towards Cyber-Peace Initiatives

After a comprehensive study of states, security, and warfare in the context of cyberspace, the discussion on developing sustainable peace in the domain shall not be ruled out. Consequently, this last chapter, "Towards Cyber-Peace Initiatives" will discuss the theory and practice of digital peace initiatives in the international system. By referring to peace thinkers including Immanuel Kant, Johan Galtung, and Mahatma Gandhi, the chapter will explore the possibility of constructing a theory of "cyber peace" to contribute to the academic debate on cyber-peace development. Various aspects of cyber peace will be discussed along with the concept of conflict prevention, peace making, peace keeping, peace enforcement and peace building. Different cyber peace initiatives taken at various levels, global, regional, national, subnational, local, and individual, will be addressed in this chapter. Subsequently, the Indian peace approach to cyberspace at the internal and external dimensions with negative and positive peace agenda will be analysed. Addressing the concluding remarks of this chapter, a combined summary of all five separate conclusions (given in each chapter) will also be highlighted in this section. A way forward or looking ahead will also be incorporated as the final remarks of the book. In addition, there are research areas (deep study on emerging technologies) that are beyond the scope of this book and they will be highlighted as a suggestion for future study by interested scholars.

Note

1 Today, cyberspace has become one of the strategic agendas for national and international security, involving a wide range of stakeholders including practitioners, scholars, strategists, military people, technocrats, lawyers, police, economists, sociologist, and the public.

Acknowledgements

State, Security, and Cyberwar: The Quest for Digital Peace is a revised and updated product of the doctoral thesis titled "State, Security, and Cyberwar in the Age of Globalisation", completed by Thangjam K. Singh under the supervision of Professor Sanjay K. Jha at the Department of Security Studies, School of National Security Studies, Central University of Gujarat (CUG), Vadodara, India. Both authors would like to express their heartfelt gratitude to the various academics, non-academics, and well-wishers, both within and beyond the university, who supported them throughout this journey, from the inception of the research idea to the publication of this book.

Within the university, during the course of this research work, immense support and guidance were received from higher authorities, colleagues and friends. Amongst the competent authorities of the CUG, Prof. Rama Shankar Dubey, Vice Chancellor of the university is highly honoured for his valuable encouragement and support. The support from the administrative officials and the examination office at CUG is highly appreciated. In the School of National Security Studies, profound appreciation is extended to Prof. Arun Vishwanathan, Head of the Department of Security Studies, and Dr Vishwas Raval, Head of the Department of Strategic Technologies, for their warm help and encouragement. This book is also deeply indebted to my colleagues, Dr Kishore Jose, Dr Mohandas Nongmaithem, Dr Manasi Singh, Dr Shrish Tiwari, Dr Sourabh Kumar, and Dr Amit Mukherjee, whose motivation and inspiration were invaluable throughout the writing process of this book. A warm appreciation is also extended to well-wishers from other departments of CUG, including Prof. Atanu Bhattacharya, Dr Khaikholen Haokip, and others, whose encouragement was instrumental in encouraging morale and energy during difficult times.

Sincere appreciation is extended to the external experts from the strategic and academic community for their evaluation of the PhD thesis "State, Security, and Cyberwar in the Age of Globalisation". Their assessments and recommendations for revision and publication were instrumental in transforming the thesis into this book. In particular, appreciation is honoured toward Lt Gen. (Dr) Konsam Himalay (Retd), former Chairman of the Manipur Public Service Commission, and Prof. M. Amarjeet Singh, Director of the Centre for North East Studies and Policy Research, Jamia Millia Islamia, for their insightful contributions.

Dr Ajey Lele, Deputy Director General, Manohar Parrikar Institute for Defence Studies and Analyses (MP-IDSA); Shri Sudhir Saxena, Senior Fellow, Vivekananda International Foundation; Dr Cherian Samuel, Research Fellow, Strategic Technologies Centre, MP-IDSA, and Dr Sameer Patil, Director, Centre for Security, Strategy, and Technology, in Observer Research Foundation, are deeply appreciated for their invaluable support and readiness to engage in discussions on the subject. Gratitude is also extended to the anonymous reviewers whose insightful contributions significantly enhanced the quality of this book. Special acknowledgement is given to Mr Aakash Chakrabarty and Ms Brinda Sen from Routledge for their dedicated efforts and continuous correspondence throughout the publication process.

The authors assume full responsibility for the content of this book and the views expressed do not necessarily represent the official stance of their affiliated institution.

Thangjam K. Singh and Sanjay K. Jha

List of Abbreviations

5G	Fifth Generation Mobile Network
AI	artificial intelligence
ASEAN	Association for Southeast Asian Nations
BARC	Bhabha Atomic Research Centre
BD	big data
BECIL	Broadcast Engineering Consultants India Limited
BHIM-UPI	Bharat Interface for Money-Unified Payments Interface
BRICS	Brazil, Russia, India, China, and South Africa
BSNL	Bharat Sanchar Nigam Limited
C&IS	Cyber and Information Security (Division), India
CAD	Cyber Armed Division
CAF	Canada Armed Forces
CBI	Central Bureau of Investigation
CCDCE	Cooperative Cyber Defence Centre of Excellence
CCS	Cabinet Committee on Security
CCTNS	Crime and Criminal Tracking Network and System, India
CCTV	closed-circuit television
CD	Cyber Diplomacy
CDC	Cyber Defence Command
CDD	Cyber Diplomacy Division
CERT	Computer Emergency Response Team
CHS	Cybersecurity Strategic Headquarters
CIA	Central Intelligence Agency
CIIs	Critical Information Infrastructures
CISA	Cybersecurity and Infrastructure Security Agency
CISO	Chief Information Security Officer
CMS	Central Monitoring System
CRS	Congressional Research Service, US
CSC	Common Service Centres
CSD	Cyber Strategic Division
CSE	Communication Security Establishment
CSIS	Canada Security Intelligence Service
CV	Condition Variable
CWD	Cyber Warfare Doctrines

CYBERCOM	Cyber Command
DCA	Defence Cyber Agency
DCIO	Defence Chief Information Officer, Canada
DCMS	Department for Digital, Culture, Media, and Sport
DHS	Department of Homeland Security
DIA	Defence Intelligence Agency (India)
DIH	Defense Intelligence Headquarters (Japan)
DND	Department of National Defence
DoI	Directorate of Information
DPRK	Democratic People's Republic of Korea or North Korea
DRDO	Defence Research and Development Organisation
DSCI	Data Security Council of India
DSI	Directorate for Signals Intelligence
DST	Department of Science and Technology
DV	dependent variable
EFF	Electronic Frontier Foundation
EMMC	Electronic Media Monitoring Centre
ENISA	European Union Agency for Cybersecurity
EU	European Union
FATA	Iranian Cyber Police
FINnet	Financial Intelligence Network
FIU-In	Financial Intelligence Unit-India
FSTEK	Federal Service for Technical and Export Control
GB	gigabytes
GCHQ	Government Communication Headquarters, UK
GCI	Global Cybersecurity Index
GDP	gross domestic product
GGE	Group of Government Experts
GIL	Gujarat Informatics Limited
HTS	Hay'at Tahrir al-Sham
I4.0	Industry 4.0
I4C	Indian Cyber Crime Coordination Centre
ICT	information and communication technology
IDF	Israel Defence Forces
IDS	Integrated Defence Staff, India
IISS	International Institute for Strategic Studies
INCD	Israel National Cyber Directorate
IntV	intervening variable
IoT	Internet of Things
IPA	Information-Technology Promotion Agency
IR	International Relation
ISA	Israeli Security Agency
ISACs	Information Sharing and Analysis Centers
ISP	internet service provider
ISPC	Information Security Policy Council

IT	information technology
ITS	information technology services
IV	independent variable
J&K	Jammu and Kashmir
JFCyG	Joint Forces Cyber Group (UK)
JNC	Joint Network Center
KPA	Korean People's Army
KWP	Korean Workers' Party
LAN	local area network
LWE	left wing extremism
MEA	Ministry of External Affairs
MeitY	Ministry of Electronics and Information Technology
MI&B	Ministry of Information and Broadcast
MoC	Ministry of Communication
MoD	Ministry of Defence
MoF	Ministry of Finance
MoL&J	Ministry of Law and Justice
MS&T	Ministry of Science and Technology
NASSCOM	National Association of Software and Service Companies
NATO	North Atlantic Treaty Organization
NCB	National Cyber Bureau, Israel
NCB	Narcotics Control Bureau, India
NCCC	National Cyber Coordination Centre, India
NCCRP	National Cyber Crime Reporting Portal
NCSA	National Cyber Security Authority, Israel
NCF	National Cyber Force (UK)
NCIIPC	National Critical Information Infrastructure Protection Centre
NCRD	National Crime Records Bureau
NCSA	National Cyber Security Authority, Israel
NCSP	National Cyber Security Programme
NCSP	National Cyber Security Policy (India)
NCSS	National Cyber Security Strategy
NE	North East (India)
NEST	New, Emerging & Strategic Technologies
NGO	non-government organisation
NIC	National Informatic Centre, India
NMW	New Media Wing
NOCP	National Offensive Cyber Programme
NSA-USA	National Security Agency (USA)
NSA-I	National Security Advisor (India)
NSC	National Security Council
NSCS	National Security Council Secretariat
NTRO	National Technical Research Organisation
NTS	non-traditional security

NYPD	New York Police Department
OEM	Original Equipment Manufacturer
OEWG	Open-Ended Working Group
ORF	Observer Research Foundation
PMO	Prime Minister's Office
RBI	Reserve Bank of India
ReBIT	Reserve Bank Information Technology Private Limited
RGB	Reconnaissance General Bureau, North Korea
SAARC	South Asian Association for Regional Cooperation
SCC	Supreme Council for Cyberspace, Iran
SCO	Shanghai Cooperation Organisation
SMWIPM	Suzanne Mubarak Women's International Peace Movement
SORM	System for Operative Investigative Activities
TCS	Tata Consultancy Services
TOR	The Onion Router
TRAI	Telecom Regulatory Authority of India
UCB	Urban Corporative Banks
UK	United Kingdom
UN	United Nations
UNCCT	United Nations Counter Terrorism Centre
UNCTAD	United Nations Conference on Trade and Commerce
UNODC	United Nations Office of Drugs and Crime
US	United States
WFS	World Federation of Scientists
WGIG	Working Group on Internet Governance
WSIS	World Summit on the Information Society
WWW	World Wide Web

1 Cyber Affairs in the International System

Introduction

After the end of the Cold War and as Industry 4.0[1] (I4.0) begins, the role of cyberspace has increased not only for communication and economic means but also for the states' military services and supremacy. Unlike the physical world, the virtual world is multipolar in nature, with numerous players participating in digital power games. Any nation with or without nuclear capabilities can be a potential player in cyberspace. Even a smaller nation with technological capabilities can challenge a bigger power, taking advantage of the lack of international cyber laws, the cost-benefit of cyberattacks, and lesser chances of kinetic response from the opponent. Big or little, states with stronger technology (cyber skills) could influence the geopolitical structure of the world more effectively. Great powers such as the United States (US), Russia, and China are vying to control the world's electronic system by becoming "cyberpower"[2] nations. Global digital platforms could be dominated by any potential state, and whoever holds control of these platforms shall have the advantage to influence the anarchic international system. This book, however, examines the position of middle powers, including the UK (Europe), Canada (North America), and Japan (Asia), with their behaviour in cyberspace. This study will also look at the state of international concerns with countries, such as Israel, Iran, and North Korea, that have the ability to challenge the middle and major powers in the cyber sphere.

India, standing between great and middle powers acknowledged cyberspace as a domain of strategic affairs and aspires to be an influential power in international cyber politics. Meanwhile on the domestic front, it promotes national growth and development through cyber means along with security mechanisms. Since the early part of the century, India has been increasingly involved in cybersecurity activities in both technical and non-technical aspects,[3] and at external and internal levels. At the external level, India improved its digital diplomacy by actively participating in the United Nations (UN) initiatives to encourage member states to respect international norms in cyberspace. At the domestic level, not only has India enhanced its software and hardware capabilities, but it also introduced new cyber laws and policies or amended existing ones from time to time. Indian ministries associated with electronics and technology, communication, defence, finance, home affairs, science and technology, and external affairs have introduced domestic cyber policies, guidelines, standards, doctrine, command, and echelons (positions) with respective mandates to secure the cyber ecosystem of the state.

Cyberspace and the International System

The advent of cyber technology plays a critical role in the economic growth[4] and political development in the international system. According to the International Telecommunication Union (ITU), about 68 per cent (5.5 billion people) of the world's population will have used the internet[5] by 2024 (ITU, 2024), and 4.5–15.5 per cent of the world gross domestic product or GDP is contributed by the digital economy, depending on the definition of the digital economy (UNCTAD, 2019). In comparison with only one website on the internet in 1990, there were 1.88 billion websites in the middle of 2021 (Armstrong, 2021). About 15.37 per cent of all computers using the internet in the world are at least affected by one malware-class assault[6] (Kaspersky, 2022). The first industrial revolution (I1.0, 1780–1900) transformed the state's economy from agriculturally based to large-scale industrial mechanised and factory products. This was followed by the second industrial revolution (I2.0, 1900–1970), which was based on electricity and advanced manufacturing of steel for automobiles and weaponry systems. The third industrial revolution (I3.0, 1970–2000) was associated with computers and automation, the substitution of manpower by machine. I4.0, which began in 2000, is an era based on information and communication technology. Some scholars claim that I5.0 has also started in 2020 as an advanced form of I4.0 when human and cyber-physical systems are closely knitted by the application of artificial intelligence (AI) and quantum technologies. According to Barry Buzan, these technological changes not only brought development to civil society but transformed military affairs drastically. His book, *Military technology and international relations*, illustrates how these several industrial revolutions brought about a revolution in military affairs. Some of the significant changes that the revolution brought in the defence sectors are the radical impact of firepower, self-protection systems (bulletproof, armoured vehicles and other materials), speed in mobility of automobile systems (land, air, and sea), communication systems and their flexibility, and intelligence gathering methods through advanced electronic technology (Buzan, 1987). These transformations are particularly evident in recent conflicts, such as the Russia-Ukraine war, the Israel-Hamas and Hezbollah conflicts, and the Syrian civil war. For instance, Israel's use of sophisticated cyber tools and pager explosives against Hezbollah affiliates (Laila, 2024), Russia's strikes against Ukraine with Oreshnik hypersonic missiles (Starchak, 2024), and the role of the Syrian Electronic Army and Branch 255 in countering rebel forces (Baezner, 2017). These developments underscore how modern technology has reshaped the strategies and dynamics of contemporary warfare.

Cyberspace as a part of the industrial revolution emerged during I4.0, which is based on the information and communication industries (though it can be traced back to the previous I3.0 when computers and the internet were introduced in a limited capacity to the world). According to Lucas Kello, the revolution in cyberspace presents both opportunities and challenges to society, necessitating an appropriate response from policymakers (Kello, 2013).

To study cyberspace in the international system, it is first necessary to study the structure of the domain. Similar to traditional and non-traditional concepts of security studies, the structure of cyberspace can be examined through a two-tiered strategic or security approach, including technical (traditional) and non-technical (non-traditional) notions. The traditional or technical aspect deals with the natural or scientific elements of computer-related technologies or facilities, such as software and hardware, that enabled computers to operate. Computer facilities, including the emerging technologies of 5th Generation (5G), cloud computing, quantum computing, AI, big data (BD), and the internet of things (IoT), which make the computer world physically powerful, could be part of the technical classification. The non-technical aspect of cyberspace could be the governing system of the cyber world, which includes its executive, legislative, and administrative policies, rules, guidelines, behaviours, and business, as well as management of threats (cyberwar, cyberterrorism, cybercrime, etc.) that affect the global order.

The concept of cyberspace can further be discussed in three features (hardware, software, and users), that provide the framework on which cyberspace depends to function. In other words, this has been described as three layers, the "physical, logical, and social" of cyberspace by the *Tallin Manual*[7] *2.0 on the International Law Applicable to Cyber Operations*. The first layer, physical or hardware, is based on computer devices, cables, routers, and servers, which are the object material of the cyber ecosystem. The second layer, logical or software, is the technicalities, algorithms, programs, protocols, and data that connect or make the functioning of the physical system. It acts as the fuel of these cyber engines and makes cyberspace run. The third layer, the social or the user, is the individuals behind the machine that control the cyber systems or the groups that engage with the cyber operations (Schmitt, 2017). A few scholars tried to add another layer, known as "information", which operates between the software and the user, or between logical and social layers, according to the *Tallin Manual* (Relia, 2015, p. 9). Information is made of data, a mixture of binaries (0 and 1), generated by the combination of both hardware and software. Data are transferred or stored in the form of text, picture, sound, and video. However, they are non-physical as long as they remain within the realm of cyberspace. Although "information" isn't classified as software or a physical component, according to the *Tallin Manual*, it makes more sense to classify it at a logical layer.

Despite the fact that states usually recognise cyberspace as the fifth domain of warfare after sea, land, air, and space, it lacks a comprehensive global legal framework unlike the other four domains. Taking advantage of this lawlessness, great powers are actively involved in stealing from and targeting the critical data of other states in the digital space. Similarly, smaller nations (Iran or North Korea) with cyber potential took advantage of these grey areas to contest or challenge powerful nations through the cyber domain. The participation of multiple powers in the cyber domain and competition amongst them (states or actors) led to a cyber arms race posing threats to political stability in the world order. Hence, the establishment of the multipolar system in the cyber world reveals the beginnings of a potential global cyber conflict. Consequently, establishing universal norms and principles for cyber governance has become one of the most pressing challenges in shaping the global order of the 21st century. This emerging trend not only indicates how technology shapes the world but also reflects how it influences diplomatic relations of nation-states in the anarchic system. Meanwhile, the concept of cyberspace and its security threats can be understood from the following flowchart. While cybersecurity is a component of cyberspace, vulnerable threats such as cyberwar, cyberterrorism, and cybercriminal activities and espionage are sources of cyber insecurity. In other words, cybersecurity can be divided into four main categories: cyberwarfare, cyber terrorism, cybercrime, and cyber espionage (Shackelford, 2013, p. 1273).Following Figure 1.1 illustrates the

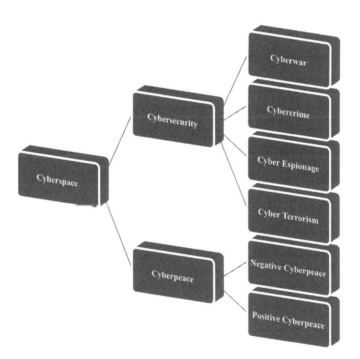

Figure 1.1 Concept of Cyberspace (Security, Threat, and Peace).
Source: Author.

concept of cyberspace, highlighting both its elements of threats/security and dimensions of peace within the domain.

Theory of Cyberspace in Security Studies

The theories of International Relations (IR)[8] or security studies including realism, liberalism, liberal realism (English School), rationalism, constructivism, securitisation theory, critical theory, and feminism could be used to discuss the context of cyberspace. Classical realists (Hobbes or Morgenthau) would view human nature as selfish and believe that it strives to maximise power through the use of technology. The domain of cyberspace itself is anarchic in nature, where there is no single authority (international governance), and states accordingly prepare themselves to be free from "cyber fear" and threats. Neo-realists (Kenneth Waltz or John Mearsheimer) would hold that the structure of the international system is anarchic without a supreme authority (sovereign), and hence states or non-state actors using their potential would exploit cyberspace as a platform to accrue power by using legal or illegal means. Meanwhile, classical liberals (John Locke or Immanuel Kant) would consider that international conflict or conflict over cyberspace can be avoided by using the domain as a medium for people to interact and cooperate with each other. Neo-liberals (Robert Keohane or Joseph Nye) believe that cyberspace is a domain of opportunities for commercial and economic benefits, by acknowledging the significant role of private industries, as well as threats posed by non-state actors such as terrorists and criminals.

Seeking common ground between the two (liberalist and realist), liberal-realist (English School scholars including Hedley Bull) would recognise cyberspace as a medium of both threat and collaboration where international society (among states) or world society (among individuals) interact to share ideas and norms (Buzan, 2004, p. 10). Rationalists (James Fearon) would assume states can negotiate instead of choosing war in cyberspace and international bodies (UN) can play an active role by introducing universal laws for international digital networks systems. Constructivists (Nicholas Onuf or Alexander Wendth) may consider the idea to maximise states' power through cyberspace as a construct of strategic actors in world politics (see McDonald, 2008, p. 60). Critical theorists or the Frankfurt School (Jurgen Habermas or Ken Booth) would believe cyberspace is a platform not only to acquire power and integrate cooperation but a "public sphere" that supports the democratic process with people having fair debate on governance and politics. Cyberspace is used by members of society to mobilise against (the Arab Spring) and for (election campaigns) states. However, the Copenhagen School (Barry Buzan and his colleagues), which has not included cyberspace (technology) within sectoral securitisation theories, would believe it to be a new domain that perceives existential threat that requires the extraordinary attention of the state (referent object) and public. Meanwhile, the contributions of feminist perspectives to fostering peace and addressing the victimisation of women in cyberspace cannot be ruled out while discussing the security dimensions of cyberspace in contemporary international affairs.

Referring to the works of Augustine, Spinoza, Niebuhr, and Morgenthau, Kenneth Waltz identified that men's evilness and improper behaviour led to war and that this practice is unlikely to change (Waltz, 2001, pp. 39–41). Consequently, states persist in vying for dominance in cyberspace, often resorting to unlawful practices and disregarding ethical norms. This raises the question of how cyberwarfare might fit into the way that security, conflict, and war are currently understood. Meanwhile, as India is in the process of digitisation, it must reasonably conceptualise the challenges, dilemmas, and opportunities produced by the cyber realm. Subsequently, it must integrate cyberwar into its national security matrix, and cyber capability should not be simply seen as just another technological revolution, a force multiplier or a weapon. The intricate relationship between cyberspace and other domains of warfare requires in-depth analysis to understand how digital operations influence and integrate with traditional war-fighting strategies across land, sea, air, and space. Hence, India must incorporate cyberwar into its national security framework, and cyber capabilities should not just be viewed as another industrial revolution, tool, weaponry, or force multiplier.

States and Cyberspace

Cyberspace is a state creation and a domain to cooperate and compete at various levels. Held (1992, p. 88) explains that the important components of a state are territoriality (fixed borders); control of violence (military coercion); impersonal structure of power (sovereign political order); and legitimacy (state right). However, unlike land, sea, air, and space, cyberspace has no physical borders despite occupying a virtual territory. In contrast to a state, Barlow[9] (2019), in his widely quoted article "A Declaration of the Independence of Cyberspace", claimed that the domain possesses authority but no elected governments. Even if people connect and communicate in this domain, there is no presence of human bodies in cyberspace; therefore, there is no discrimination based on culture, caste, or religion. Additionally, there is no actual sovereignty for human races in this place. He further expressed that cyberspace does not adopt the legal concept of "property, expression, identity, movement, and context" as the state does in real world. As its universe has no bodies (humans), it cannot obtain world order by physical coercion (data does not fight each other without a force behind the machine). Barlow stated that while states attempted to thwart computer viruses by establishing "guard posts" (firewalls) at the boundaries of digital networks, the prevention of the contagion could only be temporary and would not endure for long because cyberspace would soon be overspread. A human civilisation of mind (technology) has emerged in the cyber domain, which, in Barlow's opinion, is more human and trustworthy than the actual anarchic world.

A state is assumed to have a variety of forms, such as absolutist, socialist, and Islamic states. However, in contemporary debate, the nature of the state has largely focused on the model of the state found in Western societies, i.e., liberal democratic states (Heywood, 2016). Due to differences in ideologies, different states utilised or approached cyberspace differently. Western countries or democracies have less restriction on the public using the cyber domain. Countries such as China, North Korea, and Iran maintained restrictions on public network access. Similarly, Russia controls online communication on state-run cyber platforms. Based on their national interest, technological capabilities, and need to accrue national power, states engage in illegal operations against other countries. Some of the classic cases are the Chinese attack on the Pentagon (Moonlight Maze, 1999), Israeli-associated US attack on Iran's nuclear reactor (Stuxnet, 2010), and Russia's attack on Ukraine (NotPetya, 2017). Hence, states have tried to maximise their muscle through the digital world. India, a developing country among other developed or developing countries, has been a victim of cybercrime from its capable neighbours China and Pakistan. To have greater offensive and defensive capabilities, it has also taken part in the "cyber arms race".

Security and Cyberspace (Securitisation of Cyberspace)

Buzan, Waever, and de Wilde (1998) of the Copenhagen School, in their book, *Security: A New Framework for Analyses* have added four new sectors in security studies to traditional studies of military affairs. The four new sectors are environment, economic, societal, and political security, which perceive threats from an internal or external factor. Ralf (2016) further discussed this in his work on "Securitization", a chapter of the book, *Contemporary Security Studies* edited by Alan Collins. Ralf outlines the process of securitisation, from a non-politicised issue to one that is politicised and then successfully securitised. Securitising a domain or sector requires few important elements such as actors, a referent object, and audience. Securitising actors include governments, bureaucrats, political leaders, lobbyists, and pressure groups who securitise a domain by declaring something ("referent object") is threatened in reality and truly exists. Referent objects are those sectors that are extremely threatened and have the natural right to survive, such as a state (military security), sovereignty (political security), identities (societal security), and habitats (environmental security). The relevant audience is the civil society or general public that view a domain as a genuine threat and necessitates extraordinary measures (sanctioning of funds and creation of new rules and policies) to address the danger.

Cyberspace, initially introduced to the public as a non-political medium primarily for communication, gradually underwent politicisation and eventual securitisation, transforming it into a critical security concern in the modern era. In the securitisation process, the state or its critical infrastructure associated with cyberspace becomes the referent object, perceiving imminent threats from both internal and external elements. Any disruption or damage to this infrastructure is viewed as a potential cause of significant risk to the state. Every critical asset of any state has a legitimate right to survival and protection as rooted in natural law. Critical information infrastructures of those in defence, banking, energy, communication, transportation, and health are essential functionaries of a state that have the right to survive and be protected. Any disruption to these facilities will have a debilitating impact on the state's digital ecosystem. Recognising the strategic importance of cyberspace, actors including governments, bureaucrats, political leaders, lobbyists, and pressure groups have prioritised its protection as a critical strategic issue. Consequently, extraordinary measures, including the introduction of new regulations and increasing investment in cybersecurity, are being implemented to ensure its resilience. Subsequently, a significant segment of the general public is increasingly aware of cybersecurity challenges and recognises the potential threats it poses to national security.

In India too, cyberspace, which was earlier a non-security issue, has gradually evolved into a critical strategic domain. Cyberspace became a part of the national security debate and the government subsequently introduced new strategies and policies on cybersecurity. India perceives threats in the digital networks of both civil and military sectors. The civil sector includes banking systems, energy installations, communication systems, transportation networks, and health segments. Hence, civil laws, including *Information Technology (IT) Act-2000* (amended in 2008), and the *National Cyber Security Policy-2013* (Hatfield, 2017) were introduced to address these cyber vulnerabilities. In the military sector, the *Indian Army Doctrine-2004*, *Basic Doctrine of the Indian Air Force-2012*, *Joint Doctrine: Indian Armed Forces-2017*, *Land Warfare Doctrine-2018*, and *Joint Doctrine for Cyberspace Operations-2024* were released by the Ministry of Defence (MoD) and recognised the importance of cyberspace in military affairs. To challenge external aggression, a military command known as the Defence Cyber Agency (DCA) was established in 2018 and has been functioning since 2019. In the beginning, it was developed at an agency level but now operates at the level of command. While India was late in developing it, similar cyber commands were already established in the US, China, Russia, and a few other developed countries in the first decade of the 21st century. With immediate threats it perceives from neighbouring countries such as China and Pakistan, and with its aspiration to expand its position in global politics, India is likely to increase its cyber potential in the decades ahead.

Interstate War and Cyberwarfare

Cyberwar has become one of the contemporary strategic concerns for national security. This concept can be traced back to 1993 when John Arquilla and David Ronfeldt tried to develop the concept of "cyberwar" and "netwar" through their article, "Cyberwar Is Coming!" published in the journal *Comparative Strategy* (Craig, 2018, p. 86). Though the definition of war is subjective, Clausewitz, in his book, *On War*, explains war as a duel fought on an extensive scale. It is an act of violence compelling an opponent (country A) to fulfill the will of another (country B), directed by political motives and morality. The *Oxford Dictionary* defines war as "a situation in which two or more countries or groups of people fight against each other over some time" for a strategic or political objective with tangible or non-tangible results. Meanwhile, in the same lexicon, warfare is referred to as "the activity of fighting a war, especially using particular weapons or methods". Similarly, cyberwar can be understood as a form of aggressive action executed by a nation-state or organised non-state actors through the deployment of cyber weapons with an aim to disrupt, harm, or destroy the adversary's computer systems or information networks, with the ultimate goal of achieving strategic, political, or personal objectives.

Consequently, cyberwarfare is a method deployed for the short or long term in the digital space by state or an organised non-state group to disturb or win over their opponent for a targeted cause, which could be political, economic, or strategic. Cyber warfare involves actions carried out by a state or international organisation[10] to attack and attempt to damage another nation's computers or information networks through, for example, computer viruses or denial-of-service attacks (RAND, 2020). In the contemporary global conflict situation, a state chooses different forms of means and methods to fight against its enemy. States such as Syria and Iraq illegitimately select chemical and biological warfare as a means to attack and defeat their opponents. Subsequently, in the age of the digital world, potential states. including great (US and China) and small (Iran and North Korea) powers with their technical capabilities. select cyber warfare as a preferred method to damage their opponents and achieve national objectives.

Throughout history, states have engaged in various forms of warfare conducted across land, sea, air, and space. However, with the end of the Cold War and the dawn of the 21st century, cyberspace has emerged as a new domain of warfare. However, the concept of "cyberwarfare" has different understandings among individuals, institutions, and states. To differentiate cybercrime, cyberterrorism, cyber espionage, propaganda campaigns (social media mobilisation such as the Arab Spring) or any other cyber violence from cyberwarfare often depends on the perception of the parties involved. Beyond the domestic sphere, when such activities are carried out at the transnational level with the involvement of state actors aiming to accumulate power or achieve a strategic objective, then it could be classified as an act of (cyber) "war" depending on the perception of the concerning state (leaders). Meanwhile, there has been no outbreak of war in the digital platform (e.g., a cyber world war) that can be termed a "cyber hot war", which is internationally declared or recognised, where a scholar can even theorise (*ex post facto* of the cyberwar). However, cyberattacks occurred in Estonia (2007), Georgia (2008), Stuxnet (2010), and a few other symbolic digital incursions have been permanently set as an example or a reference point of cyberwarfare. All cyber incursions cannot be considered as cyberwar. To qualify it as a war requires a discussion of war elements including actors, economy, doctrines, command structure, weaponry, and rationale on why states engage in cyberwar (See, Fearon, 1995).

While traditional wars are fought to increase territorial control or national power, cyberwars are carried out to dominate digital space with other associated implications for physical space. For instance, these digital conflicts target critical infrastructure, disrupt communication networks, and influence the socio-political environment, blurring the boundaries between virtual and physical domains. Power in natural science is considered "force" and "energy",; in social science, it is the ability to achieve the desired outcome or a form of control that makes a person obey another (Heywood, 2016). In the international system, power politics, or the distribution of power among states, has been one of the key driving forces for fundamental causes of war and the stability of the system (Buzan & Hansen, 2009). Barry Buzan and Lene Hansen stated that bipolarity has ended with the end of the Cold War and replaced by unipolarity. However, John Mearsheimer, with the re-emergence of Russia, the rise of great power such as China, and other great players (having a strong economy, stable political status, nuclear capability, and large population) questions the re-appearance of multipolarity in the global order. Meanwhile, technology plays an important role in the power games ranging from Cold War nuclear missile capabilities to post-Cold War cyber potentials. The internet, which was originally developed during the Cold War as a military technology (distributed network) to transmit information under nuclear attack (Buzan & Hansen, 2009), continues to be used for strategic purposes apart from opening it for civil affairs. Consequently, states are inclined to become "cyberpower nations", resulting in a new era of technological (cyber) arms race in the globalised world. India too has joined the race to be able to protect its digital ecosystem from its counterparts, including China and Pakistan.

Meanwhile, Kaldor (1999, 2013) argues that a new form of warfare has replaced the traditional Clausewitzian model following the Cold War. In this new type of conflict, state actors are replaced by non-state actors, the war is funded through clandestine means, and the strategies employed are inherently asymmetric in nature. Over time, cyberspace also emerged as a new domain of warfare, gaining attention and actively discussed within academic communities. Subsequently, cyberwar has emerged as an imperative component of the contemporary international system, with the relationship between states and cyberspace growing increasingly complex. Cyberspace serves not only as a platform for communication and economic activities but also as a tool for military purposes and the expansion of power (by nation-states). States with more technological (cyber) capabilities can play a better role in the global world order. Hence, big powers such as the US, Russia, and China are in the race to become a cyber-power nation with intentions to control the global electronic system. Cavelty (2016) in military discourse discussed the concepts of cyber offence, cyber defence, and cyber deterrence. She expressed that fancy concepts such as cyber deterrence to avoid digital warfare are otherwise a common mechanism of information assurance. However, it can be considered that the referent object of the cybersecurity concept (threat) is the technology that directly or indirectly supports the political, economic, social, and military sectors of a state. Any harm to these critical sectors (infrastructures) will have severe consequences for the nation. Hence, the state needs to have proper cooperation and consider a common policy on cyber "peacebuilding" with special attention on cyberwarfare.

Cyber-Peace Formation (Quest for Digital Peace)

Considering the vulnerabilities in cyberspace, digital "peacebuilding" distinct from "cybersecurity" and the development of means or strategies to prevent war in this domain are essential. While cyberwar and digital threats have been discussed broadly, debate on theories and practice of cyber peace in the academic realm is still minimal. Hence, discussion on developing a sustainable order for peace in the domain is needed for contemporary cyber-world order. This must begin with a conceptual and theoretical clarity of what peace represents in the non-physical world of cyberspace. Classic insights of peace theorists such as Immanuel Kant, Johan Galtung, and Mahatma Gandhi must be thoroughly evaluated to comprehend the theory of cyber peace, as this book discusses in its fifth chapter.

In the contemporary world order, cyber threats are pervasive, and no state is immune to digital vulnerabilities. Therefore, these issues must be addressed with urgency and seriousness through international cooperation and institutions. In 1998, for the first time, as an initiative for international cybersecurity, Russia proposed a draft resolution on *Development in the Field of Information and Communication Technology for International Security* at the United Nations General Assembly's First Committee on Disarmament and International Security (UNIDIR, 2017, p. 15). Cyber networks are global and interconnected with threats capable of emerging from any part of the globe. This lack of clear boundaries underscores the need for a "Cyber Westphalia" model, where nations acknowledge and respect the sovereignty of each other's digital territories in the international system. Chris Demchak and Peter Dombrowski (2016) explained that establishing a border for cyberspace and sovereignty over it would be "nonlinear, dangerous, and lengthy" (Dombrowski, 2013–2014, p. 33). Consequently, to have better regulation of digital (internet) systems, the UN-sponsored World Summit on the Information Society (WSIS) was held with delegates from 175 countries in Geneva in 2003. While the agendas discussed at the WSIS were unable to be implemented, it was able to create the Working Group on Internet Governance that submitted its report at the next WSIS summit held in 2005 in Tunis (Bharadwaj, 2013, p. 221).

12 *State, Security, and Cyberwar*

As cyberspace became an issue for international security, setting up an international working body to look after the welfare of interstate digital affairs was necessary. Hence, the UN developed the Group of Government Experts or UNGGE (members limited to a few countries) in 2004 and established the Open-Ended Working Group or UNOEWG (open to all nations and other stakeholders including non-government institutes) in 2018 and implemented in 2020. The primary aim of the group is to ensure member states behave responsibly in cyberspace and not disturb international security through digital space. The first session of the UNGGE was held in July 2004 (UN, 2004) and the UNOEWG took place in June 2021 in New York (UNOEWG on Information and Communication Technologies, 2023). Separately, the UN General Assembly developed an Ad Hoc Committee "on countering the use of information and communication technology for criminal purpose" (with the participation of public and private stakeholders) in December 2019 (UN General Assembly, 2020). While the first organisational session was supposed to be held in August 2020, it occurred in May 2021 because of the COVID-19 pandemic (UNODC, 2023). A new convention on preventing the use of information and communications technology for criminal purposes is now being negotiated by member states.

On the same approach, bilateral and multilateral cooperation is also instituted by member states at the individual level. A comprehensive support system is required from regional and international organisations. Safeguarding cyberspace would be deficient without active cooperation from the private sector as well. Though absolute peace may be difficult to achieve in the international anarchic system, cooperation amongst states can help reduce war in cyberspace. Meanwhile, the option of using deterrence, cyber armistice, and other applicable concepts and practices towards peace should be kept open to bring peace to the international cyber ecosystem. India has been a member of the UNGGE since its inception and encourages member states to have universal norms on cyber warfare. Separately, an Indian non-government organisation (NGO), the CyberPeace Foundation, is a world-famous organisation working on "initiatives to build collective resilience against cybercrimes and global threats of cyberwarfare" (www.cyberpeace.org).

Conclusion

In light of the above debate on state and cyber affairs, this book is an in-depth study and systematically explain state behaviour on the domain of cyberspace by using flexible, non-systematic, and unstructured methodologies. Considering the gaps or the lack of existing works on the relationship amongst state, security, and cyber warfare in the globalised world, this book studies the characteristics of these three elements in three dedicated chapters (Chapters 2–4). This will be followed by a study on cyber peace, as the aspect of peace cannot be discounted in the study of interstate war and domestic violence. Appropriate research questions on theories of state, cyberspace, cybersecurity, digital warfare, and peace will be evaluated to solve their problems systematically. The objective and findings of this research will not only be useful for cyber researchers but for practitioners who are involved in making policy on digital affairs. The research method of this study is designed in the simplest form and allowed to be flexible enough so that the work continues efficiently and does not hold it in the absence (non-availability) of any specific data.

Notes

1. Industry 4.0 (I4.0) is the industrial innovation (revolution) of digital technology of the current era, which comes after Industry 3.0 (computer and automation); Industry 2.0 (electricity and mass production); and Industry 1.0 (steam power and mechanisation) (Boz ena Gajdzik, 2021).
2. "A country that is world-class in safeguarding the cyber health of citizens, businesses and institutions; has the legal, ethical and regulatory regimes to foster public trust; and the ability to project cyber power to disrupt, deny or degrade adversaries" (Julia Voo, 2020).
3. The concept of technical and non-technical aspects of cyberspace has been highlighted in the section *Cyberspace and the international system*.
4. The World Bank predicts about 60 per cent of the global gross domestic product (GDP) will rely on digital communication technologies by the year 2022 (World Bank, 2022).
5. The following terms "internet", "cyberspace", "digital space", and "information/communication networks" are used interchangeably in this book to reduce the redundancy of the terminology in the contents. However, the terms are carefully used according to their suitability and meaning in the context.
6. The data is based on the assessment period of November 2021 to October 2022 provided by Kaspersky (2022).
7. *The Tallinn Manual*, originally titled *Tallinn Manual on the International Law Applicable to Cyber Warfare* is a non-binding document detailing how international laws apply to cyber operations and digital warfare. It was developed by a group of experts working for the Cooperative Cyber Defence Centre of Excellence and North Atlantic Treaty Organisation (NATO) and published in 2013 by Cambridge University Press. While its second volume, *Tallinn Manual 2.0* was published in 2017, the subsequent volume of *Tallinn Manual 3.0* is yet to be released.
8. This book uses the term "International Relations" (capitalised) to refer to the academic discipline or field of study, and "international relations" (lowercase) to denote the general concept of relationships among nations.
9. John Parry Barlow was an American Republican, rock lyricist, and cattle rancher. He sold his ranch in the late 1980s and became a telecommunication enthusiast (Sterling, 1992). He was the co-founder of the Electronic Frontier Foundation (EFF) in 1990.
10. For example, an international organisation such as NATO for the safety of the European digital ecosystem can declare cyberwar against Russia.

References

Armstrong, M. (2021). *How Many Websites Are There?* Retrieved from Statista. https://www.statista.com/chart/19058/number-of-websites-online/

Barlow, P. (2019). A declaration of the independence of cyberspace. In J. Boyle (Ed.), *The past and future of the internet: A symposium for John Perry Barlow* (pp. 5–8). North Carolina: Duke University School of Law.

Baezner, M., & Robin, P. (2017, October). The use of cybertools in an internationalized civil war context: Cyber activities in the Syrian conflict. Zurich: Center for Security Studies, ETH Zürich. Retrieved from https://css.ethz.ch/content/dam/ethz/special-interest/gess/cis/center-for-securities-studies/pdfs/Cyber-Reports-2017-05.pdf

Bharadwaj, S. (2013). Security in cyberspace: India's multilateral efforts. In P. B. Mehta & B. J. Pratap (Eds.), Shaping the emerging world: India and the multilateral order (pp. 217–236). Washington, D.C.: Brookings Institution Press.

Buzan, B. (1987). *An introduction to strategic studies: Military technology and international relations.* London: Macmillan Press.

Buzan, B. (2004). *From international to world society? English School theory and the social structure of globalisation.* Cambridge: Cambridge University Press.

Buzan, B., & Hansen, L. (2009). *The evolution of international security studies.* Cambridge: University Printing Press.

Buzan, B., Waever, O., & de Wilde, J. (1998). A new framework for analysis. London: Lynne Rienner Publisher.

Cavelty, M. (2016). Cyber-security. In A. Collins (Ed.), Contemporary security studies (4th ed., pp. 401–415). Oxford: Oxford University.

Craig, A. J. S., & Valeriano, B. (2018). Realism and cyber conflict: Security in the digital age. In D. Orsi, J. R. Avgustin, & M. Nurnus (Eds.), *Realism in practice: Apprisal* (pp. 85–101). Bristol, England: E-International Relations Publishing.

Dombrowski, C. D. (2013–2014). Cyber Westphalia: Asserting state prerogatives in cyberspace. Georgetown Journal of International Affairs, 15(1), 29–38.

Fearon, J. D. (1995). Rationalist explanations for war. International Organization, 49(3), 379–414.

Gajdzik, B., Grabowska, S., & Saniuk, S. (2021). A theoretical framework for industry 4.0 and its implementation with selected practical schedules. *Energies*, 14(4), 940.

Hatfield, J. M. (2017). Social engineering in cybersecurity: The evolution of a concept. Computers & Security, 73, 102–113.

Held, D. (1992). The development of the modern state. In S. Hall & B. Gieben (Eds.), Formation of modernity (pp. 71–126). Cambridge: Polity Press.

Heywood, A. (2016). *Political theory: An introduction.* London: Palgrave.

ITU. (2024). *Measuring digital development: Facts and figures 2024.* Retrieved December 13, 2024, from https://www.itu.int/itu-d/reports/statistics/2024/11/10/ff24-internet-use/

Julia Voo, I. H. (2020). *National cyber power index 2020.* Cambridge: Harvard Kennedy School.

Kaldor, M. (1999). *New and old wars: Organised violence in a global era.* Stanford: Stanford University Press.

Kaldor, M. (2013). In defence of new wars. *Stability*, 4(1&2), 1–16.

Kaspersky. (2022, December 01). *Kaspersky security bulletin 2022. Statistics.* Securelist by Kaspersky. Retrieved from https://securelist.com/ksb-2022-statistics/108129/

Kello, L. (2013). The meaning of the cyber revolution: Perils to theory and statecraft. International Security, 38(2), 7–40.

Kumar, R. (2011). *Research Methodology: A step by step guide for beginners.* London: Sage.

Laila, B. (2024, September 18). Israel planted explosives in Hezbollah's Taiwan-made pagers, say sources. *Reuters.* Retrieved from https://www.reuters.com/world/middle-east/israel-planted-explosives-hezbollahs-taiwan-made-pagers-say-sources-2024-09-18/

McDonald, M. (2008). Constructivism. In P. D. Williams (Ed.), Security studies: An introduction (pp. 59–72). London: Routledge.

Ralf, E. (2016). Securitization. In A. Collins (Ed.), Contemporary security studies (4th ed., pp. 168–181). Oxford: Oxford University Press.

RAND. (2020). *Cyber warfare*. Rand Corporation. Retrieved July 08, 2020, from https://www.rand.org/topics/cyber-warfare.html

Relia, S. (2015). *Cyber warfare: Its implications on national security*. New Delhi: Vij Books India Pvt Ltd.

Schmitt, M. N., & Vihul, L. (Eds.). (2017). Tallinn Manual 2.0 on the international law applicable to cyber operations. Cambridge: Cambridge University Press / NATO Cooperative Cyber Defence Centre of Excellence. Retrieved from NATO Cooperative Cyber Defence Centre of Excellence.

Shackelford, S. J. (2013). Toward cyberpeace: Managing cyberattacks through polycentric governance. *American* University Law Review, 62(5), 1273–1364.

Starchak, M. (2024, November 29). *Russia's hypersonic missile attack on Ukraine was an attempt at blackmail*. Carnegie Endowment. Retrieved from https://carnegieendowment.org/russia-eurasia/politika/2024/11/russia-oreshnik-nuclear-blackmail?lang=en

Sterling, M. B. (1992). The hacker crackdown: Law and disorder on the electronic frontier. New York: Bantam Books.

UN. (2004, December 16). Developments in the field of information and telecommunications in the context of international security (A/RES/59/61). Retrieved June 20, 2022, from https://documents-dds-ny.un.org/doc/UNDOC/GEN/N04/479/92/PDF/N0447992.pdf?OpenElement

UN. (2023, January 21). *Open ended working group on information and communication technologies*. UN Office for Disarmament Affairs. Retrieved from https://meetings.unoda.org/open-ended-working-group-on-information -and-communication -technologies-2021

UNCTAD. (2019). Digital economy report 2019: Value creation and capture – Implications for developing countries. United Nations. https://unctad.org/system/files/official-document/der2019_en.pdf

UNGA. (2020, January 20). *Resolution adopted by the general assembly on 27 December 2019*. United Nations General Assembly. Retrieved from https://documents-dds-ny.un.org/doc/UNDOC/GEN/N19/440/28/PDF/N1944028.pdf?OpenElement

UNIDIR. (2017). The United Nations, Cyberspace and International Peace and Security: Responding to Complexity in the 21st Century. Geneva.

UNODC. (2023). *Ad* Hoc Committee to elaborate a comprehensive international convention on countering the use of information and communications technologies for criminal purposes. Retrieved from https://www.unodc.org/unodc/en/cybercrime/ad_hoc_committee/home

Waltz, K. N. (2001). *Man, the state and war: A theoretical analysis*. New York: Colombia University Press.

World Bank. (2022, October 6). *Digital development*. World Bank. Retrieved from https://www.worldbank.org/en/topic/digitaldevelopment/overview

2 Characteristics of States and Cyberspace

Introduction

Both before and after the creation of modern states,[1] technology has played a major role in the advancement of human civilisation. As technology evolves along with the progress of nation-states, the former has been used or misused by the latter for political, military, economic, and social purposes. Likewise, the domain of cyberspace (part of Information and Communication Technology, ICT), which was developed during the Cold War, became a significant determinant for interstate affairs. As Buzan concludes, states are objects of security, the same is true of cyberspace. History clearly demonstrates the role of technology in securing victory in war and the advance of cyberspace has an impact on the security dynamics of the international system, particularly in terms of power and military capabilities. Given the significance of cyberspace in the global order, this chapter explores the behaviour of nation-states in the realm of cyber politics. It briefly touches upon the theory of states' elements, population, territory, governance, sovereignty, and legitimacy, along with the connection of cyberspace, comprising its concept, operation (governance), actors involved (population), functioning jurisdiction (territory), and cyber prowess (sovereignty). The study will also explore the cyberspace policy followed by great, middle, and small powers (countries).

This chapter will discuss the role of technology, particularly cyberspace, in shaping the emergence of India as a powerful state in the international system by comparing it with other countries. India's expanding ICT skills have led to its development as a "cyber power nation" in the contemporary world order. While India attempts to grow its presence in the global cybersecurity platform (UN initiatives), it has developed various institutes and policies to challenge digital menaces at the domestic level. India is a member of the UN Group of Government Experts (UNGGE), which advocates for appropriate guidelines for national governments to adhere to in the area of cyberspace. At the domestic level, India has introduced the *Information Technology Act-2000* (amended in 2008), the *National Cyber Security Policy-2013*, and other national cybersecurity standards, guidelines, and centres along with a national cybersecurity coordinator.

Theory on the Origin of States and Cyberspace

The characteristics of both the state and cyberspace are shaped by theories of their origin and the elements involved in their formation. The origin of states has been discussed by several scholars from ancient to modern times by proposing different theories. While five different theories are discussed below on the origin of states, an attempt has also been made to construct similar theories on the formation (origin) of cyberspace. Both the state and cyberspace are the creation of people (as data for cyberspace), within a territory (jurisdiction of a digital network), through governance (computer algorithms, logics, programming), and with sovereignty (technological power of computers). However, both have differences in their own character, as discussed below.

Origin of States

The origin of states indicates that they are the creation of human conglomerates thorough political process. Based on the political thoughts and philosophies developed since the ancient period from Plato to John Locke, the theories on the origin of states include the natural theory, patriarchal theory, force theory, divine right theory, and social contract theory. The natural theory says that states are formed by the natural process of human beings as a social creature and their desire to live together as a community for a common purpose, which later developed into a social political institute (*polis* or state). In his popular book *Politics*, Aristotle proposed that the state originates from the union of individuals (male and female) forming a family, which grows into a village and eventually evolves into a state. Patriarchal theory suggests that states evolve through the expansion of the family under parents (father as the head) as elders and authority, which later developed into the form of a tribe, kingdom, or state. Force theory illustrates that states are formed through the use of force or coercion, involving acts such as waging war, invading and conquering new territory and populations, a practice predominantly observed in the ancient period. The divine right theory posits that the state is established by a supernatural entity, such as God, and that past rulers (kings or queens) governed as divinely ordained representatives of the state, wielding absolute power over the population and territory. Finally, social contract theory, regarded as the foundation of the modern political system, suggests that a state is formed when people voluntarily choose a ruler or government to serve and protect their collective interests. This same populace retains the authority to remove the ruler if they become corrupt or fail to serve the public.

Though states are created through various methods and processes, German scholar Ratzel in his *Politische Geographic* (1903) explained that in the evolution of the state, each state passes through three stages of village-state (*Dorfstaat*), city-state (*Stadtstaat*), and country-state (*Landstaat*). Meanwhile, states have four key elements in which two of them are physical and the other two are non-physical aspects. While population and territory are the core physical components of a state, governance and sovereignty are the basic non-physical components. To consider itself a state, every political body (state) should have these four elements and any absence means it cannot be called a state. The corresponding comparison of the state and cyberspace is discussed in the following section.

Origin of Cyberspace

Similar to the theories of the origin of state, the origin of cyberspace can also be comparatively analysed. Just as the concept of the state was developed by people, cyberspace is likewise a human construct. However, the world of the state is based on population, territory, governance, and sovereignty, but the world of cyberspace (an electronic medium for communication) is designed based on data, networks, algorithms, and powerful tools. Unlike the state, which was created through anthropological (mortal or living being) aspects, cyberspace was invented with mechanical (immortal or non-living being) features (supported by humans). While the philosophy of state was developed centuries ago, the domain of cyberspace was developed in the middle of the 20th century.

If the "natural theory" on the origin of states is to be applied in the development of cyberspace, there are possibilities for cyberspace to be naturally evolved as communication systems advance with the development of computers (or computing devices). Digital communication (cyberspace) can be considered an advanced version of previously existing telegrams (text) or telephones (voice), which were invented to connect users (population) within a network (territory) under an authorised principle (governance). Like states, this digital domain was developed based on the human desire and need-basis for social interaction through a natural process supported by technology. While humans are the creators of cyberspace, the cyber domain is maintained by machines (hardware) and programs (software), as Barlow has also explained. Technically, even without human beings (external force), cyberspace can survive and function for a "period". However, it cannot endure without the mortals who manage and control these systems. Ultimately, the power to govern and regulate cyberspace lies in human hands, much like the control of states is exercised by humans.

The patriarchal theory of cyberspace believes that the current form of cyberspace was created through early foundational tools (abacus, calculator, telegram, telephone) and chips (valves, transistors) that can be considered as "parental" machines of today's cyber platform. Like a family expands into a society, the number of microchips and cyber tools exponentially increases (the number of transistors in a microchip doubles every two years increasing computing power and efficiency, as per Moore's law) to establish a complete cyber network. The force theory of cyberspace suggests that digital networks (territories) can be forcibly seized using powerful tools or programs. Like a state wages war against another, a digital system (computer) can attack another cyber network and occupy it for political or other interests. This can manifest in various forms such as hacking, holding networks hostage, defacing systems, detaining data, snooping, conducting surveillance, or engaging in espionage.

The "divine right" theory of cyberspace in could be explained in mechanical terms in that the domain of cyberspace is controlled by traditional technologies (old systems, less risk), not by cloud computing, artificial intelligence (AI), internet of things (IoT), and big data (BD). For instance, storing one's data in old storage devices such as a floppy disk, or external drive would be safer than saving it in the cloud. As the US is the creator of cyberspace, it has the ordained mandated or "divine right" to have more power to influence the domain of cyberspace in the international system. Viewing cyberspace from the perspective of social contract theory, which is premised on an agreement between two groups, the government and the public, to function as states, cyberspace is also built on the interactions of circuits and transistors through electronic medium. This input-output mechanism, governed by programming, creates a functional network system (cyberspace) that mirrors the collaborative framework underlying the social contract. These tools can also detect corrupt systems and ignore them. The concept that firewalls and antiviruses are designed to protect from corrupt and malicious threats aligns well with such a philosophy. Cyberspace in the international system is administered by both the government and private companies whose corrupt powers can be challenged by the public (users or subscribers).

Elements of States and Cyberspace

The characteristics of states and cyberspace are determined by their origins and the elements associated while creating them. States have different theories of origin and four key elements (population, territory, governance, and sovereignty) that make a human society into the form of a "state". Similarly, the origin of cyberspace could be analysed through state theories as to how it was created with what elements. Referring to the *Tallin Manual 2.0*, the layers of cyberspace can be studied at two levels: the *logical layer* (the virtual world) and the *social layer* (the physical world with human activities), as indicated in Table 2.1. In the logical layer, data refers to the state population, electronic medium as territory, algorithms/programming as governance, and AI or machine learning capabilities as sovereignty. In the social layer or the physical world, population refers to the number of internet users in a country, territory is the area of internet coverage in a state, governance signifies the national cyber laws, and policies, and sovereignty is the cyber power or the digital strength of a nation. The following is a comparative discussion on the elements of state and cyberspace where the focus is given more to the theoretical aspect of the logical layer than the social layer of cyberspace.

State Population and Cyber Data

Population is the foundation of every state system. It serves as the most essential element, and the other components, such as territory, governance, and sovereignty (power), are inherently dependent on it. Population has three important aspects: size, distribution, and type, which can affect the state's domestic affairs and international relations. The "size" of people living in a state has political and economic implications in both national and international affairs. Plato, in his writing, also reflects the ideal size of a state by providing a number as specific as "5,040". Meanwhile, Aristotle proposed that a state should neither be too large nor too small. However, it should be sizable (large) enough to be self-sufficient and accurate (small) enough to be well governed. In ancient times, states often believed that population size directly influenced the outcome of wars, as larger populations meant more soldiers for combat. This perception made demographic strength a critical factor in military success. Even in the modern world, population continues to play a significant role in determining a country's economic and strategic power. For example, populated nations like India and China benefit from large labour forces, substantial economic output, and potential military manpower, giving them considerable advantages in terms of wealth and influence.

As indicated in Table 2.1, the population of cyberspace can be seen in two aspects, the logical layer and the physical layer, where the concept of the former needs more clarification. The *logical layer* of the digital world pertains to digital information and data such as "text, video, audio, or other" in the cyber environment. Interestingly, like the population of a state, digital data

Table 2.1 Comparison: Elements of States and Cyberspace

Sl No.	States	Cyberspace	
		Logical layer (Virtual world)	*Social layer (Physical world)*
1.	Population	Data (information of voice, text, audio, video, etc.)	Population of internet users in a country
2.	Territory	Specified electronic medium where cyber networks function (internet jurisdiction)	Cyber network coverage within a geography (country)
3.	Government	Software functioning principles, its designs, and guidelines (programming, algorithms, etc.)	Cyber governance (IT Act and cyber laws, cyber policies, etc.) of a country
4.	Sovereignty	Technical machine-learning power (AI, decision-making capabilities)	Cyber power or m

Source: Author.

has a size (data volume), distribution (networks), and type (file type). John Parry Barlow was probably the first cyber theorist who tried to compare cyberspace with the elements (theory) of state. He explains who or what represents the population, territory, government, and sovereign system in the virtual world or cyberspace. In his essay, "Crime and Puzzlement" published on 8 June 1990, Barlow explains that cyberspace at that time has certain similarities with that of the wild west in the 19th century. He defines cyberspace as "vast, unmapped, culturally and legally ambiguous, verbally terse, hard to get around in, and up for grabs" (Barlow, 1990). It is a perfect breeding ground for both outlaws and new ideas about liberty. Further, on 9 February 1996, another essay, "A Declaration of the Independence of Cyberspace" (Barrow, 1996), which became more popular[2] than his previous essay, detailed the characteristics of cyberspace. In his "declaration" (essay), the following excerpt followed by an analysis seems to be relevant for the study of "population" as in who or what exists in the world of cyberspace.

> Governments of the Industrial World, you weary giants of flesh and steel, I come from Cyberspace, the new home of Mind. On behalf of the future, I ask you of the past to leave us alone. You are not welcome among us. You have no sovereignty where we gather ... Cyberspace consists of transactions, relationships, and thought itself, arrayed like a standing wave in the web of our communications. Ours is a world that is both everywhere and nowhere, but it is not where bodies live.

Though he was not clear about its identity, whether it was a living or non-living organism, Barlow's "I" and "us" in the given excerpt represent the "population" of cyberspace. While he expressed that cyberspace is a home for "new minds", it was not clear if he was referring to the minds of humans or robots (artificial neurons that have thinking capabilities). He further confirmed that the sovereign power of humans is not applicable where the "population" of cyberspace exists. It was vividly mentioned that no bodies of human flesh live in the domain of cyberspace, which indicates it is a world of steel and wires (tools and machines). Like humans, these elements ("population") of wire and steel have relations, connections, and transactions that form an electronic network or web as a society (Barlow, 1996). Since cyberspace is an electronic medium for information exchange (communication), bits that represent various forms of data, including text, audio, pictures, and video are being transferred and moved. It, in short, is a binary world populated and ruled, governed, and designed by zeros and ones.

The ontological perspective of cyberspace likens it to an essential domain tied to electronic chips and transistors, comparable to water for fish, land for humans and animals, and air for birds, and outerspace possibly for microorganism. While humans inhabit the land permanently and can physically navigate and operate—whether for commerce or warfare—within the realms of the sea, air, and space, they cannot physically traverse cyberspace. Instead, their presence in cyberspace is limited to manoeuvring and conducting both military and non-military activities within this virtual domain.

Bruce Sterling discussed the origin of the term "cyberspace", which was coined by a science fiction writer William Gibson in 1982 (Sterling, 1992). Sterling explains cyberspace as an indefinite, virtual environment where communication occurs, such as telephone conversation. Though it is not a "real" physical space, it is a "genuine place" with real and significant effects that influence individuals and events. Since the 1960s, the world has been blended with computers and televisions, yet the concept of cyberspace has remained absent. While modern society has become deeply intertwined with cyberspace, people often still struggle to fully understand how to exist within it. Despite established practices, rules, and guidelines, life is far from perfect in the physical world. Similarly, in cyberspace, individuals are still adapting to new norms and practices along with new and evolving technologies (Sterling, 1992, pp. 16–20). Sterling believes humans are now living in cyberspace as they are so dependent on and influenced by this domain.

Meanwhile, the *social layer* of cyber population pertains to the usage of the internet (cyberspace) by the population of a specific place or country in the real world. It represents the number of people accessing the internet in an area. It also considers the utility of the service for urban and rural populations. That is why every country maintains a record of the population using cyberspace. Though cyberspace is a place of unreal or non-physical consequences, it has become a genuine place of consequences where humans are involved too much and they act or become a part of its population (Sterling, 1992). People may not fully comprehend the domain of cyberspace, but they are undeniably dependent on it, as it has become an integral part of daily life, shaping how they communicate, work, and engage with the world.

State Territory and Cyber Jurisdiction

The second important physical element of the state is territory, which includes land, water, and airspace where people can live, move, and travel through various international standards and rules. Spykman suggests "geography is the most fundamental factor in foreign policy because it is the most permanent" (Spykman, 1942, p. 41). The territory of a state is generally a geographical phenomenon where different states are divided by mountains, the sea, deserts, forests, or other natural barriers (e.g., India and China divided by mountains). It is also sometimes demarcated by political factors (India and Pakistan divided by political decision) rather than a geographical factor. Hence, it is the sense of the identification of the people that plays a crucial role in defining the territorial boundary. For example, China developed a unique cultural, political, and social identity, shaped by its distinct historical experiences and philosophical traditions, setting it apart from its neighbouring countries including India. An attempt to reallocate the territory could result in the amalgamation or detachment of different states or the emergence of new states. Territory merely resembles the population, as the former has no standard of life cycle that involves birth and death (Buzan, 1983).

Meanwhile, people who belong to the territory permanently reside there and exercise their power that is authorised by the state. It signifies the space of sovereignty that the state can exercise. Territory provides natural resources, as the population provides human resources to sustain the state. Sometimes, scarcity of resources or unequal distribution of them lead to conflict in the international system. Territory provides a sense of security and belonging to residents, creating an emotional bond amongst the people to commonly worship or adore their state as a motherland. This encourages people to protect their territory and develop a sense of patriotism, even though they belong to different religions, languages, and cultures.

Referring to the *logical layer* of cyberspace, the territory of cyberspace could be considered as the virtual province or area (space) covered by an internet network in a specific location (town, district, country, etc.). This is the medium where the "cyber population" (data) exists and electronic communication occurs. According to Barlow, it is a place that is both "everywhere and nowhere", where living beings do not exist. While cyberspace, unlike land, water, and airspace, has no physical border or boundary, it has a specific jurisdiction or separation between states, defined by the walls of bandwidth, language, and filters. In connection with this, the laws of cyberspace or cybersecurity are introduced and implemented within the borders of nation-states (Wu, 2006, p. viii). Cyberspace, though available worldwide and connected universally, is distributed through different states (zones or regions) where the host nation has the ability to control its functioning within the state itself. Meanwhile, the extensive networks of the internet (cyber) are controlled through "internet kill switches". This is why an internet network can be selectively suspended in a specific location, such as a district experiencing protests or unrest, while other areas within the same state continue to function normally. Such incidents are commonly observed in conflict-prone areas like Jammu and Kashmir, the northeastern regions, and other parts of India. However, the overall global cyber network system is largely managed by the Internet Corporation for Assigned Names and Numbers (ICANN) that coordinates and manages the technical elements of the global Domain Name System (DNS). The DNS ensures that all internet users are identifiable through their unique Internet Protocol (IP) addresses, facilitating seamless communication and data exchange across the global network. These services were earlier operated by the US government under the Internet Assigned Numbers "Authority", but now are the responsibility the non-profit organisation ICANN (ICANN, 2022).

Like people of the physical world who permanently reside in and exercise power over their territories, data inhabits and operates within the virtual world, exerting its influence and functionality through cyber networks. This analogy highlights the emerging concept of sovereignty in cyberspace where control over data and information networks reflects a form of authority simlar to that in the physical world. This electronic medium (cyberspace as a territory) provides a space for other communication technologies to interact and help[the cyber ecosystem endure. The absence of cyberspace would have a significant impact on the world of ICT. Without cyberspace, computers would lose their interconnectivity, effectively reducing them to standalone devices with limited utility, much like typewriters or tape machines. Just like territories in the physical world provide resources, such as oil in the Gulf region, the scarcity of technological infrastructure creates variations in networking systems, resulting in differences in internet speeds. Since it is a non-physical world, the emotional bonding that the territory of the physical world provides is missing in the cyberworld (as Barlow also says it is a world of no caste, creed, or colour). Nonetheless, as humans of the different religions, languages, and cultures combine, the same technology is used in the world of cyberspace. The independent language or algorithms of *Facebook* can understand only its own application and specific programs, not that of *WhatsApp* or some others (*Twitter, YouTube, LinkedIn*, etc.).

Meanwhile, in the *social layer*, normally a state has its own digital network spreading throughout its country. Whichever place the digital network physically covers within the geography of a state could be considered the "territory of cyberspace" of that particular nation. The areas where cell towers are installed, lines of cable stretch, the distance covered by the network communication within the geography of a state could be considered as features of cyber territory in the social layer or physical world.

State Governance and Cyber Algorithms

Government is the third fundamental element of the state, established to ensure the state's effective and organised functioning. No state functions in the absence of a government. C.F. Strong states that the government is the highest authority of the state that makes laws to enforce. J.W. Garner explains that government is the agency through which public policies are made to regulate common affairs and promote collective interest (Garner, 1928). The government is responsible for making laws and checking their implementation for public services including defence, diplomacy, internal affairs, transport, power, health, and education. A state without government would be a lawless society, a disjointed population with no common aims, interests, or organisation. Citizens of any state must abide by the laws implemented by the government. Meanwhile, any interactions, including war and conflict, between different states take place through their governments.

A government is not treated as a state, though both are closely connected. While a government is part of the state, its power is drawn from the state. Unlike the state, which is abstract and invisible, a government is concrete and visible but temporary as it comes and goes. Governments may rise and fall, but the state does not unless its established constitution and customs are dissolved. India, as a state, remains constant regardless of whether it is governed by a coalition or a single-party government, which may either strengthen or weaken its authority. However, a state will lose its identity if it is occupied or suppressed by a foreign power and suspended from its original structure, system, or government like those operated by the British in India in the 19th century (Buzan, 1983, p. 54). The right to form a government by the original population will disappear if they are suppressed by a strong power. However, in the world of cyberspace, any new structure causes the old ruling system or the software principles to dissolve or be repressed (first generation (1G) to fifth generation (5G) network system).

The governance of cyberspace can be discussed in two aspects: the logical layer and the social layer. Cyber governance in the *logical layer* refers to the principles and algorithms run by communication devices (computing machines) in the virtual world. These software and algorithms serve as the rules and norms for the smooth functioning of the virtual world. For example, the Java programming language operates based on principles that allow it to interact only with its own ecosystem, not with C++ programs. Similarly, a Portable Document Format (PDF) viewer can open PDF files but cannot process Microsoft Word documents. When the "governing system" of these devices is disrupted by internal factors, such as algorithm failures, or by external or foreign forces, such as hackers, the system malfunctions. This is akin to how punishments, like imprisonment, are imposed on individuals who break the law in the physical world. An interesting example is the explosion of the US Mariner 1 spacecraft in 1962, which occurred due to a missing "overbar" over the letter "R" in its computer program. This overbar, representing radius ("R-bar" or $\bar{R}$), acted as a critical rule in the program (Fishman, 2019). The failure to address this rule led to the spacecraft's malfunction and eventual destruction, effectively serving as a "punishment" for the error in the system. While human error in managing the cyber logical layer cannot be ruled out, attempts by external elements, such as hackers, to compromise this governing system can be mitigated with robust security measures. Strong antivirus and firewalls function as enforcement mechanisms, safeguarding digital operations and maintaining the integrity of cyberspace's governing systems.

In Barlow's philosophy, he describes the cyberworld as having its own "social contract" system, where governance will grow by itself. It will emerge not by physical coercion but by "ethics, enlightened self-interest, and commonwealth". He further suggests that a "civilization of mind" is created in cyberspace and the laws (governance) are more human and fairer than the real world of humans (Barrow, 1996). Unlike human civilisation, the norms of digital technologies in cyberspace are impartial, adhering strictly to their programmed design. They function without favouritism or bias, unless influenced or altered by the humans operating the machines.

If the governance (or laws) within cyberspace are analysed through C.E. Shannon's "mathematical theory of communication", they can be understood as the rules established between the transmitter and the receiver to ensure effective and accurate communication. These include the transmission of signals emitted by a transmitter through a channel to a receiver to reach its

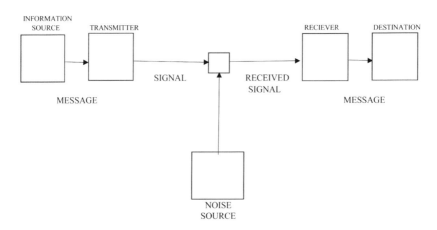

Figure 2.1 Schematic Diagram of a General Communication System.
Source: Shannon, 1948.

destination.[3] A transmitter sends a signal over a channel that is suitable to transmit a message. While the receiver reconstructs the message that emits from the signal, the destination is the device or person that receives the end product. The channel acts as the medium to transmit the signal from a transmitter to a receiver. This process is what cyberspace has created in today's computer system, however, in other contexts (telegram, telephone), they are wires, cables, radio frequencies, microwaves, and beams of light. Cyberspace encompasses activities such as numerical calculations, designing relays, creating electronic filters for communication, translating between computer languages, and making logical deductions (Shannon, 1948). Therefore, the virtual governing system of cyberspace is composed of software programs that serve as rules or laws, enabling interaction between transmitters and receivers across computer devices. In other words, cyberspace is a converging world of binary digits.

Meanwhile, governance in the *social layer* is based on the rules and guidelines introduced by the state government to govern cyber activities in the real world. For instance, the Indian *IT Act 2000*, the *National Cybersecurity Policy 2013*, and other digital safety guidelines (documented and implemented) introduced in the state could be considered as the governing principles of cyberspace implemented in the social and physical world. Similarly, every nation establishes its own distinct policies, laws, and regulations to safeguard and manage its cyber environment.

State Sovereignty and Cyber Power

Sovereignty is an element with the most potential in the state. It is the supreme legitimate power or right exercised by a state government to formulate laws, ensure their enforcement, and make political decisions aimed at achieving national objectives. Sovereignty represents the ultimate authority over its state and territory. The authority is represented by the government, the power of the government is provided by the state's sovereignty, and sovereignty is power sanctioned by the state. By virtue of its sovereign authority, the state controls its citizens' behaviour and penalises offenders through the government (domestic affairs). Similarly, using its sovereign rights, a state acts unilaterally against other states, including in times of peace and conflict (external aspects). The state has the ultimate authority to employ force or violence against other institutes or belligerents. The right to use this legitimate coercion is the exclusive prerogative that the state enjoys in its own rights. The US invasion of Afghanistan (2001) or Iraq (2003) was a sovereign decision taken by the United States, though they were opposed by the other UN member states.

Cyber sovereignty can be discussed from the perspectives of both logical and social layers. The *logical layer* pertains to those capabilities of cyber technologies that are inherent within the electronic medium. This includes the significant role played by artificial neural networks or digital brains, which possess independent-thinking and decision-making abilities. It also encompasses the autonomy of machines or systems to regulate and control their own activities within the electronic domain. While modern drones have increasingly advanced in targeting systems, efforts to enhance their ability to distinguish between military and civilian targets remains a challenging issue. The concept of cyber devices portrayed as challenging human authority (sovereignty) by controlling all man-made electronic systems (IoT) has been dramatised in films like *Eagle Eye*. Although the idea of machines possessing their own sovereign power is not yet a reality, advancements in AI and emerging technology could make such scenarios plausible in the future.

Meanwhile, cyber sovereignty in the *social layer* refers to the digital capabilities exercised by individual states to fulfill their national objectives, encompassing strategic, economic, political, and other dimensions. These digital capabilities or authorities are exercised within a state's territorial boundary. Within their geographical limits, states hold the sovereign power to enforce laws and regulations governing cyberspace, ensuring security and effective management of digital activities while protecting their national interests.

A state has the right to control and protect its own cyber activities and infrastructure against foreign interference. As per the UNGGE Report 2021, and the UN Open Ended Working Group (UNOEWG) Report 2021, the sovereignty of the physical world applies to information and communication technologies (cyberspace) and states have jurisdiction over cyberspace within their territories. Member nations are asked to respect and refrain from taking any measures that would hurt the sovereignty of cyberspace.

States and Digital Behaviour

States operate in cyberspace either independently or collaboratively to advance their national interests by formulating national cyber policies and engaging in international cooperation. States that play a significant role in the international cyber system can generally be classified into three categories: great powers, middle powers, and states of concern. While the role of weak states cannot be ruled out, its role in cyber affairs is minimal. The states of great powers in the cyber realm include the US, China, and Russia and the middle powers are the UK, Canada, and Japan (Julia Voo, 2022). Although relatively small in global power dynamics, digitally advanced countries such as Iran, North Korea (DPRK), and Israel, often classified as states of concern, play a crucial role in global cyber affairs. Fragile or weak countries, including Afghanistan, Myanmar, Somalia, etc., are merely important in international digital security affairs. Meanwhile, multilateral organisations such as the UN, North Atlantic Treaty Organisation (NATO), and South Asian Association for Regional Cooperation (SAARC), are actively involved in international cyber diplomacy. While the important initiatives taken by regional organisations and small powers cannot be ignored, this chapter focuses specifically on the cyber norms and digital behaviour of the great powers, middle powers, and the states of concern.

Therefore, cyber-related elements including internet users (population), networks and space (territory), cyber policies (governance), cyber capabilities, and power (sovereignty) of these powerful nations are worthy of analysis. The International Telecommunication Union (ITU) estimated that 5.5 billion people of the world population (8 billion) used internet in 2024, which is approximately 68 per cent of the global population (ITU, 2024). While the number of users has increased by 3 per cent from the previous year, 2.6 billion people, which is one-third of the global population, survives without internet access. In high-income countries, around 93 per cent of the population has access to the internet, approaching near-universal connectivity. On the contrary, in low-income nations, only 27 per cent of the population is online, highlighting a significant digital divide (Ibid.). Meanwhile, the *Digital Economy Report-2021* released by the United Nations Conference on Trade and Commerce (UNCTAD) suggests that about 80 per cent of the global internet traffic is related to videos, social networking, and gaming. The monthly global data traffic is also likely to increase from 230 exabytes in 2020 to 780 exabytes in 2026.

Table 2.2 highlights the elements of cyberspace for nine key players in the international (cyber) system. While data on the number of internet users is readily accessible, obtaining precise figures on the geographic extent of network coverage across countries is challenging. To address this, network coverage is categorised as follows: "wide" (where over 90 per cent of the population uses the internet), "near wide" (80–90 per cent), "above average" (50–80 per cent), and "nil" for countries lacking publicly available

Table 2.2 Components of Cyberspace

States	Population (percentage of internet users in a country)*	Territory (network coverage area per country seize)	Governance (state behaviour along with their ranks, ITU)	Sovereignty (cyber power ranking of countries)
Great power				
United States	97% (2022)	Wide	Tier 1	1st Rank (HC, HI**)
China	77% (2023)	Above average	Tier 2	2nd Rank (HC, HI)
Russia	92% (2023)	Wide	Tier 2	3rd Rank (HC, HI)
Middle power				
UK	95% (2022)	Wide	Tier 1	4th Rank (HC, HI)
Canada	94% (2022)	Wide	Tier 2	13th Rank (HC, HI)
Japan	85% (2022)	Near wide	Tier 1	16th Rank (HC, LI)
States of concern				
Iran	82% (2022)	Near wide	Tier 3	Rank (NA***) (LC, HI)
Israel	92% (2022)	Wide	Tier 2	19th Rank (HC, LI)
North Korea	Nil	Nil	Tier 5	Rank (NA) (LC, HI)

Source: Compiled by author from various sources.
H = Higher; C = Capability; L = Lower; and I = Intent. * Data based on "Individuals Using the Internet (% of population)", provided by the World Bank Group. ** Method based on the National Cyber Power Index-2020 report released by the Belfer Center for Science and International Affairs (Julia Voo, 2022). *** "Not Available (NA)" indicates an absence of data for ranking certain countries. The National Cyber Power Index-2022 evaluated only 30 nations globally, in which North Korea and Iran are apparently not in it.

data on network coverage. On the governance part, the assessment (good, average, and ordinary) is provided based on the ITU *Global Cybersecurity Index-2024*. The ITU ranks countries based on their commitment and participation in protecting the cyber ecosystem at both national and international levels. This assessment is made based on five pillars: legal framework, technical measures, organisational structures, capacity building, and cooperation initiatives. Countries are categorised into five tiers based on their score: Tier 1 (called the Role Model, scoring at least 95/100), Tier 2 (Advancing, scoring 85/100), Tier 3 (Establishing, scoring 55/100), Tier 4 (Evolving, scoring 20/100), and Tier 5 (Building, scoring below 20/100). Cyber sovereignty, which represents the digital power of states, is evaluated using specific indicators, including their economic and military capabilities. The *National Cyber Power Index-2022* released by the Belfer Center for Science and International Affairs is referred to, to assess the capability of competing nations.

Great Powers

Powerful nations including the United States, China, and Russia are struggling to become a cyber superpower nation. By taking strategic interest in cyberspace, they have been trying to exert their influence on digital affairs at a global scale. They not only want to strengthen their economic, military, and political power by using cyber resources, they also want to intimidate middle and small powers into following their interests in the international cyber system. The following are analyses of these countries referring to cyber elements including internet users, cyber networks, internet governance, and cyber power.

United States

After China and India, the United States is the third-largest country with 298.8 million (2021) internet users (CIA, 2022). According to the ITU record, approximately 90.9 per cent of the US population used the internet in 2020 (ITU, 2022). It was the first country to produce the internet with the early Advanced Research Projects Agency Network project conducted under the authority of the US Department of Defense in the 1960s. Today's global (public) cyber network actually originated from this military project. The United States has the highest number of internet service providers (ISPs) with 7,000 of them (CIA, 2010). Some of the top-level domain names hosted in the US include *.edu*, *.gov*, *.mil*, *.com*, *.net*, and *.org* all launched on 1 January 1985, and *.us* on 15 February 1985. Though challenges remain in rural areas and tribal lands, the US has a large, technologically advanced, multipurpose communications system with reliable internet services. Both at the domestic and international level, it has a wide array of networks implemented through large fibre-optic cables, microwave radio relay, coaxial cables, satellite carriers, etc. The EXA Atlantic submarine cable systems (previously known as the GTT Atlantic system) provides international connectivity to Europe, Africa, the Middle East, Asia, Southeast Asia, Australia, New Zealand, the Pacific, the Atlantic, the Indian Ocean Islands, Central and South America, the Caribbean, Canada and US[4] (CIA, 2022).

Being the founder of cyberspace, US has the best and oldest experience in cyber governance. The cyber-governing system in the US is highly pluralistic concerning both human and technical challenges and involves key stakeholders including business, academics, government, state authorities, defence interests, and privacy protection groups. Cyber policies in the US are implemented by various institutes such as intelligence communities, military services, and departments of homeland security, defence, justice, commerce, energy, and transport. They are coordinated by the National Security Council supervised by the president, and its Principals Committee chaired the National Security Advisor (IISS, 2021). In the civil sector, the White House, Department of Homeland Security, Cybersecurity and Infrastructure Security Agency, and Information Sharing and Analysis Centers, take an active role in governing cyberspace. On the military front, it has a dedicated cyber command (CYBERCOM) under the Department of Defence with defensive and offensive capabilities. It coordinates cyberspace planning and operations to defend and advance national interests by collaborating with domestic and international partners (Cybercom, 2022). It has a series of well-developed strategic documents including the *National Security Strategy of the United States 2017*, *Cyber Strategy of the United States 2018*, and the *Department of Defense Cyber Strategy 2018*.

The US has strong sovereign power over the global cyber system. Though its power has been challenged by other great powers such as China and Russia, it still dominates the cyberworld in terms of digital economy, ICT innovation, data surveillance, and cyber diplomacy. It has organisations such as ICANN that manage the world's internet domains and function under the state's law of California (ICANN, n.d.). In 2019, the digital economy made up 9.6 per cent ($2,051.6 billion) of the current-dollar gross domestic product ($21,433.2 billion) of the US (BEA, 2022). Innovation from Apple, Google, and Microsoft in the US has made history in cyberspace and still shapes its future through investment in research and development (IISS, 2021). The US National Security Agency (NSA) conducted mass surveillance of domestic and foreign internet traffic through various operations including the Planning Tool for Resource Integration, Synchronization, and Management (PRISM). Meanwhile, the US has made several bilateral and multilateral agreements with different countries, and can influence the decision-making process of global cyber policies.

China

China has the highest number internet users in the world with a record 939.8 million users in 2020 (CIA, 2022), which is more than three times the record figure of the US. China has the widest network and heaviest traffic in the cyberworld today. It has maintained a robust governance framework and policy infrastructure since the transformation of its ICT sector in the 1990s and now aspires to lead the global cyberspace by 2030. Intending on becoming a cyber superpower nation, China has a reliable national cybersecurity strategy, along with great influence in global digital diplomacy and cyber politics.

Cyber governance in China is conducted through foreign and domestic digital policies. It mainly focuses on the protection of the spread of Western culture and ideologies through the internet in China and promoting the country's digital safety through collaboration. Though the President of China holds the highest authority in the chain of cyber command across both the civil and military sectors, it has a dedicated institute to deal with cyber affairs. This is supported by independent ministries, alongside a comprehensive framework of policies and laws to regulate and oversee digital operations effectively. The Cyberspace Administration of China, established in 2014, is the national agency responsible for overall internet censorship, regulation, oversight, etc. Meanwhile, the Ministry of Industry and Information Technology, the Ministry of Public Security, and the Ministry of State Security are powerful authorities that control the cyber facilities of the state. China introduced the national *Cyberspace Security Strategy* and *Cybersecurity Law* in 2016 and 2017, respectively, to strengthen the smooth functioning of cyber activities. Various documents, including the *Chinese Military Strategy 2015* and *International Strategy of Cooperation on Cyberspace 2017*, were released to support the digital governing system in the country.

China is expanding its cyber capabilities in both domestic and international systems. Since 2003, it has influenced the UN to give states more sovereign power over cyberspace and reduce US domination in the realm. In 2003, China implemented the *Golden Shield Project,* which is also known as the Great Firewall of China. It is a well organised internal surveillance and censorship program that forbids the use of foreign (US based) applications such as *WhatsApp, Twitter, Facebook*, and *YouTube.* This is how China exercises its sovereign power. Meanwhile, China's interest in military cyber capabilities can be traced back to the 2000s when the (policy of) "Winning Local Wars under Informatised Conditions" was introduced in 2004. This has been substantiated by the release of China's White Paper series in 2010. Chinese interest in cyber strategy began as it perceived threats from the US using cyber support in the 1999 Kosovo military campaign and the 2003 invasion of Iraq. Participating in global cyber affairs since 2002, China has been encouraging the UN to establish international norms for state behaviour in cyberspace. Being a member of the UNGGE, it supports the agreement on international law to be applied to cyberspace. To increase its decision-making capacity, China proposed reforming the UN Internet Governance Forum. In addition to its active participation in international forums, China has entered into bilateral and multilateral agreements with various nations, including India, and even the United States, to promote safety and security in cyberspace.

Russia

Russia is the eighth-largest internet user in the world with 124 million (2021) people accessing it or 84.99 per cent (as of 2020) of the total population of the country. While public access to the internet is high in urban areas, it is lower in the rural areas (CIA, 2022). Russia's governing system is centralised, hierarchical, and under personal presidential control (IISS, 2021). On the diplomatic front, Russia is the first country to propose safety and security measures for the international cyber system at the UN, against the alleged US dominance in the domain. Russia has actively leveraged its sovereign cyber capabilities to conduct offensive operations, which has been particularly evident during its ongoing conflict with Ukraine since 2022. Russia consistently modernises its digital infrastructure and technology to maintain parity with its global competitors.

Like China, Russia's governance on cyberspace focuses mainly on protecting its domestic information infrastructure and preventing the dominance of Western countries, particularly, the US, in global cyber systems. The president of Russia is the highest authority in the chain of command to control the domain. The state governs the domain through various domestic and foreign policies including military strategies, with cooperation from other states and organisations. To address the illegal access of computer information and cyber networks in the country, the *Criminal Code of the Russian Federation* was introduced in 1996. In 2006, Russia implemented *Federal Law N. 149-FZ on Information, Information Technologies, and Information Protection* to regulate the activities of the right to seek, receive, transmit, produce, and disseminate information, and the application of information technologies and ensure the protection of information. The Ministry of Digital Development, Communications, and Mass Media of the Russian Federation, established in 2018, takes overall responsibility to develop and implement national policy and legal regulation on telecommunication and information technology (Ministry of Digital Development, 2022).

Meanwhile, the sovereign power or operational activities in cyberspace are conducted through the state's security council.[5] The Federal Service for Technical and Export Control, established in 2004 under the Ministry of Defence, looks after the safety of critical information infrastructures and defends foreign technology-based operations. Established in 2014, the National Defence Management Centre in Moscow serves as Russia's strategic command force and fusion hub, operating 24/7 to collect data and coordinate communications across all branches of government. Russia has a surveillance mechanism to monitor online activities by using the operational investigative measures system (system for operative investigative activities), which is a set of rules that controls the internet service providers in the country (IISS, 2021, p. 106). At the global level, as a representative of the UNGGE on *Developments in the Field of Information and Telecommunications in the Context of International Security*, Russia actively engages in discussions about state behaviour in cyberspace. It expressed its views as a participant of the Open-ended Working Group on Security of and in the Use of Information and Communications Technologies 2021–2025. On cyber diplomacy, it also maintains bilateral ties with nations including China, India, Japan, Thailand, South Africa, France, and others.

Middle Powers

Middle powers in the digital world order can be defined as nations whose cyber capabilities position them between the great powers and smaller states. It comprises European nations such as the United Kingdom, France, and Germany that once held a position of global power in the world but currently have a diminished status. Additionally, developing nations with strong political, military, and economic systems, such as Argentina, Brazil, Canada, Mexico (continental America), and Japan, Australia, and India (in the Asia Pacific region), can also be placed in this middle power category. Though these states do not compete like the great powers in international cyber politics, they play an important role in the digital development sector. Consequently, in this section, three states, UK, Canada, and Japan, are selected from each continent to study their behaviour in cyberspace. India, often classified as a middle power, can be positioned between the great and middle powers due to its significant economic and military strength. Its cyber capabilities merit a separate, detailed discussion and will be addressed at the end of this chapter.

United Kingdom

The United Kingdom is the 16th-largest internet user (next to Iran) in the world with 65.32 million (2021) users, which is 94.82 per cent (2020) of the country's population (CIA, 2022). While it has one of the largest cyber networks in Europe, the UK is a highly committed country with the top cyber governing system in the world. According to the ITU *Global Cybersecurity Index*,[6] the UK ranked first among all nations in 2018 and subsequently secured the second position in 2020, following the United States (ITU, 2021). The UK has a strong operational (offensive) capability not only in the civil sector, but also in the military system. Meanwhile, the UK plays an influential role in global cyber diplomacy.

The governance of the information system in the UK can be traced back to the early 20th century marked by the establishment of the Government Communication Headquarters (GCHQ) in 1919. Initially formed to ensure the protection of information for the state's public and armed forces, GCHQ has since evolved into a critical organisation for cybersecurity and intelligence in the digital era. The prime minister, along with other key cabinet members, hold the highest position to give directions and make cyber policies. Various state ministries, including home, defence, foreign affairs, and digital/technology, play an active role in ensuring the security and resilience of the UK's digital infrastructure. Some of the notable structures (institutes, bodies, programs, guidelines) involved in governing the UK cyber domain are the Department for Digital, Culture, Media and Sport (DCMS), the Joint Forces Cyber Group, the National Cyber Force, the National Cyber Security Centre, the National Cyber Security Programme, the *National Cyber Security Strategy*, and the National Offensive Cyber Programme. Meanwhile, the

UK introduced legislation such as *The Network and Information Systems Regulations 2018*, *Electronic Communications Act 2000*, and *Computer Misuse Act 1990* to secure critical IT systems, facilitate electronic communication, and protect against the misuse of computers.

In both domestic and international cyber matters, the UK utilises its sovereign capabilities to secure the digital domain independently or in collaboration with other nations. It has a national military doctrine that is used to deter and take offensive measures against terrorists, criminals, and other foreign or domestic threats. The Ministry of Defence and GCHQ take a lead role in offensive efforts related to cybersecurity. In global cyber participation, the UK not only takes an active role in UNGGE initiatives, but it also leads in other forums such as the Commonwealth on cybersecurity related issues. The UK is a signatory of the Budapest Convention, an international treaty involving 65 countries that serves as a coordination forum to combat cybercrime. The UK maintains bilateral and multilateral cyber cooperation agreements with countries including Singapore, Saudi Arabia, Poland, Italy, Japan, Australia, France, China, India, and the US.

Canada

Canada is a cyber middle power nation (IISS, 2021, p. 39). Though its digital capabilities are low compared to countries such as the US or UK, its intent to become a digitised global player is high (Julia Voo, 2022, p. 13). It has 36.89 million (2021) internet users, which is 96.5 per cent (2022) of the total population of the state. Canada governs its domestic and foreign cyber systems through national strategic policies, government institutes, legislation, and cooperation with other countries. Its sovereign power over cyber affairs is notably reinforced by its military offensive capabilities. Some of the notable cyber support systems in the state include the Canadian Armed Forces (CAF), Department of National Defence, Communication Security Establishment (CSE), Canada Security Intelligence Service, and Defence Chief Information Officer.

The head or command of the Canadian cyber structures flows from the prime minister of the state, who supervises the duties of Canada's key positions, including the Minister of Public Safety and Emergency Preparedness, Minister of National Defence, and Minister of Foreign Affairs. Canada regulates its cyberspace through various legislative measures, including the *Criminal Code of 1985*, which was amended in 2017 to address issues related to unauthorised access to computer data and digital services. Section 342.1 talks about fraudulently obtaining any computer services in direct or indirect form, section 342.2 addresses the unauthorised use of computer systems or mischievous activity conducted through devices, and section 430.1.1 discusses the protection of computer data (Justice, Criminal Code 1985, 2017). Meanwhile, the federal law, *Personal Information Protection and Electronic Documents Act (PIPEDA)-2000*, which was amended in 2015, directs organisations to protect, secure, and safeguard private data in the cyber domain. It will "support and promote electronic commerce by protecting personal information that is collected, used, or disclosed in certain circumstances by providing for the use of electronic means to communicate or record information or transactions" (Justice, Personal Information Protection and Electronic Documents Act, 2000).

Canadian sovereignty over cyberspace is mostly the responsibility of the national armed forces and strategic documents such as *Strong, Secure, and Engaged: Canada's Defence Policy* (2017) of the National Defence Ministry. The document addresses the fact that the most sophisticated cyber threats came from the intelligence and military services of foreign nations. It further explains that potential enemies, including non-state actors and proxies, exploit the Canadian military system "command, control, communications, computers, intelligence, surveillance, and reconnaissance" (Canadian Armed Forces, 2017). Accordingly, it develops offensive capabilities to maintain a secure and resilient cyber ecosystem for the country. It also embraces cooperation and agreements with different nations and foreign institutes to protect its critical infrastructures and develop research innovations in the areas of AI, IoT, and quantum computing. Not only is Canada a party to the Budapest Convention, but it also participates in the UNGGE on global cybersecurity initiative. As a member of NATO, Canada maintains close ties to strengthen its cyber capabilities with fellow members and other countries including the US and India.

Japan

Japan is one of the global leaders in the digital commercial sector, though its application in the security sector began only a few years ago. It has 117.4 million internet users, which is 83 per cent (2021) of the total population. Japan governs its cyberspace in multiple ways by implementing legislation, setting up civil and military institutions, conducting cyber diplomacy, and maintaining bi and multilateral cooperation. Its sovereign power in the cyber domain (offensive capabilities) is being developed through support from its allies, such as the US and UK. To manage the state's cyber-related affairs, several strategy documents and organisations have been periodically established. While some of the fundamental aspects of Japan's cyberspace regulation are covered in here, further details on the cybersecurity of Japan are covered separately Chapter 3.

As a means of regulating cyberspace and safeguarding its digital environment, the National Diet of Japan (National Assembly of Japan) first enacted the *Act on Prohibition of Unauthorized Computer Access* in 1999 and amended later in 2013. The purpose of the act was to officially define the illegal use of computer facilities, outline the functionalities of local and national government agencies in the cybersphere, maintain communication sector lawfulness and stop computer-related crimes committed through digital networks, prohibit unauthorised use of computers, and explain criminal liabilities for unauthorised access to digital networks (Japan, 2013). Additionally, the *Common Model of Information Security Measures for Government Agencies* was published by the Japanese Government in 2016 and revised in 2018 to implement a common framework on information security policies by Japan's administrative bodies (NISC, 2018). Agencies including the National Center of Incident Readiness and Strategy for Cybersecurity, Cybersecurity Strategic Headquarters, Information Security Policy Council (ISPC), Information-Technology Promotion Agency (IPA), National Institute of Information and Communications Technology, and Japan Computer Emergency Response Team Coordination Center (JPCERT/CC) are responsible for addressing the safety and security of the cyber ecosystem in Japan. Meanwhile, central positions, including the Ambassador in Charge of Cyber Policy and Deputy Assistant Minister for Cyber Security and Information Technology Management in the Ministry of Foreign Affairs, take active roles in cyber diplomacy.

Japan does not have a separate cyberwar doctrine on cyber sovereignty, however, Chapter 3 of the *Defence of Japan 2020* (Annual White Paper) addresses how to respond to cyber threats and attacks. The Cyber Defence Group, which was formerly known as the Cyber Defence Unit, was created in 2013 to safeguard the defence information infrastructure. Military institutes including the Defense Intelligence Headquarters and Directorate for Signals Intelligence support the cyber offensive aspect of the state. At the global level, Japan actively participates in the UNGGE and, as one of its core members, closely cooperates with the G7 Cyber Expert Group. To promote international cooperation on cybersecurity, the ISPC established the *International Strategy on Cybersecurity Cooperation* in 2013. It also has bilateral relationships with nations including Vietnam, Singapore, the United Kingdom, India, South Korea, China, Australia, and France. It is a party to the Budapest Convention as well.

States of Concern

Despite their relatively smaller economies or military capabilities, states like Iran, North Korea, and Israel—although Israel is notably more robust—are highly competitive in cyberspace and possess significant cyber capabilities that make them a concern for global security. Based on their strategic interests, they choose cyberspace as a battleground to challenge their enduring rivals. Because they are comparatively weak to physically fight their powerful enemies, they seek to balance power by challenging them through cyberspace. In cyber conflict, it is easy to obscure the attackers' identity (unattributable), it is cheap (economical), the effect of network attacks is cascading (high impact), and the advantage of cyber weapons is overhauled (quick recovery). Cyberspace could be a strategic domain where the power of equilibrium can be maintained between weak and great powers. Weaker nations can challenge great powers in the digital domain.

Iran

After suffering the worst effects of the Stuxnet strike in 2010, Iran's policy on cyberspace is mostly oriented towards defending against digital rivalry from the US and Sunni Arab countries. Iran has 69.52 million internet users in the country (2021), which is 79 per cent of the total population (2021). While the area of network coverage is expected to be high, except in a few interior rural areas, its cyber governance is done through various stakeholders involving the military and civil sectors. Its sovereign capability (offensive) in cyberwarfare is relatively high and is built on a well-developed foundation, though it lacks technical sophistication. Nonetheless, Iran is one of the top leading countries in selective areas of scientific research, including AI (IISS, 2021, pp. 118–120).

In the chain of cyber command, the Supreme Council for Cyberspace (SCC), led by the Iranian president, holds the highest authority. Established in 2012, the SCC has the power to make decisions on national digital internet policy. The governance of cyberspace is supported by legal frameworks such as the *Computer Misuse and Cybercrime Act 2003* (Act No. 22 of 2003), the *Computer Crimes Act or Law No. 71063 2009*, and the *Declaration of General Staff of the Armed Forces of the Islamic Republic of Iran Regarding International Law Applicable to the Cyberspace 2020*. These three laws deal with cybercrime, data confidentiality, and guidelines related to the cyber military forces of Iran. Including the SCC, other civil government organisations such as the Ministry of ICT, the Iran Information Technology Organisation, and the National Cyberspace Centre (proposed to be established under the SCC), were set up to manage the functioning of cyber-related affairs in the country. Meanwhile, to prevent illegal cyber activities or domestic cybercrime within the country, the Cyber Police of the Islamic Republic of Iran (FETA) was established in 2011.

To defend sovereignty and promote national cyber goals, a Cyber Defence Command was established under the Passive Civil Defence Organization, Joint Staff of the Iranian Armed Forces, in 2010. Along with the Islamic Revolutionary Guard Corps-Intelligence Organisation, the Cyber Defence Command in Iran has been involved in carrying out offensive cyber operations against adversary states. The Ministry of Intelligence and Security, which oversees signal intelligence, is also involved in cyber defence activities. On the digital diplomatic front, Iran actively participates in multilateral and bilateral digital cooperation. It provided its perspective on how international law may be applied to the UN Secretary-General Annual Report on "Developments in the Field of Information and Telecommunications in the Context of International Security" in 2013 (UNGA, 2013, p. 11). Iran participated in the UNOEWG on "Developments in the Field of Information and Telecommunications in the Context of International Security" (2019–2021). Iran discussed and made agreements on cyber affairs with countries including Russia, South Africa, Thailand, Armenia, and Uganda.

Israel

Though geographically small, Israel is one of the most technologically advanced nations that recognised cyberspace as a tool or domain of warfare. As a cyber-potential nation, it has been using cyberspace for military purposes. Despite having lower cyber capabilities compared to superpowers such as the US or China, its intention is high in achieving strategic goals through the cyber domain (Julia Voo, 2020). Israel's focus is on the supremacy of the digital network in the West Asian region, even if it intends to compete at the global rank. According to the ITU *Cybersecurity Index 2021*, Israel ranks 36th, scoring 91/100. It had 7.68 million internet users in 2021 (CIA World Factbook report). Like other countries, Israel governs its cyberspace through legal frameworks, digital policies, and bi and multilateral cooperation. Based on the disturbing geopolitical dynamics in the region, it exploits its sovereign cyberspace capacity to carry out offensive actions against its rivals.

Israel is a technologically advanced nation that adopted *Computers Law* as early as 1995 to protect against computer crimes. Other legal guidelines include *Resolution 3611 on Advancing National Cyberspace Capabilities 2001*, *Government Resolution No. 2443 2015*, and *Resolution 2444 on Advancing the National Preparedness for Cybersecurity 2015* to secure and safeguard the cyber environment of the state. Additionally, many government organisations periodically release strategic documents on cybersecurity, notable ones include *Resolution No. 3611 2011*, *Israel National Cybersecurity Strategy 2017*, and *Resolution No. 3270 2017*. Key advisory bodies such as the National Cyber Bureau and National Cyber Security Authority under the prime minister's office and chief positions such as the Head of National Cyber Defence Authority were set up to play a significant role in cyber governance. The Israel National Cyber Directorate, Knesset Subcommittee for Cyber Defense, and Department of Emergency, Information Security and Cyber, and State Attorney's Office support the system in civil cyber affairs and prosecution of cyber criminals. It also maintains cyber cooperation with states including Australia, Armenia, Germany, and the US.

The sovereignty of Israel's cyberspace, or the protection of digital threats from foreign elements, is largely the responsibility of the Israeli Defence Forces (IDF). It developed the *IDF Strategy* in 2017 to protect against cyber threats, promote global leadership in technological innovation, and actively participate in international digital initiatives (PMO, 2017). It will strengthen its cyber capabilities apposite to its existing air, naval, and intelligence superiority. Improving its cyberwar capabilities, the IDF will collect information and conduct operations through cyberspace. The military will prepare and be ready to act against any challenge in cyberspace by increasing its proficiencies, ability to function under cyberattacks, and intensified strategic deterrence capability. The *IDF Strategy* gives permission for the establishment of a powerful cyber army for the Israeli military force (IDF, 2016).

North Korea

Because it is a closed society, information on ICT-related reports or cyber policies of North Korea are not easily available in the public domain. Although the number of internet users is unknown, it is known that only a very small number of families, who are trusted members of the ruling elite or government officials, are allowed to access global internet facilities (Insikit Group, 2020). Otherwise, DPRK has a separate intranet service known as *Kwangmyong*. It is estimated that about 3–5 million devices are connected to internal mobile networks via the *Kwangmyong* service (IISS, 2021, p. 125). While the country has low sovereign (cyber) power or capabilities, it has high intentions to achieve its national objectives through cyber means. It is the most secretive country and the least transparent in even sharing general information on military and intelligence matters (Julia Voo, 2022). North Koreans use the internet for governance or revenue generation but also exploit it to collect information on technical knowledge and skill on prohibited nuclear and ballistic missile programs. It uses internet services for other key operations including banking activities, cryptocurrencies, and financial crime (Insikit Group, 2020).

Cyber governance in the DPRK is not clear, as no formal structure is revealed in the open sources. However, control of the digital system (civil/military) is maintained by the armed forces under the direction of the Korean Workers' Party, headed by the supreme leader Kim Jong Un. As the Chairman of the National Defence Commission, and by using his sovereign power, he directs the Reconnaissance General Bureau (RGB) to conduct cyber offensive operations. RGB, also known as Unit 586, is the main intelligence organisation, established in 2009 under the General Staff (of the armed forces). Other cyber operational units include Unit/Bureau 121 (Cyber Warfare Guidance Unit), Unit 91, Unit 180, and Lab 110. Unit 121 of DPRK focuses on cyber intrusions targeting enemy digital systems, while Unit 91 is dedicated to safeguarding national critical infrastructure, including nuclear and weapons-related technologies. Unit 180 specialises in financially motivated cyberattacks. Lab 110 conducts similar operations to Unit 121 and also contains subunits like Office 98 (monitoring defectors), Office 414 (supporting espionage for China), and Office 35 (developing malware and cyber weapons) (IISS, 2021, p. 127).

The DPRK is a member of the ITU and UN, and hence can share the platform of international forums, including the World Summit on the Information Society, however, its participation is minimal. Based on the ITU survey and responses given or ignored by the member states, the ITU ranks North Korea as last (181st position) in the *Global Cybersecurity Index 2020*. Nonetheless, it always votes along with China and Russia in the UN General Assembly on annual resolutions on cyberspace issues. Against the will of the West, DPRK in 2018 voted to support a UN resolution to establish the UNOEWG on international security aspects of ICT developments, backed by Russia and

China. It first convened in 2019, and all member states, including the DPRK, were invited to participate (UNOEWG, 2022).

India and Cyberspace

In the preamble to India's *National Cyber Security Policy-2013*, cyberspace is defined as "a complex environment consisting of interactions between people, software, and services, supported by worldwide distribution of ICT devices and networks". India, as an emerging nation, seeks to assert itself as a regional cyber power in South Asia and expand its influence globally. Given its geopolitical concerns and aspirations, India is working towards strengthening its cyber capabilities to enhance national security, economic growth, and political standing on the international stage. Meanwhile, threats from the neighbourhood, such as China and Pakistan, are a source of strategic anxieties for the state. India's approach to cyberspace is multifaceted, addressing both civil (business and cooperation) and military (conflict and war) dimensions. This dual approach reflects the complexity of cyberspace, with India balancing liberal perspectives on international cooperation and economic growth with the realist perspective of ensuring national power and strategic interests. This comprehensive approach enables India to navigate challenges and opportunities in cyberspace, balancing economic growth and enhancing power through digital means. India governs and controls its cyber ecosystem by structuring various policies at internal (domestic) and external (foreign) levels. India's approach to elements of cyberspace are discussed in the next section.

India's Perspective on Cyberspace

According to Indian records, cyberspace has been recognised as a medium connected to economic development, social transformation, global communications, institutional cooperation, strategic achievements, military warfare, as well as criminal activities. It also indicates that India's approach to cyberspace as a state behaviour is realistic and liberal. As a liberal, it believes cyberspace is a domain where people/states cooperate and get benefits from each other to avoid conflict and differences. Being a realist, it considers the digital system as a realm to accumulate power, where states, as the main actors, act selfishly and achieve goals by intimidating others. Before discussing the elements of Indian cyberspace, it is worth discussing how the country manages cyberspace at the domestic and global level along with civil (non-strategic) and military (strategic) approaches.

Domestic Dimension

India's concerns in cyberspace span across several key domestic sectors: the political sector (cyber politics), the economic sector (cyber economy), and the societal sector (social connectivity). These sectors represent the interplay between cyberspace and national governance, economic development, and social relations influencing India's approach to digital sovereignty, security, and growth. Cyberspace plays a crucial role in the domestic politics of nation-states, as it assists nations (governments) in encouraging nationalism by sharing ideals and beliefs with the citizens. While political parties utilise the internet to attract voters, it also helps in maintaining political stability in the state. At the same time, it has the potential to disturb the integrity of the nation by sharing negative feelings among people. The serial anti-government demonstrations of the Arab Spring (2011) were a prime example of how the internet was essential to a regime change or political disorder. Even in India, the role of cyberspace (as a medium of social interaction) in public demonstration against the Citizen (Amendment) Act was observed in 2019.

The Indian economy is greatly influenced by the IT sector. The IT industry has improved since the beginning of the *Digital India* program initiated in 2015 and contributed 8 per cent of India's Gross Domestic Product (GDP) in 2020. The e-commerce sector has also grown from US $25 billion in 2017 to $52 billion in 2022. Next to China, India has the second-highest internet connectivity in the world with 1.37 billion users, which is 47 per cent of the total Indian population in 2021 (Basuroy, 2022). Most of them are active on social media platforms such as *YouTube, Facebook, WhatsApp, Instagram, Facebook Messenger, Twitter, LinkedIn, and Telegram*. Though they help in external communications, domestic interactions are considerably high in India. Meanwhile, to control irregularities in these cyber-connected sectors (political, economic, and societal), various policies and guidelines, including the *National Cybersecurity Policy 2013, IT Rule 2000*, and *IT (Amendment) Act 2008* were implemented in India.

Global Dimension

India intends to play a larger role in the cyber world order. Its global leadership relies on the improvement of the digital economy (economic sector), cyber diplomacy (political sector), and cyber power (military sector), which are India's primary concerns. As there is no widely accepted definition of digital economy, the UN faces difficulty in measuring the exact digital economy of the world. However, the *UNCTAD Report 2019* revealed that, depending on the definition and estimates, the digital economy contributes 4.5 to 15.5 per cent to the world GDP. While the exact figure of India's contribution is not disclosed, the report suggests that India shares the highest digital economy among developing countries. The US and China share 40 per cent of the global digital economy.

India believes cyber diplomacy is a part of foreign policy. Cyber diplomacy, in simple terms, can be understood as the use of the internet and information communications technology to carry out diplomatic objectives

(Sotiriu, 2015). To achieve a larger role in global leadership, India has been an active member of the UNGGE since 2004. This group studies threats and behaviour of states over cyberspace (ICT) to maintain a safer digital environment. It is also closely associated with the UN Open-Ended Working Group. Meanwhile, India also conducts bilateral and multilateral engagements with various countries on ICT-related issues. From a military aspect, India sees cyberspace as a domain in which to accumulate national power. It considers cyberspace as the fifth domain of warfare after land, sea, air, and space. While India is in the process of developing a dedicated national cybersecurity strategy, its existing military doctrines address aspects of cyberwarfare. The current *Indian Army Doctrine 2004*, *Basic Doctrine of the Indian Air Force 2012*, *Joint Training Doctrine: Indian Armed Forces 2017*, and *Land Warfare Doctrine (2018)* highlight or touch upon India's preparedness for cyberwarfare and protection of digital networks. On 18 June 2024, the Indian Armed Forces released the *Joint Doctrine for Cyberspace Operations*, a military document that focuses on the operational aspects of both offensive and defensive digital activities. While it has not yet been made public, media reports suggest that the doctrine outlines the strategic framework for managing and executing cyberwarfare (MoD, 2024). A military cyber command called the Defence Cyber Agency (DCA) was created in 2018 as a central force to command and manage cyber threats, particularly against external aggression.

India's Elements of Cyberspace

India's approach to cyberspace reflects its unique position in the global system, with distinct components. Key elements of India's cyberspace include its cyber territory, population, governance, and sovereignty, each contributing to its role in the digital domain.

Cyber Territory

Through its *Digital India* programme, India is in the process of digitisation to transform the country into a "digitally empowered society and knowledge economy" (MeitY, 2022). Geographically, India aims to develop the largest digital infrastructure (internet) to connect all the 250,000 Gram Panchayats[7] of the country with fibre-optical cables. In 2020, 151,000 lakh of them have been connected. To support e-governance and provide other e-facilities to rural areas and common citizens, 370,000 Common Service Centres (CSC) have been set up in India. Meanwhile, e-Hospital, Bharat Interface for Money-Unified Payments Interface (BHIM-UPI), online scholarships, DigiLocker, e-Courts, Tele Law, and e-Way Bills are digital services made widely available to every section of society in India to improve the living standards of the public (MeitY Annual Report 2020–2021).

Cyber Population

According to a report released by the Telecom Regulatory Authority of India, the Indian population able to access cyberspace (internet) is 757.61 million as of January 2021 (TRAI, 2021), which is 53.82 per cent of the total population of 1407.6 million. Next to China, it is the second-largest internet user in the world. It has the highest mobile data consumption rate in the world, with 12 gigabytes (GB) per user in a month (Abbas, 2021). According to the Kantar[8] report, *Internet Adoption in India (Internet and Mobile Association of India, 2020)*, in India there are 622 million (43 per cent) internet users as of September 2020 and this is expected to reach 900 million by the year 2025. It further suggests that while India has an urban population of 485 million, 323 million (67 per cent) of them use the internet at least once or more in a month. Out of the rural population of 948 million, 299 million (31 per cent) of them access the internet. Though the number of urban users is high, rural usership is growing fast at high speed. While the number of urban users increases at the rate of four per cent in a year (2019–2020), the number of rural users is growing at 13 per cent.

Internet Adoption in India further reveals that the gap between male and female (gender divide) internet users in India is almost negligible. While 58 per cent of males access it, the remaining per cent are female users. For urban areas, 57 per cent males and 43 per cent females access cyberspace facilities. Similarly, 58 per cent of males in rural areas use the internet, the remaining per cent are female users. The main activities conducted on the internet are mostly for entertainment purposes, such as watching videos, listening to music, and playing games (96 per cent of users). This is followed by communication (text, voice, and video chats, emailing, 90 per cent), social media (82 per cent), net commerce or online transactions (45 per cent), and online shopping (28 per cent).

Cyber Governance

India governs cyberspace broadly in two ways, civil (non-strategic) and military (strategic), with internal and external dimensions. It has multiple central ministries, state departments, and independent institutes to look after the technological (machine-related) and non-technological (human-related, or cyber-enabled criminal activities) aspects of cyberspace. On civil matters or non-strategic affairs, the Ministry of Electronics and Information Technology (MeitY) and Ministry of Communication (MoC) provide central policies and guidelines to maintain a secure cyber ecosystem. Meanwhile, the Ministry of Home Affairs (with its Cyber and Information Security Division, C&IS), and the law enforcement agencies take responsibility for internal matters to protect civil affairs or domestic crimes over cyberspace. The Central Bureau of Investigation, or CBI (which is an Indian nodal point for International Police, or Interpol) takes charge of those cybercrimes linked to external (foreign) elements. The Ministry of Finance is responsible for looking after online financial irregularities and the Ministry of Science and Technology (MS&T) is actively involved in digital research and innovation.

On the strategic front, the National Security Council (NSC), under the prime minister, plans cybersecurity strategies based on national threat perspectives. The National Cybersecurity Coordinator, functioning under the National Security Advisor (NSA), coordinates all the cybersecurity related matters, both strategic and non-strategic, of the country. He also heads the National Cyber Coordination Centre functioning under MeitY. The Ministry of Defence (MoD) oversees India's cyber defence efforts along with the DCA. Additionally, the National Technical Research Organisation, through its cyber defence wing, and the National Critical Information Infrastructure Protection Centre handle responsibilities related to safeguarding critical infrastructure and addressing external cyber threats, including offensive and defensive operations. Meanwhile, India has a dedicated Cyber Diplomacy Division, and the New Emerging and Strategic Technologies (NE&ST) Division under the Ministry of External Affairs to carry out diplomacy in international cyber strategic affairs.

Cyber Sovereignty

Given the threats India perceives from its neighbouring states, such as China and Pakistan, it intends to become a cyber power nation, if not for cyber supremacy but for digital stability in the region. *The Joint Training Doctrine Indian Armed Forces 2017* defines cyber power as the ability to operate in cyberspace to gain and take advantage of an adversary while denying the same to the adversary in an operational environment by applying the instruments of national power. The Indian Armed Forces aim to develop a comprehensive cyber force capable of effectively engaging in cyberwarfare and achieving dominance in network-centric operations. The recent release of the *Joint Doctrine for Cyberspace Operations 2024* marks a significant effort in advancing this objective by providing a unified framework to enhance both offensive and defensive cyber capabilities. While it has defensive mechanisms to protect its cyber territory, India has the capability of offensive strikes. The 2017 doctrine also addresses how India is to maintain a minimum credible cyber deterrence to protect against digital war through strategic and conventional means. Meanwhile, the DCA is the dedicated force for India to command and control any cyberwar affairs. The agency, now functioning at the command level, functions along with the tri-services of the army, navy, and air force. This command integrates with other forces, including aerospace and special forces, to protect cyberspace with strategic efforts.

In the cyber world order, India intends to augment its geopolitical influence and bring global governance to cyberspace within the rules-based international system. It actively participates and contributes to the formation of international norms on cyberspace. India, as a participant in the UNGGE,

UNOEWG, and the Ad Hoc Committee on cybercrime, actively promotes the establishment of international standards for responsible state behaviour in cyberspace. Through both bilateral and multilateral engagements, it encourages global cooperation to develop frameworks that ensure the security and stability of the digital domain. While the US is a close associate in this field, other partners include the UK, Japan, Brazil, Russia, Canada, China, France, Germany, Ireland, Egypt, Estonia, Jordan, Malaysia, Portugal, Qatar, Serbia, Singapore, South Korea, South Africa, Vietnam, and Tanzania (MeitY, 2019). To protect its digital interests, India engaged in multilateral forums such as the World Trade Organisation, G20, Regional Comprehensive Economic Partnership, Commonwealth, SAARC, Association of Southeast Asian Nations, World Bank, and Asian Development Bank.

Conclusion

While the state and cyberspace have distinct origins, the latter is a creation of the former, emerging as a result of advancements in technology. They are not separable from each other, as states require it for both civil and military affairs. As states have population, territory, government, and sovereignty, cyberspace has its own space for its activities, data that survives or travels in the space, programmes or logic that make the data interact, and the ability to make decisions (algorithms or AI applications), though with the support of humans. Based on their national interests and capability, great or small, every country would like to play a major role in cyberspace. By leveraging the inherently anarchic nature of cyberspace, states strategically accumulate power through digital means to advance their national interests, enhance security, and assert influence in the international system. At the same time, vulnerabilities in cyberspace are likely to be enlarged as new technologies continue to evolve.

Regarding India, persistent "physical" threats linked to "virtual" attacks, particularly from neighbouring countries like Pakistan and China, have prompted the nation to enhance its digital capabilities and strengthen its cybersecurity infrastructure. It intends not only to compete with or challenge its neighbours, but to establish itself as a significant cyber power on the global stage. By strengthening its digital capabilities, India seeks to play a larger and more influential role in shaping international cyber dynamics. Though a dedicated national document on Indian cyber strategy is yet to be released, the existing military doctrine addresses its desire to protect its digital ecosystem by addressing deterrence mechanisms and conducting strategic operations whenever necessary.

Notes

1 Though there is no universal definition of "states", and they have varied from ancient (Aristotle) to modern (Woodrow Wilson) times, it can simply be under-

stood as a populated defined territory functioning under a government having sovereign power.
2 It is one of the most popular essays on the theory of cyberspace that scholars refer to in their writing. It has 213 citations as of 13 January 2021 while searching with the title "Declaration of the Independence of Cyberspace" in the *Google Scholar* search engine.
3 See the schematic diagram of a general communication system in *A Mathematical Theory of Communication*, by C.E. Shannon (Shannon, 1948).
4 "EXA Atlantic (formerly GTT Atlantic, Hibernia Atlantic) is a 12,200 km private transatlantic submarine cable system in the North Atlantic Ocean, connecting Canada, the United States, Ireland and the United Kingdom" (Network, n.d.).
5 Under the *Information Security Doctrine* of 2016, the Security Council is mandated to provide annual reports on the state of cybersecurity affairs to the country president.
6 The rank of the countries' cybersecurity approach or development is prepared based on five pillars such as (i) legal measures, (ii) technical measures, (iii) organisational measures, (iv) capacity development, and (v) cooperation (ITU, 2022).
7 *Gram Panchayat* is a local self-government organisation of the *Panchayati Raj* system practised in India, at the village or small town level, headed by a *Sarpanch*.
8 Kantar is the world's leading agency that provides insights and actionable recommendations on data (IT) related issues (www.kantar.com).

References

Abbas, M. (2021, October 26). *India's growing data usage, smartphone adoption to boost Digital India initiatives: Top bureaucrat Read more.* https://economictimes.indiatimes.com/news/india/indias-growing-data-usage-smartphone-adoption-to-boost-digital-india-initiatives-top-bureauc. Retrieved March 29, 2022, from https://economictimes.indiatimes.com/news/india/indias-growing-data-usage-smartphone-adoption-to-boost-digital-india-initiatives-top-bureaucrat/articleshow/87275402.cms?from=mdr

Barlow, J. P. (1990, June 8). *Crime and puzzlement.* Retrieved January 12, 2022, from https://www.eff.org/pages/crime-and-puzzlement

Barrow, J. P. (1996, February 8). *A declaration of the independence of cyberspace.* Retrieved January 13, 2022, from https://www.eff.org/cyberspace-independence

Basuroy, T. (2022, June 9). Internet penetration rate in India 2007–2021. Retrieved January 28, 2023, from https://www.statista.com/statistics/792074/india-internet-penetration-rate/

BEA. (2022, January 07). *Digital economy, bureau of economic analysis, US department of commerce.* Retrieved February 11, 2022, from https://www.bea.gov/data/special-topics/digital-economy

Buzan, B. (1983). *People, states, and fear: The national security problem in international relations.* Brighton: John Spiers.

Canadian Armed Forces. (2017). *Strong, secured, engaged: Canada's defence policy.* Retrieved June 08, 2022, from http://dgpaapp.forces.gc.ca/en/canada-defence-policy/docs/canada-defence-policy-report.pdf

CIA. (2022). *The world fact book: Russia.* Retrieved February 9, 2022, from https://www.cia.gov/the-world-factbook/countries/russia/#communications

CIA. (2022). *The world fact book: United Kingdom.* Retrieved February 21, 2022, from https://www.cia.gov/the-world-factbook/countries/united-kingdom/#communications

CIA. (2022). *The world fact book: United States*. Retrieved February 2022, 9, from https://www.cia.gov/the-world-factbook/countries/united-states /

CIA. (2022). *United States: Communication*. Retrieved February 9, 2022, from https://www.cia.gov/the-world-factbook/countries/united-states /#communications

Cybercom, U. (2022). *U.S. Cyber command*. Retrieved February 10, 2022, from https://www.cybercom.mil/About/Mission-and-Vision/

Fishman, C. (2019, June 18). The most expensive hyphen in history. *Fast Company*. Retrieved from https://www.fastcompany.com/90365077/the-most-expensive-hyphen-in-history

Garner, J. W. (1928). *Political science and government*. New York: American Book Co.

Group, I. (2020). *How North Korea revolutionized the internet as a tool for rogue regimes*. Insikit Group.

ICANN. (2022). *Internet corporation for assigned names and numbers*. Retrieved June 17, 2022, from http://archive.icann.org/tr/english.html

ICANN. (n.d.). *What does ICANN do?* Retrieved February 11, 2022, from https://www.icann.org/resources/pages/what-2012-02-25-en

ICUBE. 2020. Internet in India. IAMAI. https://www.iamai.in/sites/default/files/research/IAMAI-KANTAR-ICUBE-2020-Report.pdf

IDF. (2016, July). *The IDF strategy*. Retrieved June 08, 2022, from https://www.inss.org.il/he/wp-content/uploads/sites/2/2017/04/IDF-Strategy.pdf

IISS. (2021). *Cyber capabilities and national power: A net assessment*. London: IISS.

Internet Service Providers (ISPs) - The World Factbook - CIA. (2010). Retrieved February 9, 2022, from https://www.nationsencyclopedia.com/WorldStats/CIA-Internet-Service-Providers-ISPs.html

ITU. (2021). *Global cybersecurity index 2020*. Retrieved February 22, 2022, from https://www.itu.int/dms_pub/itu-d/opb/str/D-STR-GCI.01-2021-PDF-E.pdf

ITU. (2022). *Measuring digital development: Facts and figures 2021*. Retrieved February 08, 2022, from https://www.itu.int/en/ITU-D/Statistics/Pages/facts/default.aspx

ITU. (2022). *Statistics (country data: Percentage of individuals using the internet)*. Retrieved February 8, 2022, from https://www.itu.int/en/ITU-D/Statistics/Pages/stat/default.aspx

ITU. (2024). *Global cybersecurity index 2004*. Retrieved December 14, 2024, from https://www.itu.int/en/ITU-D/Cybersecurity/Documents/GCIv5/2401416_1b_Global-Cybersecurity-Index-E.pdf

ITU. (2024). *Measuring digital development: Facts and figures 2024*. Retrieved December 13, 2024, from https://www.itu.int/itu-d/reports/statistics/2024/11/10/ff24-internet-use/

Japanese Law Translation (2013). *Act on prohibition of unauthorized computer access (tentative translation)*. Retrieved June 20, 2022, from https://www.npa.go.jp/cyber/english/legislation/uca_Tentative.pdf

Julia Voo, I. H. (2022). *National cyber power index 2022*. Cambridge: Harvard Kennedy School.

Justice Laws Website. (2000, April 13). *Personal information protection and electronic documents act*. Retrieved June 08, 2022, from https://laws-lois.justice.gc.ca/eng/acts/P-8.6/page-1.html#h-416931

Justice Laws Website. (2017). *Criminal code 1985*. Retrieved June 7, 2022, from https://laws-lois.justice.gc.ca/eng/acts/C-46/

MeitY. (2019, November 14). *Active MoUs*. Ministry of Electronics & Information Technology. Retrieved from https://www.meity.gov.in/content/active-mous

MeitY. (2022). *Digital India*. Retrieved March 20, 2022, from https://www.digitalindia.gov.in/content/introduction

Ministry of Digital Development. (2022). *General information.* Retrieved February 18, 2022, from https://digital.gov.ru/en/ministry/common/

MoD. (2024, June 18). *CDS Gen Anil Chauhan releases joint doctrine for cyberspace operations.* Press Information Bureau, Government of India. Retrieved from https://pib.gov.in/indexd.aspx?reg=3&lang=1

Network, S. C. (n.d.). *EXA Atlantic.* Retrieved February 9, 2022, from https://www.submarinenetworks.com/systems/trans-atlantic/hibernia-atlantic

NISC. (2018, July 25). *Common model of information security measures for government agencies and related agencies.* Retrieved June 2022, from https://www.nisc.go.jp/eng/pdf/kihan30-en.pdf

PMO. (2017). *Israel national cyber security strategy in brief.* Prime Minister's Office, Government of Israel. Jerusalem.

Shannon, C. (1948, July). A mathematical theory of communication. *The Bell System Technical Journal, 27,* 379–423.

Sotiriu, S. (2015). Digital diplomacy: Between promises and reality. In M. H. Corneliu Bjola (Ed.), *Digital diplomacy: Theory and practices* (pp. 33–51). New York: Routledge.

Spykman, N. J. (1942). *America's strategy in world politics.* New York: Harcourt, Brace and Company, Inc.

Sterling, M. B. (1992). *The hacker crackdown: Law and disorder on the electronic frontier.* New York: Bantam Books.

TRAI. (2021, March 17). *Telecom regulatory authority of India.* Highlights of Telecom Subscription Data. Retrieved January 31, 2021, from https://www.trai.gov.in/sites/default/files/PR_No.16of2021_0.pdf

UN. (2022). *Open-ended working group, office of disarmament affairs.* Retrieved March 20, 2022, from https://www.un.org/disarmament/open-ended-working-group/

UNGA. (2013, September 9). Developments in the field of information and telecommunications in the context of international security. Retrieved December 25, 2022, from https://documents-dds-ny.un.org/doc/UNDOC/GEN/N13/475/45/PDF/N1347545.pdf?OpenElement

Wu, J. G. (2006). *Who controls the internet? Illusions of borderless world.* New York: Oxford University Press.

3 State Security and Cyber Defence Frameworks

Introduction

In the contemporary world order, cyberspace plays a crucial role in national and international security affairs. No global system could be fully secure when a digital network is unprotected. This chapter delves into the concept of "security" (see Figure 3.1) within the international system, with a particular emphasis on cybersecurity. It examines the initiatives undertaken by both state and non-state actors to address challenges and vulnerabilities in cyberspace, highlighting their approaches and strategies to ensure digital security in an interconnected world. The concept of traditional and non-traditional security at the national and international level shall be discussed by referring to the widening and deepening aspect of security. Referring to the Copenhagen School's idea of securitisation, the transformation of cyberspace from a means of communication to a means of strategic affairs will be investigated. The reason for securitising the domain will be discussed by analysing the source of threats such as cyberwarfare, cyberterrorism, and cybercrimes. To address these threats, government agencies, non-governmental organisations, and international bodies function at multiple levels with a strong focus on cybersecurity measures. India, as a nation, has implemented numerous domestic and international initiatives to protect its digital infrastructure and cyber ecosystem. This chapter also examines India's cyber threat perceptions and its security strategies at both internal and external levels.

The concept of security in this study is analysed in connection with national and international affairs, emphasising its role within domestic and global politics. While defining the notion of security, it makes reference to academic studies of "national security" and "international security", which otherwise the meaning would be different from the actual/independent value of security itself. It shall be understood that the referent object of security for a nation (national security) is the state and the referent object of the security of the international system (international security) is the world as one unit. While the state takes responsibility to secure its elements (population, territory, government, and sovereignty), the world, as an anarchic society does not have dedicated authorities to protect itself. The objectives of national and international interest would be different. However, national and international securities are

DOI: 10.4324/9781003630319-3

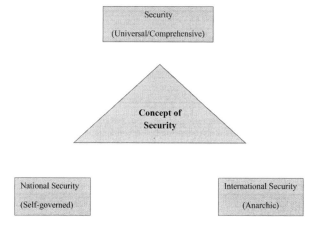

Figure 3.1 Concept of Security Agenda.
Source: Author.

linked and it is the state (including its elements) that is to be secured by the state itself for mutual survival and safety. No global security can be achieved without ensuring state security. Similarly, cybersecurity must be addressed both at the individual state level and through collective global efforts.

Security Concepts

The concept of security can be discussed in different forms depending on the ideas, culture, origins, and perception of the person. Security has a different value in different times and spaces. This section will analyse the complex concept of security, focusing on its ambiguous nature, current understanding, evolution (Cold War based), and futuristic features.

Security: An Ambiguous Symbol

The concept of "security" is ambiguous, and many describe it in regard to their best interest and role in the national and international system. Indeed, it is difficult to confirm what really qualifies as security in global politics (what it is or what it should be). Security is not a static symbol and its value keeps changing according to time and space. Consequently, the referent object of security transcends the state (traditional) to others including institutions, individuals, groups, economies, politics, environment, and biosphere (nontraditional). Meanwhile, constructivists such as Alexander Wendt believe that a threat to security is a social construct, a product of the intersubjective interactions of individuals and groups (Vaughan-Williams, 2010). However, every sector cannot be securitised, otherwise the notion of "what ought to be secured" will be replaced by "what is not to be secured".

Security has no permanent features. Today's threat or foe could be tomorrow's advantage or friend, or vice versa. Threats and security in the international system are inherently dynamic and ever-changing. For example, the US and the USSR, which were allies during World War II, became fierce rivals during and after the Cold War. Conversely, Japan, once an adversary of the US during World War II, evolved into a key ally in the post-war era. This fluidity underscores the shifting nature of alliances and threats in global politics. The United States, after years of conflict with the Taliban in Afghanistan, ultimately recognised the group as the governing authority after its takeover in 2021. Hay'at Tahrir al-Sham (HTS), designated as a terrorist organisation by the US, was also accepted by the US after HTS overthrew President Assad's regime in Syria in December 2024. Similarly, in Indian domestic affairs, insurgency, which was once a security issue in Mizoram and Tripura of Northeast India, is no more a threat today and hence lifted the military acts, such as the *Armed Forces Special Power's Act-1958*, from the region. Instead, the issue of ethnicity in the region, which was a mere political issue earlier, has now become a matter of security to the state.

Likewise, cyberspace, which was originally introduced as a means of communication, is now transformed into a strategic weapon in state politics. Even in the case of the health sector, plague, which were once a threat to human society, are now no more a predicament to mankind. Meanwhile, threats and security can vary from nation to nation or from time to time. Something that is a threat to a nation may not be a matter of security (threat) to others. For instance, hunger and disease could be a threat to weak nations such as Ethiopia and Nigeria but not for the US or the UK. However, a great power, like the US, may be suffering from a drug and crime epidemic though free from the scarcity of food and shelter. Meanwhile, joblessness and environmental safety, however, emerge as universal challenges that affect both developed and developing nations, underscoring the interconnected nature of global concerns.

Security: An Indefinite Idea

There is no universal definition of security and it is subjective in nature from ancient to recent times, groups to individuals, and states to institutes. Its origins can be traced to the wishes of early humans to be free from fear—whether from wild animals or enemies—and to ensure their survival by securing resources like food and favourable weather conditions. In ancient times, individuals used to be the referent object of security and they protected themselves without basic amenities. However, the Westphalian system came into being in 1648, where the state had to protect its territory and population from any existential threats. The referent object of security in this model is the state's territory. While this practice continues today, after the end of the Cold War, the security priorities have changed from territory to population (human). The referent object here is the individuals who must be secured from unemployment, unwanted disease, and racial discrimination. This concept of individual human security, emphasising the protection of individuals rather than the state was first introduced by the *UN Development Report* published in 1994.

The variation in referent objects over time highlights how security remains an evolving concept, adapting its priorities, meaning, and value based on historical, social, and political contexts. From early human's safe shelter to states with unthreatened, free territory, or full employment, the security agenda is set based on the interest of the actors. Besides territory and population, in contemporary international systems, sectors of security have been extended to the environment, economy, politics, and society. In the early days of humankind (e.g., in Stone Age), the responsibility of security was taken by the individual themself or groups themselves, but in the contemporary world, it is the responsibility of the state government.

Theorists or strategists including Kautilya, Sun Tzu, Thucydides, Machiavelli, Jomini, Hobbs, Morgenthau, E.H. Carr, John Mearsheimer, and Kenneth Waltz have directly or indirectly discussed state security. The debate on the subject continues with discussions by Cold War or post-Cold War scholars including Barry Buzan, Ole Waever, Richard Ullman, Mohammed Ayoob, and Ken Booth (among the notable ones). Among the contemporary scholars of security studies, Walter Lippmann is the first person to explicitly describe the notion of national security (or 'security' of a nation) in his book, *US Foreign Policy: Shield of the Republic* published in 1943 during World War II. He explains that a "nation has security when it does not have to sacrifice its legitimate interests to avoid war, and is able, if challenged, to maintain them by war" (Lippmann, 1943). In other words, security is the position in which a state should not compromise its sovereign rights to avoid a war, when it can challenge and protect its nation through a violent conflict. Lippmann's idea of security is militaristic, which that fits for the period and is a traditional method of security not fully suitable for the non-traditional world.

Arnold Wolfers agrees that the security of a state is an ambiguous symbol. He expressed security as "nothing but the absence of the evil of insecurities". He further expressed that security can be considered as a value that a nation can acquire in high and low measures. In this respect, security could be measured by the wealth that a country possesses and the power that a state accumulates. The objective of security, which is similar to the value of wealth or power of a state, is to be achieved in the absence of threats and fear (Wolfers, 1952). Therefore, security, according to Wolfers, "in an objective sense, measures the absence of threats to acquired values, and in a subjective sense, the absence of fear that such values will be attacked".

Shahin Malik, in the most basic terms explains security as the protection of values that people hold dearly and that is the reason why people are interested in achieving it. The concept of security simply refers to "protection or safety of some entity". However, the nature of the concept is multidimensional, which caused great confusion to the followers of security studies. Quoting Stephen Walt (Walt, 1991), Malik explains that the study of security (security studies) is the study of war, threat, use and control of military forces, which is a "traditional approach" in nature. He further assumed that Ken Booth's (Booth, 1991) idea on "security and emancipation are the two faces of same coin" and also a "critical security study" in approach. Too many approaches in security studies causes confusion, which can only be clarified by understanding the value of theoretical traditions that provide valuable contribution to the field (Malik, 2015).

In other non-militaristic explanations, Robert McNamara defines security (in modern society) as development. "Security is not military hardware, though it may include it. It is not military force, though it may encompass it". Security is development and without development there is no security (McNamara, 1968). This concept of security was further supported by UN Secretary General Kofi Annan in 2005 when he stated that "there will be no development without security and no security without development" (Annan, 2005). In India, the Cabinet Secretariat Resolution dated 16 April 1999, although it does not clearly define what national security is, stated that national security is "to be viewed not only in military terms, but also in terms of internal security, economic security, technological strength and foreign policy". The resolution was made to establish a National Security Council for India and identifies its constitution, roles, and functionalities (Secretariat, 1999). Strategist K. Subrahmanyam expressed that security (national) does not merely mean safeguarding India's territorial integrity, but ensures industrial growth and cohesive egalitarian and technological society in the country. And whatever comes in the way of this development, internally or externally, is a threat to India's national security. Meanwhile, the then-President of India, Abdul Kalam, believed that national security is born out of two important components that are "economic growth and prosperity; and the capability to defend the nation against all types of threats" (Kakar, 2021).

The above discussion highlights that the definition of security is inherently diverse and can only be considered unique when it is clear and less multidimensional. Without resolving conflicts in the interpretation of security values, achieving a definitive answer to the concept of security may remain elusive. Hence, a reduction of inclusiveness in security parameters could probably help in defining a better meaning of it. Meanwhile, the meaning and orientation of security is determined by the political powers and the time or situation.

Security: A Cold War Product

As Ken Booth and Eric Herring expressed, "the atomic bomb was the midwife of strategic studies", and it is apparently true that the concept of contemporary security studies is a product of the Cold War. Until the mid-1950s, the formal study of strategic issues was never developed as it is acknowledged today. The period from the mid-1950s to the mid-1960s is often regarded as the golden era of security debates, dominated by discussions on nuclear policies, arms control, and limited war (Baldwin, 1995). This was during the height of the Cold War, marked by significant events such as the 1961 Cuban Missile Crisis and the subsequent development of the brinkmanship strategy, reflecting the intense rivalry and delicate balance of power between the United States and the Soviet Union. This period was considered as the first wave of security studies that lasted for only a decade and began to decline in the second half of the 1960s. Walt attributes the decline of security studies to several factors: the lack of a well-defined research program, the failure of the first wave of scholars to train PhD students who could carry the field forward, the tendency of trained scholars to join government or consultancy roles rather than academia, and the inability of the discipline to adequately analyse and address complex events like the Vietnam War. These limitations hindered the intellectual and institutional development of security studies during that period (Walt, 1991, p. 216). However, in the next decade, the 1970s witnessed the issues of increasing oil prices, *détente* between the US and USSR, the armistice movement, and non-proliferation, which indicated the world was leaning towards cooperation and interdependence in the international system. This was a time when debates on security shifted from military to economic and corporation, a concept supported by scholars such as Robert Keohane and Joseph Nye (1977) and Kenneth Waltz (1979) (Herring, 1994).

The doom period of security studies was over soon and a renaissance began in the mid-1970s. This renaissance was influenced by the gradual conclusion of the Vietnam War and a renewed interest in academic research on security issues. Notably, the Ford Foundation, US, played a significant role by sponsoring academic programs and activities focused on security affairs. The failure of *détente* in the late 1970s and 1980s stimulates studies and national security studies were replaced by international security studies (Baldwin, 1995).

Walt identifies various reasons for the revival of such study, including rigorous historical research on the subject, critiques of deterrence theory, evolution of new nuclear weapons policy, and emerging debate on conventional warfare. The active involvement of first-wave scholars in think tanks like the RAND corporation and universities also played a key role along with greater access to security-related data outside military institutions. Additionally, the proliferation of academic journals and books, increased funding from public and private organisations, and stronger connections between security studies and the broader social sciences spurred this resurgence. The re-emergence of security studies in this phase of the Cold War is normally considered as the second wave of the discipline.

With the end of the Cold War, debates started among security scholars that the significance of military or external threats were reducing and a new era that focuses on non-military threats and domestic issues had begun.

56 *State, Security, and Cyberwar*

Military power is now no more the sole source of national security and military threats are not the only dangers that a nation experiences (Walt, 1991, p. 213). States began to prioritise the values of security towards threats associated with poverty, unemployment, health, crime, migration, and pollution. Scholars including Barry Buzan and Ole Waever from the Copenhagen School introduced new sectors to the subject, such as economics, politics, society, and the environment, that should be secured rather than territory or the state's military. Further, scholars such as Mohammed Ayoob and Mahbub ul Haq and Heidi Hudson added a new concept of human security and feminism, respectively, to security studies. The concept of security during the pre-Cold War and Cold War era primarily focused on state-centric and military agendas, forming the basis of what is known as traditional security. In contrast, the period following the Cold War witnessed the emergence of non-traditional security approaches, which expanded the scope to include issues such as economic stability, environmental concerns, human security, and transnational challenges like terrorism and cyber threats, reflecting the evolving nature of global security priorities. However, there are also dangers in sacrificing the domain of security if one commits to securitise everything perceivable as threats.

While the Cold War is widely referred to in security studies and other subjects alike including international relations IR, participants should be able to distinguish between these disciplines. Security studies centres on strategic, defence, and military policies, whereas IR focuses on diplomacy, foreign policy, and broader international interactions. As a foreign policy cannot replace a strategic policy, the role of a strategist differs from a diplomat. Consequently, the Ministry of Defence (MoD) operates independently of the Ministry of External Affairs (MEA). Sometimes, duplicating these fields not only undermines their distinct specifics but endangers the focus of the subjects. Meanwhile, as separate disciplines, the syllabi of the two should be different although they share some common ground. One subject could deal purely with foreign policy and the other could focus on security (defence/military plus) policies. However, unlike IR, the name of the subject differs from state to state. For instance, it is known as National Security Studies in the United States and Strategic Studies in British universities. The Cold War era has also made the subject focus narrowly on states and the military, as scholars began to concentrate on the nuclear revolution and Soviet Union hostilities (Malik, 2015, p. 5).

Security: An Evolving Concept (From Traditional to Non-traditional)

The concept of security keeps progressing over time. While the traditional understanding is based on war and armed forces, the non-traditional concept of security focuses on non-military related threats (see Table 3.1). Apparently, interest in the latter now seems to dominate the former. Though reduced, the value of traditional security has never been completely discarded

Table 3.1 Security Dimension

Sl No.	Definition	Traditional	Non-traditional
1.	Referent Object – the primary object that perceived existential threat	State – security is focused on the territory, its borders, and institutions	Human – concentrates on individuals, communities, and society
2.	Security Domian – the space/area that needs to be protected	Territory–emphasises on physical borders and national geography	Community – identity-based ethnic groups become key
3.	Authority and Autonomy – who exercises power and controls decisions	Sovereignty – state is the absolute authority	Human rights – emphasis on protecting individuals' right
4.	Means of Threat or Protection – how security is achieved or threatened	Military – national security is done through armed forces and hard power	Non-military – focuses on threats perceived from environment, politics, economics, society, health, migration, natural disasters, organised crimes, energy, cyber, etc.
5.	Key Scholars/Thinkers – major contributors to security thoughts	Walter Lippmann, Arnold Wolfers, Stephen Walt, Kenneth Waltz, and John Mearsheimer – focus on realism, power politics, and national interest	Barry Buzan, Richard Ullman, Mohammed Ayoob, Mahbub ul Haq, and Mely Caballero-Anthony – emphasise broader security dimensions, including human security, regionalism, and developmental concerns

Source: Author.

or substituted by the non-traditional system. The traditional value will exist as long as states continue to protect their territory using military tools. What brought in the new concept is the introduction of non-military sectors such as economics, politics, society, environment, and human security (in addition to the military) to security studies by scholars including Barry Buzan and Mohammed Ayoob, who are known as wideners. Meanwhile, other interesting concepts such as "emancipation" and feminism were discussed by Ken Booth and Spike Peterson, who are known as deepeners. While traditional (military) threat varies from state to state, non-traditional threats, such as environmental factors (climate change), are common to all states. In the contemporary international system, scholars are interested in discussing the environment (post Cold War) more than nuclear issues (Cold War).

Consequently, cyberspace is another noble area yet to be explored in regard to its security aspect fully.

Traditional SecurityThe traditional notion of security is state-centric in nature and realistic in perspective. The medium of security studies is restricted to threats associated with the military and only those related to war, conflict, violence, and force. Traditionalists such as Stephen Walt suggest that the prevention of conflict should only be done through military means such as deterrence policies, non-offensive defence, and other related means (Tarry, 1999). By limiting security studies to military issues in traditional security, this means it should be labelled as *strategic studies*, not security studies (Buzan, 1998, p. 4). Hence, according to Buzan, traditional security is synonymous with strategic studies and non-traditional security with *security studies*, as it encompasses other non-military sectors. Security in the traditional system is concentrated mostly at the top level only, i.e., at the international system level, its subsystems and units only. However, he suggested that security also needs to be done at the subunit and individual level. In his security framework, the international system includes the entire planet. Subsystems refer to groups of units such as the Association of Southeast Asian Nations (ASEAN) or the South Asian Association for Regional Cooperation (SAARC). Units are entities like states, nations, or transnational firms. Subunits include bureaucracies, lobbies, and executives. Individuals, as the smallest element, represent the foundation of security within this hierarchy (Buzan, Wæver, & de Wilde, 1998). This multilayered approach highlights the interconnectedness of various actors and structures in shaping security dynamics

Traditionalists consider the state as the only referent object and it normally rejects insecurities at the lower or individual level. By this phenomenon, even if citizens in a country are ill-treated by the government itself, it does not come into the ambit of national security. Meanwhile, issues of water sharing or an oil crisis between two states is merely a matter of security unless war breaks out between the two or the military is involved. The traditional concept of security is based on external threats with interstate concerns. However, most of the wars fought since 1945 are intrastate, be it Yugoslavia, Rwanda, Somalia, or insurgency in parts of India. Therefore, security in a traditional system is conceptually narrow concerning only conflicts amongst states or great powers (Tarry, 1999).

India is traditionally viewed as a liberal-realist state, balancing cooperation with others while striving for power in the international system. Since its independence in 1947, India has maintained a neutral security policy and decided not to join any of the two "blocks" during the Cold War. India introduced the Non-Alignment Movement, however, after a terrible experience in the 1962 war with China and multiple conflicts with Pakistan in 1965, 1971, and 1999, India was compelled to revise its strategic policy. Security doctrines and manuals were developed over time, and in 1998, the National Security Council was established to advise the government on security matters (Secretariat, 1999).

Non-traditional Security (Wideners and Deepeners)

While traditionalists restricts security to the state (territory/military) as the referent object, non-traditionalists widen and deepen the scope of security by introducing other referent objects including the economy, politics, society, environment, and humans that ought to be free from any existential threats. Over the past three decades, the risk of a major armed conflict has been reduced globally and the security challenge has shifted to threats emerging from the local as well as transnational, which are non-military in nature. This emerging concept of new security, which is also known as non-traditional security (NTS) has identified other threats as the most serious and harmful to human society than the damage inflicted by interstate wars or conflicts. Consequently, policymakers and experts have focused their attention to rethink security agendas and discover new ideas to address these emerging threats. Meanwhile, the Consortium on Non-Traditional Security Studies in Asia defines NTS issues as "those challenges that affect the survival and well-being of peoples and states that arise primarily out of non-military sources, such as climate change, resource scarcity, infectious diseases, natural disasters, irregular migration, famine, people smuggling, drug trafficking and transnational crime" (Caballero-Anthony, 2013).

While traditionalists warn of the risks involved in widening the security agenda in the form of NTS, scholars who are popularly known as wideners and deepeners (see Table 3.2) began to debate and develop theories on the subject in the 1980s (Hameiri, 2013). Wideners argue that the definition of security should not be limited to a military threat only but also extended to other non-traditional sectors for the survival of the state. Meanwhile, deepeners interestingly enquire whose security has been threatened from whom (or what) and simply disapprove of the state being the only referent object of security; humans should be considered as well (Tarry, 1999). Table 3.2 highlights the areas that the wideners and deepeners focus on with a few of their names.

Security Wideners

Scholars including Barry Buzan, Ole Wæver, Mohammed Ayoob, Michael Klare, and Daniel Thomas are scholars who worked on broadening the concept of security agendas (Tarry, 1999). In their book, *Security: A New Framework for Analysis*, Buzan, Waever, and de Wilde discuss the debate of 'wide' versus 'narrow' and explain the emerging concept of non-military-centric security studies, which is beyond the traditional obsession of nuclear issues and the Cold War. They further expressed that the rise of economic and environmental concerns in the 1970s and 1980s, along with issues of identity and transnational crimes in the 1990s, paved the way for contemporary NTS studies (Buzan, 1998). In addition to the military sector, they highlight other sectors such as the economy, politics, environment, and society that need to be freed from potential threat. Meanwhile, Mohammed Ayoob

Table 3.2 Non-Traditionalists

Sl No.	Wideners	Deepeners
1.	Environment, politics, economics, society, health, migration, natural disasters, organised crime, energy, cyber, etc.	Individual rights, poverty, oppression, racism, education, class, living standards, feminism, etc.
2.	Barry Buzan, Ole Wæver, Jaap de Wilde, Mohammed Ayoob, Mahbub ul Haq, Amitav Acharya, Kanti Bajpai, Egbert Jahn, Pierre Lemaitre, Joseph Nye, Helga Haftendorn, Neta Crawford, Michael Klare, etc.	Ken Booth, Spike Peterson, Walter Lippmann

Source: Author.

in his chapter, "Defining Security: A Subaltern Realist Perspective" in Keith Krause and Michael C. Williams (eds.) *Critical Security Studies: Concepts and Cases*, stated that the traditional definition of security has been dominated by Western literature and ignores the multifaceted and multidimensional nature of the problem of security as challenged by the majority of subaltern members in the international system (Ayoob, 1997, p. 121). Mahbub ul Haq discussed "human security" as one of the sectors for NTS studies and became a pioneer of the theme. In *Reflections of Human Development*, he argues that security should be centred on people's well-being rather than just territorial or national boundaries. He emphasises that security extends to individuals, their homes, jobs, communities, and environment. He advocates for achieving security through development rather than relying on arms, stressing the importance of addressing human needs for a broader and more sustainable sense of security (Haq, 1995, p. 115). Indian scholars such as Amitav Acharya support his idea and express that human security as an instrument of national strategic priorities has a strong domestic root (Acharya, 2021). Kanti Bajpai also expressed that the study of human security should focus on "the map of violence", which is much larger than the map of organised interstate violence (Bajpai, 2003). He suggests that human security requires attention to various forms of violence affecting individuals, communities, and societies at large, not just state-based conflicts.

Security Deepeners

Ken Booth is one of the notable pioneers who advocates for "inclusive" security or deepening the concept of security. In his book, *Theory of World Security*, he argues for the deepening of the concept of security than broadening it. He believes that broadening security is just a synonym for "updating" the security agenda (Booth, 1991). He claimed that a deep understanding in security is a good source of assumption, which later encouraged the creative idea of broadening. Broadening, if it happens, is a functioning of deepening. In other words, broadening is a by-product of deepening or deepening is a source of broadening. He explains security as a derivative concept of a "simple idea with enormous implications". The core elements of security agendas are a referent object, a danger, and the desire to avoid harm, threat, and risk (Booth, 2007, pp. 149–150). In another book, *Security and Emancipation*, Booth took the position of utopian realist that is holistic in character and non-statist in approach. Besides the military aspects, he expressed the need to include daily threats (poverty, political oppression, poor education, etc.) to the lives and well-being of most people in the security agenda (Booth, 1991, p. 318). Interestingly, the idea of personal security and emancipation was addressed by the traditionalist security scholar, Walter Lippmann, in his book, *The Good Society*, as indicated in the excerpt below.

"The road whereby mankind has advanced in knowledge, in the mastery of nature, in unity, and in 'personal security has lain through a progressive emancipation from the bondage of authority, monopoly, and special privilege" (Lippmann, 1937).

Quoting Spike Peterson, Tarry also suggested that the exclusion of feminism (or female concerns) in the security agenda is a narrow concept that decreases the security of women. This indicates that the military establishment and state institutions are patriarchal and masculine in nature. Meanwhile, the concept of world security should consider worldwide problems such as ecological imbalance, human rights abuses, widespread poverty, gender bias, and the systemic oppression of women. Meanwhile, the discrimination of lower classes and weaker sections of society is a matter of security concern for deepeners.

Digital Threats and Cybersecurity Framework

As the security agenda evolves and widens (or updates), cyberspace, having fully securitised, has become a key domain within the broader NTS framework. Though the concept of cyberspace originated during the Cold War period as a product of the US military program in the 1960s, its popularity began in the early 1990s after the world wide web (WWW) was created in 1989 (Ritchie, Mathieu, Roser, & Ortiz-Ospina, 2022). Originally developed for communication purposes, later commercialised for economic benefits, and ultimately securitised for power politics, cyberspace has emerged as a crucial strategic arena in international security affairs. Concerning the potential threats posed by cyberspace, states and multilateral organisations have begun to implement new legislation, develop strategic policies, and adopt various security measures to effectively safeguard the digital ecosystem. Meanwhile, India, as the second largest internet consumer in the world, faces several threats and challenges through this medium. Like other countries, India has established national protection mechanisms at both military and non-military levels and actively engages in international forums, including the UN, to address cybersecurity challenges and strengthen its digital resilience.

Element of Threats in Cyberspace

Due to the threats and challenges associated with it, cyberspace has been securitised (as discussed in Chapter 1) and elevated to a critical security agenda. Cyber threats come in various forms and are often interpreted differently depending on the specific needs or objectives of the interpreter. A cyber intrusion can sometimes be thought of as a cybercrime, act of cyberwar, cyberterrorism, cyber espionage, and other cyberattacks. Meanwhile, the range of possible threats in cyberspace is indeed vast affecting from governments, business, and individuals as well as machinery and infrastructure. Some of the common threats include interfering with internet networks, attacks on banking and financial sectors, breaches targeting military facilities, disruptions to energy industries, oil refineries, gas pipelines, transportation systems, and hospitals, as well as violations of commercial and individual privacy. These threats are perpetrated by a range of actors, including criminal organisations, terrorists, revolutionary groups, and hostile state entities (Myers, 2020). Concerning these aspects and based on the actors involved, this section will deal with threats related to cyberwar, cyberterrorism, and cybercrimes. It explores cyberwar or espionage conducted by state actors, cyberterrorism orchestrated by terrorist organisations, and cybercrimes, which may or may not involve state or terrorist entities but are typically carried out by civilians or non-combatants.

Cyberwar

Since there is no universally agreed-upon definition of cyberwar, it is unclear whether what type of attack or incursion in the digital domain qualifies as an act of cyberwar. However, Martin C. Libicki, who extensively writes on cyberwar issues, tries to identify "What constitutes an act of war in cyberspace?" He opined that the act of cyberwar can be explained in three aspects: universally, multilaterally, and unilaterally. The first aspect is that every member of the UN accepting a cyberattack as an act of war. The second aspect is the acceptance of any cyber intrusion as an act of war by a multilateral organisation such as NATO or a group or allies. The third refers to any state that can unilaterally declare that an attack (digital) was an act of war (Libicki, 2009, pp. 179–189). In fact, there is no universal definition of cyberwar or cyberwarfare. However, a consensual definition perhaps is required to develop a cyberwar policy (doctrine or strategy) and states must decide what resources should be devoted to the remedies. One definition[1] of war, famously articulated by Clausewitz, is that "war is a mere continuation of politics by military means to achieve a political objective". Cyberwar can also be described as an extension of politics by digital means to attain a strategic goal. If the 2010 Stuxnet attack on Iran's nuclear facilities is seen as an act of cyberwar, then it was an expansion of politics by the US and Israel against Iran to achieve the US and Israel's political goals. The 2008 Russian cyberattacks against Georgia's communication and financial system (while kinetic attacks or intense conflict were also simultaneously ongoing between the two over South Ossetia, Caldwell, 2012, p. 153) was an extension of Russian politics against Georgia for a strategic goal. As war is an instrument of state policy, cyberwar is also a means to achieve a national interest (objective).

In the anarchic international system, states adopt varied approaches to cyberwarfare, shaped by their strategic objectives, technological capabilities, and security concerns. The United Nations has already admitted that there are cyber conflicts and has sought to promote "cyberpeace" through international collaboration. Unless the definitions between a "cyberattack" and "cyberwar" are unanimously agreed upon (Talihärm, 2013), it will be challenging to establish international law on cyberwarfare. All cyberattacks cannot be described as acts of cyberwar (Schneier, 2013). War is generally understood or interpreted with literal and rhetorical meanings. While the literal meaning is associated with real war that involves, guns, tanks, and advance armies, the rhetorical meaning is associated with war on crime, poverty, terrorism, and drugs. However, cyberwar has both literal and rhetorical aspects making it a complex term to use while discussing cybersecurity and cyberattacks (Schneier, 2013). Meanwhile, super power nations such as the US state that there is no specific criteria to determine whether a cyberattack is an act of crime, terrorism, hactivism, or a state actor using a force equivalent to kinetic armed attack. Under certain conditions, the US recognised any cyber assault (even one without kinetic effects) as an element of armed conflict. Cyberattacks on US information networks during an active armed conflict would be subject to the laws of armed conflict (Service, Cyberwarfare and Cyberterrorism: In Brief 2015). This indicates that the US will proportionally retaliate with kinetic force in response to a cyberattack (Service, Use of Force in Cyberspace, 2021).

India's position on cyberwarfare has been reflected in its military documents published from time to time. It believes cyberwar is in progress and certain mechanisms on digital warfare need to be developed in the state. As a result, the cyber military command, the Defence Cyber Agency (DCA) was established in 2018 to operate in both defensive and offensive dimensions. Consequently, military doctrines were eventually developed to address India's approach to digital warfare. The *Indian Army Doctrine-2004*, addresses cyber warfare as a part of 'Information Warfare" and explains it as "techniques to destroy, degrade, exploit or compromise the enemy's computer-based systems" (Army, 2004, p. 21). The *Joint Training Doctrine: Indian Armed Forces (2017), Land Warfare Doctrine (2018), Basic Doctrine of the Indian Air Force (2012)*, and *Joint Doctrine for Cyberspace Operation (2024)* touched upon India's preparedness for cyberwarfare. The 2017 joint doctrine illuminates cyberspace as an important area of national security and expressed India's willingness to become a "cyber power" nation (IDS, 2017, p. 25). The 2018 doctrine also acknowledges cyberwar as a key factor to win future battles. It addresses India's interest in a cyber deterrence mechanism, the elimination of digital threats, and preparedness for defensive and offensive engagements (Indian Army, 2018). The 2024 document, although not publicly released, was outlined by the Chief of Defence Staff, General Anil Chauhan on the day of its release on 18 June 2024. He stated that the doctrine provides an understanding of and guidelines for commanders, staff, and practitioners in cyber operation, warfighting, and strategic planning (MoD, 2024). Indepth details on cyberwar and cyberwarfare will be discussed in the next chapter.

Cyberterrorism

Cyberterrorism, like cyberwarfare, lacks a universally accepted definition (Service, Cyberwarfare and Cyberterrorism: In Brief, 2015). Since its inception, cyberterrorism has been interpreted in different forms in several documents released by academics, business, and governments (Colarik, 2006, p. 45). The term, 'cyberterrorism' first emerged in 1996 by combining the two terms 'cyber' and 'terrorism'. It was widely accepted and popularised further by the US military forces. The first definition of cyberterrorism was in the report, *Cybercrime, Cyberterrorism, Cyberwarfare: Averting an Electronic Waterloo,* released by the US Department of Justice in 1998. The document describes, "cyber terrorism means premeditated, politically motivated attacks by sub national groups or clandestine agents, or individuals against information and computer systems, computer programs, and data that results in violence against non-combatant targets" (Janczewski, 2007). Subsequently, the US Congressional Research Service (USCRS) report on *Cyberwarfare and Cyberterrorism: In Brief,* explains that cyberterrorism is "the premeditated use of disruptive activities, or the threat thereof, against computers and/or networks, with the intention to cause harm or further social, ideological, religious, political or similar objectives, or to intimidate any person in furtherance of such objectives" (2015). These few definitions are widely accepted in academic and government circles on cyberterrorism. Other definitions also include "an attack carried out by terrorists either via the Internet or targeting the Internet that results in violence against persons or severe economic damage" (Conway, n.d.).

While the UN does not have a common definition on cyberterrorism, most of its official publications related to the subject referred to it as a terrorist's malicious acts on digital networks (information and communication technology, ICT) for harmful purposes. The UN Counter Terrorism Centre (UNCCT) expressed concern regarding the increased use of ICT by terrorists to "commit, incite, recruit for, fund or plan terrorist acts" (UNCCT, 2022). Resolution 2341 (2017) of the UN Security Council appeals to member states to strengthen cooperation with stakeholders and share information or their experience to prevent and respond to terrorist attacks against critical information infrastructure facilities. Some of the areas that the organisation focuses on are kinetic cyberattacks to critical information infrastructures and internet-of-things (IoT) devices, the spread of terrorist content, complex terrorist communication, and digital terrorist financing (Terrorism, 2022).

Since its independence, India has been suffering or tolerating terrorism in different parts of the state. Terrorists have been actively operating with the aid of cyberspace or digital networks since the introduction of the internet in India. Terrorists became more complex when they used ICT and bomb-laden drones to attack Jammu Airport on 27 June 2021. Immediately after this incident, India appealed to the UN General Assembly to focus serious attention on the possible use of weaponised drones for terrorist activities (Today, 2021). Consequently, the UN Office of Counter-Terrorism took initiatives to discuss the terrorist use of unmanned aerial systems and its developing threats in this area (Terrorism, 2022). Weaponised drones were also used to drop bombs in the ethnic conflict between the Kuki and Meitei in Manipur. The attack took place at Koutruk, Imphal West when Kuki militants killed two villagers and injured 10 others, including security personnel, by using bomb-laden drones on 1 September 2024 (Achom &Choudhury, 2024).

While India does not have a dedicated official definition of cyberterrorism, Section 66F of the *IT (Amendment) Act-2008* (amended after the Mumbai 26 November terrorist attack), addresses "Punishment for Cyber Terrorism". It states that whoever is "intent to threaten the unity, integrity, security or sovereignty of India or to strike terror in the people or any section of the society cause the denial of access to anybody's computer; penetrate or access computer resource without authorisation; or any computer activity causing the death or injury to person, damage property, or national facilities; will be punishable extendable to life imprisonment". While it addresses punishment, the meaning of "cyberterrorist" has been defined as those who intend to damage other property and the integrity of the state.[2]. Meanwhile, two sister divisions, the Counter Terrorism and Counter Radicalisation Division and the Cyber and Information Security Division, were created in the Ministry of Home Affairs (MHA) on 13 November 2017 to address issues relating to cyberterrorism, counter-radicalisation, cybersecurity, cybercrime, and information security (PIB, 2018).

Cybercrime

No society is free from criminal activities, and such behaviour has increased with the evolution of the internet or cyber networks. In one way, criminals use cyberspace to conduct their traditional illegal operations such as money heists, drug trafficking, gun running, and sex work (cyber-enabled crimes). In another way, they exploit the digital world by disseminating or deploying malware/ransomware, attacking critical information facilities and valuable digital property of the government, private citizens, businesses, and industries (Congressional, 2015; UNODC, n.d.). Cybercrimes affect not only individual rights but economic conditions that have national security implications. The global financial loss in cybercrimes[3] in 2021 was six trillion dollars, which is the equivalent of the third-largest economy after the US and China. It is expected to grow 15 per cent every year, which shall reach $10.5 trillion in 2025, and the trend is likely to continue annually (Morgan, 2020).

Cybercrime has no single definition and organisations (public or private) define it according to their objectives and interests. For the US, there is no unique definition of cybercrime that distinguishes it from other forms of cyber threat, and the term is used interchangeably with other internet-based malicious acts (Congressional, 2015). However, the US Congressional Research Service report suggested that cybercrime is the "unauthorized breaches of network and theft of intellectual property and other data, which can be financially motivated, and response is typically the jurisdiction of law enforcement agencies" (USCRS, 2015). Cybersecurity companies, such as *NortonLifeLock Inc.*, (formerly known as Symantec Corporation) defines cybercrime as any crime that occurs mostly or exclusively online and targets computer networks (or devices), including identity theft and security breaches (Norton, 2021). The UN Office of Drugs and Crime (UNODC) considers cybercrime as an "evolving form of transnational crime" that takes place in the borderless realm of the digital world and is operated by organised crime groups and other criminals. The office has developed an Open-ended Intergovernmental Expert Group on Cybercrime to conduct a comprehensive study on cybercrime issues and responses by member states, the international community, and the private sector. Between 2011 and 2021, the expert group has held seven meetings (UNODC, 2022). The UN General Assembly, by Resolution 74/247, established the *Ad Hoc Committee to Elaborate a Comprehensive International Convention on Countering the Use of Information and Communications Technologies for Criminal Purposes* and held its first meeting in New York in May 2021 (UNODC, 2022).

India has taken a dedicated initiative to address the challenges associated with cybercrime. The National Cyber Crime Reporting Portal[4] describes cybercrime in "general" as "any unlawful act where computer or communication device or computer network is used to commit or facilitate the commission of crime". The portal has identified 24 types of cybercrime including cyber espionage, drug trafficking, web defacement, data breach, sextortion, debit/credit card fraud, stalking, and bullying (Portal, 2022). Cyberwar and cyberterrorism are not on the list as both are dealt with separately in the Indian cybersecurity context. Cybercrimes are considered those offences conducted by criminals with non-political and short-term objectives, and terrorism or warfare is waged by regulated combatants with a long-term political objective. The *IT (Amendment) Act-2008*, though it did not define cybercrime, Section XI, "Offences" addresses the punishment for offences related to cybercrimes including identity theft, misuse of computers, cheating by using cyber sources, privacy violation, publishing obscene material, and child sexual exploitation. Meanwhile, in section three ("Objective") of the *National Cyber Security Policy-2013*, which does not explain what represents cybercrimes, the term, "cybercrime" is mentioned in two places (at point number 10 and 11, a few lines out of the 38 pages) related to data theft, prosecution, and enhancement of enforcement agencies.

Level of Cybersecurity Frameworks

In response to cyberthreats, states gradually developed cybersecurity frameworks (policies) at various levels of the international system. According to Barry Buzan, the level of analysis of international security (relation) was done with five systems. They are the international system (planet/world), international subsystem (regional organisation), units (states/nations), sub-units (organised groups), and individuals (citizen) (Buzan, 1998, pp. 5–6). Similarly, cybersecurity policies can also be analysed at six levels,[5] international (universal), multinational (regional forums), national (country), subnational (states, Kerala, Manipur, etc.), agencies/institutes (corporate firms), and individuals (citizen responsibility) as highlighted in Table 3.3. While the protection of the cyber ecosystem at the international level refers to the safety of collective digital networks ion the planet, the multinational level denotes the group of states territorially united with a common effort to secure the digital networks of the particular community (ASEAN, SAARC, African Union, EU, etc.).

International (Global Cybersecurity System)

As the international system is anarchic, there is no supreme authority that rules or supervises the global cyber ecosystem. Consequently, there is no universal law, policy, or strategy for cyberwar or digital security, as individual states used to have and practice for traditional war. Therefore, the main responsibility to defend or protect the digital domain is to be done by the states themselves. However, the UN, a conglomerate society of nation-states and with its brainchild, the International Telecommunication Union (ITU) supports and unites countries to adhere to international standards and laws on cybersecurity related issues. While the UN lacks a universal legal cybersecurity framework for all its member states, it has established internal guidelines and protocols to safeguard its office networks and digital infrastructure. The first discussion on information security was proposed by Russia with a draft discussion on *Developments in the Field of Information and Telecommunications in the Context of International Security* in 1998. Further, a series of initiatives were taken up by the organisation on the safety of the global cyber ecosystem. A report of the General Secretary titled, *Information and Communications Technology in the United Nations* (A/69/517), released on 10 October 2014, discussed the development of a cybersecurity strategy for the organisation. The strategy was designed "to

Table 3.3 Cybersecurity Framework (Level of Analysis)

Sl No.	Level	Entity	Framework/Policy/Guideline
1.	International	The whole world (UN)	*Developments in the Field of Information and Telecommunications in the Context of International Security*
2.	Multinational	Group of nations (NATO, SAARC, Shanghai Cooperation Organisation, SCO)	*Agreement on Cooperation in Ensuring International Information Security between the Member States of the SCO*
3.	National	Individual states (great, middle, small powers)	*National Cyber Strategy of the United States of America* (US)
4.	Subnational	State (Kerala, Telangana, Gujarat, etc.)	*IT Policy 1998* (Kerala)
5.	Agency	Organisational setups	*Key Roles and Responsibilities of Chief Information Security Officers (CISOs) in Ministries/ Departments and Organisations managing ICT operations* (CERT, MeitY)
6.	Individual	Personal device protection and leadership, professionals, non-professional, citizens	*A Handbook for Adolescents/ Students on Cyber Safety* (MHA, India)

Source: Author.

strengthen, and provide a common vision for, the delivery of ICT in the UN through modernisation, transformation and innovation and by providing a framework for improved governance, strong leadership and optimal use of ICT resources" (UNGA, 2014). Consequently, the report on "ICT strategy endorsed" was released on 26 February 2015 focusing on five pillars: modernisation, transformation, innovation, government, and optimisation of ICT (UN, 2015).

Besides the ITU, there are several offices dealing with cybersecurity in the United Nations. For instance, the United Nations Institute for Disarmament Research (UNIDR) launched the *Security and Technology (SecTec) Programme* in 2019 working on cybersecurity, autonomous technology, and AI, emerging technologies for a peaceful purpose. The UN Office on Drugs and Crime (UNODC) provided assistance to capacity building, promoting awareness, international cooperation, data collection, and research and analysis on cybercrime. The Office of Information and Communications Technology (OICT) takes charge of developing a strategic direction for

ICT and the UN secretariat. The United Nations Office for Disarmament Affairs, established in 1998, looks after ICT-related multilateral discussions including the United Nations Group of Government Experts (UNGGE) on *Developments in the Field of Information and Telecommunications in the Context of International Security*. Meanwhile various regulations and reports have been released related to ICT cybersecurity for international security (UN, 2022). Notable resolutions include *Resolution on the Right to Privacy in the Digital Age (A/RES/68/167)* in 2013; *Resolution on the Creation of a Global Culture of Cybersecurity and Taking Stock of National Efforts to Protect Critical Information Infrastructures (A/RES/64/211)* in 2009; and *Resolution on Combating the Criminal Misuse of Information Technologies (A/RES/56/121)* in 2002.

A series of cooperative activities were initiated by the United Nations for the safety and security of cyberspace. These include the *Secretary General's High-level Panel on Digital Cooperation that* convened on 12 July 2018 to propose member states strengthen their cooperation in cyberspace amongst public and private sectors, civil societies, multilateral organisations, academic communities, and other related stakeholders. Other notable programs also commenced to increase the efficiency and effectiveness of cybersecurity cooperations. They include the *Annual Cyber Stability Conference under UNIDR* started in 2012; *World Summit on the Information Society (WSIS) Forum* started in 2016; *Arria-formula Meetings on Cyber-Attacks Against Critical Infrastructure Combatting Cybercrime* and *Tools and Capacity Building for Emerging Economies*; project on the *Global Cybersecurity Index*; *United Nations Group on Cybercrime and Cybersecurity*; the *Digital Blue Helmets Programme*; and the *Global Programme on Cybercrime*.

Multinational (Regional Cybersecurity System)

While individual states are responsible for securing their national cyberspace, allied nations cooperate with each other to be free from and protect themselves from digital threats. Multilateral organisations such as the European Union (EU), ASEAN, Caribbean Community (CARICOM), the Commonwealth, Group of Seven (G7), North Atlantic Treaty Organization (NATO), Organisation of Islamic Cooperation (OIC), Organization for Security and Co-operation in Europe (OSCE), Organization of American States (OAS), Shanghai Cooperation Organisation (SCO), and South Asian Association for Regional Cooperation (SAARC) are an amalgamation of like-minded countries that share experiences and take collective measures to protect their digital networks. Though the cybersecurity policies of all the organisations are important, initiatives taken by NATO, SAARC, and SCO are discussed below. NATO is selected as one of the powerful politico-military unions in the West and SAARC is selected as a group of developing countries lead by India and studied from an Indian context. The cybersecurity initiative of the SCO will also be an interesting organisation to study as competitive countries such as China, India, and Pakistan who blame each other (India-China and India-Pakistan) for cyber intrusion are all together in the same organisation.

North Atlantic Treaty Organization

As a conglomerate of 32 member nations, NATO, a political and military organisation, has reliable policy, legislation, structure, and cooperation. NATO's policy on cyber defence originated at the *Wales Summit Declaration* held on 5 September 2014. The policy recognises the application of international law in cyberspace and affirms cyber defence as part of the organisation's key agenda of collective defence (NATO, 2014). A *Cyber Defence Pledge* was taken by the allied heads of state and government to ensure their alliance keeps peace and they are able to protect cyberspace (NATO, 2016). In the *Brussels Summit Declaration* held on 11 and 12 July 2018, NATO affirmed that cyber threats were becoming "frequent, complex, destructive, and coercive". Identifying it as one of its core tasks, NATO promised to operate effectively in cyberspace as it does in the air, land, and sea (NATO, 2018). NATO's Cyber Security Center, functioning under the Communication and Information Agency, provides special services to prevent, detect, respond to, and recover from cyber security threats (NATO, 2022). The Cyber Defence Committee, NATO Cyber Defence Management Board, and Director, NATO Cooperative Cyber Defence Centre of Excellence (CCDCOE) are dedicated structures created with the NATO's cybersecurity interest. It also conducts several cooperative exercises and talks including the NATO Annual Cyber Coalition Exercise, International Conference on Cyber Conflict, NATO Information Assurance Symposium, and Executive Cyber Seminar. NATO has signed a memorandum of understanding with many countries on cybersecurity related affairs (UNIDR, 2019). Interestingly, the CCDCOE, which is an affiliated institute but not part of the NATO structure, plays a significant role in cybersecurity. It focuses on domains related to law, operations, strategy, and technology in cyber defence. One of its renowned contributions in international cyber affairs is the release of the *Tallin Manual* series, a comprehensive document on the rules and regulations of cyberwar. This document has become a cornerstone in discussions on cyber defence and security.

South Asian Association for Regional Cooperation

The eight-member organisation, SAARC, is a cooperative organisation working for the welfare and development (economic, social, cultural, technical, and scientific fields) of the South Asia region (SAARC, 2022). Unlike NATO, it does not have a military formation and its approach to cybersecurity is non-military centric. SAARC acknowledges that cyberspace threatens the economic, social, and cultural sectors, which are its focus areas. The organisation takes civil (non-military) initiatives to restrict the menace, especially cybercrime (not cyberterrorism or cyberwar). The Working Group on Telecommunications and ICT (WGT&ICT) was established in January 2004 to work on a comprehensive strategy to enhance and expand ICT facilities, minimise disparities among member states, use ICT for social and economic uplift, reduce digital divides, and encourage cooperation in technology transfer. Though the first (2004) and second (2008) meetings did not discuss digital threats, the third conference mentions "cybersecurity" as a major issue in its agenda (SAARC, 2020). In the 18th SAARC Summit held at Kathmandu in November 2014, it established a "cybercrime monitoring desk" to support handling criminal activities occurring in the region. While the development of the desk was uncertain,[6] SAARC is involved in organising cybersecurity conferences in collaboration with other institutes. For instance, the Information Security Media Group (ISMG) conducted a series of seminars on "India and SAARC Submit" in 2021 (23 and 24 March) and 2022 (17 May, New Delhi). Since cybercrime has been a core agenda of the organisation, SAARC established a separate body to deal with regional cybersecurity policies involving law enforcement agencies to challenge digital threats and improve ICT activities in the region.

Shanghai Cooperation Organisation

The SCO is an intergovernmental organisation made up of six nations, including China, Russia, and four other Central Asian republics. It was founded in 2001 to increase mutual confidence between its members. With the historic entry of India and Pakistan in 2017, the group has eight members now (SCO, 2022). Though the group has no specific policy on cybersecurity, it has taken different initiatives to support and coordinate the safety of cyberspace at the regional and international level. The SCO Expert Group on International Information Security commenced in 2006 as an agreement to coordinate and take preventive measures to ensure the peace, security, and stability of cyberspace in the international system (SCO, 2018). A cyber expert group of the Regional Anti-Terrorist Structure (RATS) under SCO considered developing a Protected Information and Telecommunications Security System to improve cybersecurity collaboration among member states in counter-terrorism (SCO, 2019). Article 2 of the *Agreement on Cooperation in Ensuring International Information Security between the Member States of the SCO (2019)* addresses major threats to the international information system including information weapons, information warfare, information terrorism, and information cybercrime.[7] The other initiatives include the conduct of the *Anti-Cyber-Terrorism Joint Drill* to improve and share experiences on counter-cyberterrorism among the member states in 2017. It also held the *International Cloud Security Conference,* for participants to secure and protect their international cyber ecosystems in 2017.

National (Country Cybersecurity System)

As cybersecurity becomes a top priority for national security, it is exclusively the responsibility of individual states to safeguard their digital ecosystems. In the contemporary world order, states are categorised into great, middle, and small powers. Likewise, cybersecurity policy in this section studies the initiatives taken by these three different powers. Among the great powers, the US, Russia, and China, along with their cyber policies, structures, legislature, and cooperation, will be examined. Consequently, national cybersecurity programs implemented by the UK, Japan, and Canada as middle powers and Iran, North Korea, and Israel as small powers will be assessed. Iran, North Korea, and Israel are chosen from among other small powers because they are considered as states of concern in the global cyber systems and are potentially active in the field of cyber affairs. India is consequently placed between the major and middle powers, and its cybersecurity system will be covered individually in a later portion of this chapter.

Great Powers

The *United States*, being the sole superpower amongst the great powers and the creator of cyberspace, has the most comprehensive (civil as well as military) cybersecurity policies in the world. In 2018, the White House introduced the *National Cyber Strategy of the United States of America*, and the Department of Homeland Security implemented its *Cybersecurity Strategy* to promote prosperity in American's lives and reduce cyber threats, respectively. In the same year, the Department of Defence (DoD) released *The DoD Cyber Strategy-2018* to ensure, strengthen, and expand cyber-related activities and defend or secure against cyber threats (DoD, 2018). The Cybersecurity and Infrastructure Security Agency, under the Department of Homeland Security takes the responsibility to protect and respond to cyberattacks in the country. Under the National Security Agency, the United States Cyber Command (CYBERCOM) was established in 2009 to carry out defensive and offensive operations in cyberspace. The *National Cybersecurity Protection Act of 2014* and the *Cybersecurity Act 2015* were also enacted to prevent, detect, analyse, and mitigate threats in the digital world. Meanwhile, the United States is involved in several multilateral and bilateral cooperations including the Budapest Conventions, UN cybersecurity processes, and several other agreements with individual countries.

Meanwhile, *Russia* prefers to use the term 'information technology' instead of using the term 'cyberspace' or 'cybersecurity' in their official documents. Most of its policies covering cybersecurity are published in the name of information security. Russia, under its president-led security council introduced the *Doctrine of Information Security* in 2016 to ensure, upgrade, forecast, promote, and counter cyber-related threats and affairs of the state

(Federation, 2008). While the Security Council of the Russian Federation is responsible for making critical decisions on cybersecurity policy, the Department of International Information Security is involved in international cybersecurity initiatives and internet governance. Russia has different laws related to the protection of social (internet) media, critical information infrastructure, and cybercrimes. Notable laws include the Federal Law N. 149-FZ on Information, *Information Technologies and Information Protection*, which was amended in 2017 and issued provisions related to information (cyber) security. It engaged with multilateral forums and was the first country to propose a UN discussion on *Developments in the Field of Information and Telecommunications in the Context of International Security* in 1998. In response to Russia's suggestion, the UN established the UNGGE, of which Russia has been a member since 2004. It also maintains bilateral agreements and cooperation on cybersecurity with countries including India, Thailand, Japan, France, etc.

China, with its objective to become a global cyber power nation, implemented the *National Cyberspace Security Strategy* in 2016 to manage cybersecurity, protect the cyber ecosystem, and utilise the domain for peaceful purposes. In 2017, it developed the *International Strategy of Cooperation on Cyberspace* to safeguard sovereignty, promote cyber governance and cooperation, and develop international rules in cyberspace. In 2020, China introduced the *Global Initiative on Data Security* for all stakeholders, especially UN member states, to encourage dialogue and cooperation in cyberspace for peace, security, and orders (Ministry of Foreign Affairs, 2020). In 2014, the Cyberspace Administration of China was established and later in 2018 converted its name to the Central Cyberspace Affairs Commission. It makes national decisions on cybersecurity and internet policies. In 2016, under the Communist Party of China, the Cyber Security Association of China' was created to connect with major stakeholders and promote network security and development. The People's Liberation Army and its Strategic Support Force along with the General Armament Department (GAD) and General Political Department are responsible for cyberwarfare, space, and electronic combat. In 2014, the Cyberspace Strategic Intelligence Research Centre under GAD was established to conduct cutting-edge research on internet intelligence, data tracking, and digital network analyses. China has strong legal frameworks such as the *Cybersecurity Law (2017)*, *Data Security Law (2021)*, *Regulation on Protecting the Security of Critical Information Infrastructure (2021)*, and *Personal Information Protection Law (2021)* to control crime and irregular activities in cyberspace. China, as a member of the UN and a regional organisation (the SCO), actively participates in cybersecurity initiatives and developments. Individually, it also maintains bilateral relations with countries including the US, Australia, UK, Japan, South Korea, etc.

Middle Powers

The *United Kingdom* has a comprehensive cybersecurity policy with national structures, strategies, legal framework, and bi and multilateral cooperation. In 2016, to reduce cyber threats against critical sectors, industries, and the public sphere, the National Cyber Security Centre (NCSC) headed by a chief executive officer was established under the Government Communications Headquarters (GCHQ). Other establishments include the Office of Cyber Security and Information Assurance and the Cabinet Office (2009) to provide strategic directions on cybersecurity, the National Cyber Crime Unit and National Crime Agency (2013) to respond to cybercrime, and the National Cyber Security Centre Incident Management, GCHQ (2014) to contribute technical advice and guidance to stakeholders. In order to secure cybersecurity in the defence supply chain system, the Ministry of Defence launched the Defence Cyber Protection Partnership in 2021. As a strategic document, the *National Cyber Security Strategy 2016–2021* was released by the Cabinet Office in 2016 and later updated in the successive year (Government, 2017). Similarly, in 2021, the *National Cyber Strategy 2022: Pioneering a Cyber Future with the Whole of the UK*, was released with five main pillars to strengthen, make prosperous, lead, advance, and detect/disrupt/deter the security aspect of cyberspace. The UK has established distinct cyber, computer, and electronic laws to ensure the safe use of digital networks and to safeguard its cyber ecosystem. Some of the notable laws include the *Network and Information Systems Regulations 2018, Computer Misuse Act 1990*, and Electronic Communications Act 2000. As a member of the UNGGE on *Advancing Responsible State Behaviour in Cyberspace in the Context of International Security*, the UK actively participates in the UN cybersecurity process, and is a signatory of the Budapest Convention. It also preserves bi and multilateral relations on cybersecurity affairs with Poland, Lithuania, Italy, France, Australia, China, US, etc.

Given its success in the field, *Japan* is regarded as one of the best ICT nations in the world. It provides multiple forms of support to other nations due to its extensive capacity for industrial developments in ICT sectors[8] (Ministry of Internal Affairs and Communications, 2022). The National Diet of Japan adopted the *Basic Act of Cybersecurity* in 2014 (enforced 2015) to promote the cybersecurity policy (measures, principles, regulation) for national and local government by establishing a Cybersecurity Strategy Headquarters (CSH) under the cabinet secretariat. The CSH was established in 2015 to coordinate with government agencies including the IT Strategic Headquarters and the National Security Council (Japan) to take measures on information and cybersecurity affairs. Further, the National Centre of Incident Readiness and Strategy for Cybersecurity (NISC[9]) was created as the secretariat of the CHS to coordinate the cybersecurity strategy, policy of critical information infrastructures, common standards, human resource development, and research and development. In 2021, the Digital Agency was created to work with cybersecurity headquarters to reform and make new policies on the culture of the state digital program. Under the Self Defence Forces, Ministry of Defence, Japan, the Cyber Defence Group, formerly known as the Cyber Defence Unit, was developed as a joint structure to protect the infrastructure of the military services in 2013. Meanwhile, the *Cybersecurity Strategy 2021* was released with a target to secure cyberspace in three years. In December 2021, the CSH published the *Basic Policy on Cybersecurity Capacity Building Support for Developing Countries* for capacity building in the realm of cybersecurity. A series of policy documents including the *International Strategy on Cybersecurity Cooperation 2013*, *General Framework for Secure IoT Systems 2016*, and *The Cybersecurity Policy for Critical Infrastructure Protection 2022* were released for the safety of Japan's digital networks. It also put collaborative efforts on cyber resilience by having multi and bilateral relations with other countries as highlighted in Chapter 2.

Canada has a dedicated government department on cybersecurity to educate the public about the risk associated with internet activities and to ensure their safety while connecting to cyber networks (Canada, 2022). Major contributors to the state's cybersecurity architecture are the Communications Security Establishment (CSE) and its brainchild the Canadian Centre for Cyber Security (also known as the Cyber Center). While the CSE acts as a national cryptologic agency, providing the government with IT security and foreign signals intelligence (Canada, 2022), the Cyber Center is a conglomerate of experts from various organisations that serve as a nodal agency to respond to and mitigate cyber-related events in the country (Canada, 2022). The Cyber Center works based on five pillars: information, protection, development, defence, and action on cybersecurity related affairs. They are also supported by the Cyber Crime Fusion Center (it operates under the Royal Canadian Mounted Police) that analyses and provides assessments on cyber threats and cybercrimes. Subsequently, the Cyber Threat Evaluation Center, a unit of the CSE, is composed of technical and analytical experts to identify and discuss threats over national key networks. Meanwhile, the *National Strategy for Critical Infrastructure*, released in 2010, aims to build partnership, share, protect, and manage CIIs. In 2015, the Royal Canadian Mounted Police published the *Royal Canadian Mounted Police Cybercrime Strategy* to prioritise the prevention of cybercrime through intelligence collecting and analysis. In 2018, the *National Cyber Security Strategy: Canada's Vision for Security and Prosperity in the Digital Age* was implemented to promote CIIs, protect rights, encourage business, collaborate across sectors, and adapt new technologies on cybersecurity issues. The *Action Plan 2010–2015 for Canada's Cyber Security Strategy*, which outlines the state's goals for a digital security strategy, was also put into effect in 2013. Canada also cooperates and signs Memorendum of Understandings (MoUs) with countries including India, Sweden, and the US.

Small Powers (States of Concern)

The cyber capabilities of *Iran* were highlighted in the report, *Iranian Government-Sponsored Actors Conduct Cyber Operations Against Global Government and Commercial Networks* released on 24 February 2022 by a collaborative group of Western cybersecurity agencies.[10] The report suggested that a group of mercenaries known as *Muddy Water*, sponsored by the Iranian government, conducted cyber operations (espionage and persistent malware attacks) against public and private information systems in Asia, Africa, Europe, and North America (CISA, 2022). By taking advantage of the ambiguous and lawless nature of cyberspace, small powers such as Iran could challenge greater powers through digital networks and attacks, which may not be possible out of the cyberworld (physical space). Iran has been attacking the US since 2009, when the Iranian Cyber Army vandalised the homepage of *Twitter*. Other incursions have since taken place, including distributed denial of service (DDoS) attacks on US banks in 2012 (Operation Ababil) and an alleged cyberattack targeting a Saudi petrochemicals factory close to a US base in 2017 (Hanna, 2019). Soon after the Stuxnet incident, the Cyber Defence Command was created in 2010 under the Passive Civil Defence Organization of Iran (Joint Staff of the Iranian Armed Forces) and has the potential to act in both offensive and defensive dimensions. Iran has strengthened its cybersecurity capabilities by establishing a national supreme authority known as the Council of Cyberspace in 2012 to make central decisions regarding internet policy. Iran has actively expressed its opinions over UN cybersecurity procedures and has continued bi and multilateral relations with other nations.

Because of the threat posed by the Arab World and the technical prowess *Israel* possesses, it is one country that has a comprehensive cybersecurity setup in the world (though small in size). The Israel National Cyber Directorate (INCD) (PMO-Israel), published a dedicated *National Cyber Security Strategy* in September 2017 with the goal of making Israel the "leading nation in leveraging cyberspace as an engine of economic growth, social welfare, and national security". To achieve its vision, Israel wants its cyber ecosystem to be safe and secure from potential threats. Through this strategy, Israel will contribute its leadership and technical knowhow in the world cyber affairs (Directorate, 2017). The INCD is a "national security and technological agency" that operates at the national level to defend the country's cyberspace and achieve cyber power in the world. It will prevent, detect, identify, and respond to any cyber threat (internal/external) against Israel. It designs the state's strategy and policy on the digital domain along with the responsibility to advise the prime minister and government of the country (INCD, 2020). The INCD was created in 2017 by uniting the National Cyber Bureau (NCB) and National Cyber Security Authority (NCSA). While the NCB was founded in 2011 to advise the prime minister and develop a strategy (or policy) on cyberspace affairs, the NCSA was created in 2016 to take responsibility for national cyber defence, respond to cyberattacks, and strengthen resilience in sectors of economic growth. Meanwhile, the Cyber and Technology Division of the Israeli Security Agency[11] (ISA) initiates, develops, and produces advanced technologies for intelligence collection, counter terrorism, and espionage through cyberspace (ISA, 2022). Being a signatory of the Convention on Cybercrime (Budapest Convention), it made agreements on cybersecurity matters with countries including German, Armenia, Japan, and Australia.

The cybersecurity policy of *North Korea* (DPRK) officially remains obscured from the public sphere. The world's attention was drawn to its cyber capabilities when the digital facilities of Sony Pictures Entertainment was attacked by North Korean hackers in 2014 because of a movie *(The Interview)* that allegedly insulted their supreme leader Kim Jong-un. Because the DPRK is not connected to the global internet and relies on its own national intranet, *Kwangmyong*, the government can more easily keep an eye on or monitor the online environment. While a few elites and foreign visitors are allowed to access the internet in the country, the DPRK is extremely vigilant and closely monitors it (CRS, 2017). The narrative around cybersecurity in North Korea differs from that of other nations that internationally disclosed their digital policies. While countries are concerned about other countrys' cybersecurity, countries are is more concerned with the DPRK's cyber capabilities. Instead of observing how the DPRK protects its cyberspace, the world debates more on the threat it poses or about the crimes (cyber) it commits. Most of the cyber-operational planning and attacks are carried out by the state's Reconnaissance General Bureau (RGB) and The Korean People's Army (KPA) General Staff. More than 6,000 cyber operatives are estimated to be actively engaged in state-sponsored cyber offense operations, most of which are carried out by the RGB and KPA General Staff. While these offices are mostly known for their offensive dimensions, their involvement in the protection of its national cyberspace is imminent. Besides the Sony Picture Entertainment attack, other globally known infamous digital attacks attributed to the DPRK are the *WannaCry* ransomeware attack (2017), the Bangladesh bank heist (2016), the South Korea bank attack (2013), etc. (CRS, 2017).

Subnational (Cybersecurity at the State Level)

The protection of cyberspace also extends to the subnational or individual state level, and hence the US federal government provides certain autonomy to local government to develop state-wide guidelines or policies for cybersecurity. For instance, in *New York* technology companies play an important role in its economic sector, supporting its growth rate. Similar to California's Silicon Valley', New York has Silicon Alley', a hub for information technology businesses that concentrate on software development, new digital media, financial technology, cryptocurrency, telecommunications, and the internet, all of which are connected to cyberspace and necessary for the protections that follow. Subsequently, the Government of New York State introduced cybersecurity policies, laws, and regulations to be implemented within the state only. In 2002, to permit the authority to establish cybersecurity or IT-related policies, it implemented the *NYS-P08-002 Authority to Establish State Enterprise Information Technology (IT) Policy, Standards and Guidelines*. The Office of Information Technology Services (OITS) was created in 2012 to provide IT services, develop technology solutions, give strategic direction, and develop IT policies. (Services, 2022). The Chief Information Security Officer (CISO) as the head of OITS is in charge of protecting the state government infrastructure, coordinating policies and standards related to cybersecurity, giving direction, governance and vision to the OITS, developing partnerships, and capacity building (OITS, 2022a). The OITS introduced cybersecurity policies including the *Information Security Policy 2003*, *Secure Use of Social Media 2010*, *802.11 Mobile Device Security 2014*, *Wireless Network Security 2015*, and *Digital Identity Policy 2020,* including many others (OITS, 2022b). Meanwhile, the Special Investigations Division and Grand Larceny Division of the New York Police Department is involved in cybersecurity and cybercrime incidents (NYPD, 2022).

While all states in India have dedicated departments to govern and regulate information and communication technology within their states, Kerala and Gujarat have been chosen for this study as Kerala is the best state in public governance and Gujarat is where a research institute resides. With 46.4 million internet users in March 2021 (TRAI, 2022), *Kerala* is the best governed state of India (ETGovernment, 2021). In 1995, the first IT Park (Technopark) of India was established in the state creating jobs for 64,000 IT professionals. While the Infopark was developed in Kochi in 1995, employing 51,000 people, the Cyber Park (Kozhikode Cyber Park) was established in 2009 providing more than 1,000 jobs. Under the Kerala *IT Policy 1998*, the Department of Information Technology was developed in 1999 "to address the changing needs of IT development in the state". Another *IT Policy 2017* was introduced with objectives to create a cybersecurity framework to promote digital activities including privacy and freedom of the Internet, encouraging safe e-transactions, and conducting cyber awareness programs (Kerala, 2017, p. 12). Meanwhile, to control crime associated with cyberspace, the Cyber Crime Police Station was established in 2009. It investigates complex cybercrime issues with its forensic capabilities (Police, 2020). Kerala Police established the Cyberdome as a centre of excellence for cybersecurity with the vision of educating people about digital space; defending cyberspace; protecting state CIIs, e-governance, and civilian business; and creating a cybersecurity platform to secure cyberspace for society (Police, 2022).

With 70.36 million internet users in March 2021 (TRAI, 2022), *Gujarat* is a leading industrial area that is globally and nationally recognised by its state-of-art infrastructure. Out of Gujarat's total export, the IT sector contributed $433 million in the year 2018–2019.[12] Most of the information and communication technology related affairs in the state are the responsibility of the Directorate of Information (DoI) and Department of Science and Technology (DST). While the DoI provides general services on communication activities (radio, television, media, and natural disaster information) (DoI, 2022), the DST is responsible for the growth and development of emerging technologies and formulating and implementing key ICT policies of the state (DST, 2022). As promoting ICT is one of the core agendas of the department, the DST publishes state IT policies from time to time. The first *IT Policy 2006–2011* was released on 1 November 2006 with an objective to attract investors and create employment in the IT sector in Gujarat (DST, 2006). It also calls to strengthen the Cybercrime Detection cell functioning under the police department to provide the highest level of security for information technology and its enabled services (Section 11 of the released policy). This was followed by a series of policy publications including *IT Policy 2014–2019*, *IT/ITeS Policy 2016–2021*, and *IT/ITeS Policy 2022–2027*. The Directorate of ICT and e-Governance and Gujarat Informatics Limited support DST in monitoring and managing e-governance and the procurement of IT-related facilities. While there is no separate policy on cybersecurity, criminal activities on the digital ecosystem or cyber-enabled physical offences are the responsibility of the law enforcement agencies of the state. Gujarat Police has set up a dedicated Cybercrime Cell "to monitor and support cybersecurity across the state". Defining the meaning of cybercrime and listing the types of cyber offences,[13] the body has different units with diverged responsibilities. These units include the Cybersecurity Lab, Cybercrime Incident Response Unit, Cybercrime Prevention Unit, and Anti-Cyber Bullying Unit (G. Police, 2022).

Organisation (Cybersecurity of Companies and Industry)

A government runs its state with the support of administrative functionaries and public institutions (ministry, department, etc.) and private organisations (company and industry). With the development of ICT, no sector (political, economic, social, military, or any offices) operates without cyber networks. Therefore, every organisation needs to maintain digital standards and adhere to protective procedures in order to function in a safe and secure environment free from digital threats. The *National Cyber Security Policy* (NCSP)-2013 in its "Para A (Creating a secure cyber ecosystem) of the Section IV (Strategies)" ensures every institution (public or private) must nominate a senior representative as CISO to be responsible for cybersecurity efforts and initiatives of public institutes and private industries (Meity, 2013). The CISO will make cybersecurity policies suitable for their institutions and businesses and implement them as per international best practice. Establishing standards and mechanisms for handling, storing, and transferring data; performing risk assessments; and implementing advanced security measures and forensic-enabled information infrastructure are part of the CISO's duties (Technology, 2013). Separately, addressing the detailed guidelines of the CISO, the Computer Emergency Response Team-India (CERT-In) on 14 March 2017 released a document entitled the Key Roles and Responsibilities of Chief Information Security Officers (CISOs) in Ministries/Departments and Organisations managing ICT operations. To strengthen the cybersecurity ecosystem, the Ministry of Electronics and Information Technology (MeitY) organised a training program for CISOs along with technical heads and IT staff from various ministries, departments, and organisations from central and state governments and bank organisations (PIB, 2021).

Below are three examples of organisations at national, state, and sub-state (district) levels that demonstrate the implementation of cybersecurity frameworks and initiatives. These organisations are chosen based on their relevance and suitability for this study rather than their prominence or perceived importance. This approach offers a diverse perspective on cybersecurity efforts prepared at multiple administrative levels.

National Organisation

Referring to national-level institutes, and taking the Indian Ministry of External Affairs (MEA) as an example (referent object), the MEA has a dedicated division, known as the E-Governance and Information Technology Division to look after the overall cybersecurity and computer-related activities of the ministry. The division is headed by a joint secretary, who also serves as the CISO. He is supported by two Officers on Special Duty with military backgrounds and two undersecretaries (MEA, 2022). It protects its institutional ICT (computer/internet) setups through trusted companies (outsource) and contracts. Vendors are invited to tender for annual maintenance of computers (soft and hardware), digital networks, servers, communication equipment, and internet cabling for the ministry. Different levels of technicians (seniors and juniors) from the approved company will be responsible for maintaining "switches, Unified Threat Management (UTM) Devices, Servers, Firewall Managers (FMs) and also coordination with Original Equipment Manufacturer or OEM (Firms) for support of IT devices". The company will also take charge of repairing or laying internet cables and maintenance of computer facilities including firewalls, troubleshooting, formatting, installation of operating systems, browsers, antivirus, and office software (Division, 2018). Strict rules and regulations are enforced for contract technicians, including thorough identity verification and defined duty durations within the ministry. While the overall cybersecurity aspect is controlled by the authorities of the MEA, the management and protection of the digital system are responsibility of the outsourced vendors.

State Organisation

At the state institutional (departmental) level, this section examines the cybersecurity system of the Finance Department, Government of Gujarat.

The state finance institute plays an important role in the development and management of the state's financial sector, ensuring fiscal stability, formulating budgets, and implementing policies (Department, 2013). The ICT (or cybersecurity) unit of the department and its role are not published in the open domain and it functions in a confidential manner.[14] Cybersecurity is viewed by the agency as a complex component of its services. Interacting with department staff, it was learned that Tata Consultancy Services (TCS) had been contracted to manage the institute's computer and cyber-related matters. With the help of TCS, the department conducts its activities through an "intranet" facility for secured networks. TCS provided various services including "cybersecurity, enterprise applications, cognitive business operations, analytics and insights, blockchain, AI, cloud computing, digital engineering, etc." It helps the Finance Department in the design and development of its IT architecture, network security, and enables executing business operations (TCS, 2022). It continuously augments, replaces, and upgrades the IT infrastructure of the institute. It not only ensures the compliance of the cyber network, but also mitigates various types of risk and combats sophisticated threats (TCS, 2022). While the organisational requirement and policy is the responsibility of the department, TCS is in charge for the overall ICT system of the department.

Substate Organisation

The cybersecurity framework conducted at the national and state organisational level is illustrated in the previous two paragraphs. In the same order, while the next study should be undertaken with a substate office at the district level (for example, the cybersecurity system of a collector's office), the cyber protective mechanism of the Central University of Gujarat (CUG) is being examined.[15] Though CUG does not disclose information about its dedicated ICT department in the university bulletin or website, the division has existed since the inception of the university in 2009. The department functions under the supervision of a CISO of the institute. The institute does not have a separate recruitment process for a dedicated position of the CISO, instead, the role is assigned to a teaching faculty member with a technical background. However, at lower ranks, technical assistants from eligible computer backgrounds are hired as the institute's full-time employee (CUG, 2021). While Bharat Sanchar Nigam Limited (BSNL) officially provides the internet, wi-fi, and local area network (LAN) including the cables and installation of facilities in the campus, the technicians of the university take the responsibility of managing and operating all the cyber (internet and other digital) related matters of the campus. They involve day-to-day cyber activities, network management and monitoring; web design and maintenance; server and data security; web technologies and data analyses; and installation and management of operating system.[16] The cybersecurity approach in the CUG campus is done collectively by the technicians working in the institute with support from the vendor (BSNL), under the direction of the CISO who sets the institute's policy requirement.

Individual (Personal Cybersecurity)

The individual plays a significant role in politics (state formation) and war (security). Individuals are the source of both the Aristotelian theory of the state and the Clausewitzian theory of war. The security of the digital environment begins with personal awareness and safety, much as the saying goes, "Charity begins at home". Cybersecurity at the individual level can be perceived in three aspects: defensive, non-offensive, and cyber volunteer (contribution at personal level).

Defensive

The first step in personal cybersecurity is to safeguard one's own gadgets, which is defensive in nature. This includes the measure taken at the individual level for the safety of one's computer, mobile phones, and associated networks by updating antivirus and changing passwords. The NCSP 2013, in its Para-K of Section IV, "Creating Cyber Security Awareness" promotes nationwide awareness and develops programs on cybersecurity. In order to inform the public and raise their level of understanding on digital security, it also emphasises the importance of encouraging public campaigns on cybersecurity through electronic media. Seminars and workshops along with certifications as encouragement of young and old on cybersecurity issues are mentioned in the document (MeitY, 2013). The MHA released *A Handbook for Adolescents/Students on Cyber Safety* for everyone, especially students above the age of 13, to create awareness about various cyber threats and how to protect themselves from cybercrime (MHA, 2018). To report cyber associated crimes and action to be taken by states authorities, the ministry released the *User Manual for Reporting Cyber Crimes* on 30 August 2019 (MHA, 2019).

Non-offensive

Being non-offensive in cyberspace is not the same as being defensive in the domain. While the former is to take a stance that an individual not disrupt other users' digital systems (with or without using protective mechanisms), the latter is based on safeguarding personal computer systems by taking personal preventive measures. This cybersecurity aspect warns that either on moral or legal grounds, an individual should never be involved in any digital-offensive or cyber-criminal activities. In simple terms, whether one protects his computer or not, he must never disturb others cyber or information facilities. Disobeying and committing any digital crimes (by citizens) is punishable according to the law of the land or the *IT (Amendment) Act 2008*. Section 66 and 67 of the Act deal with the subject and cybercriminals will be punished with imprisonment and fines for stealing computer resources (66B), identity theft (66C), cheating and impersonation by computing device (66D), violation of privacy (66E), cyberterrorism (66F), publishing/transmitting obscene material (67), child pornography (67B), and retention of information by intermediaries. When utilising computers, the internet, and social media, citizens are warned about illegal content that could harm India's essential values. Citizens should avoid any content that would violate or disturb the sovereignty and integrity of the nation, defence of India, security of the state, friendly relations with foreign states, public order, communal harmony, and child sex abuse (MHA, 2022).

Cyber Volunteer

This third category of individual cybersecurity can be discussed from the perspective of the contribution made by leaders, academics, scientists, and activists at the personal level for the betterment of the cyber ecosystem at the national level and beyond. This class of individuals are those who, beyond their personal cyber safety, contribute to the digital security agenda of society. Leaders and stakeholders (public and private community) in their personal capacity can persuade policymakers to introduce new national cybersecurity strategies and programs. Meanwhile, individual scientists who develop new technology, software, and applications, as well as their contribution to society, cannot be disregarded. Cyber academics who promote the development of public policy and who write insightful books and articles on digital security should be taken into account. Cyber awareness among the populace is also promoted by the knowledge sharing of cyber activists and their useful contributions on blogs and social media. Common citizens are even requested and permitted by the state authorities to provide support on handling cybercrimes and safe cyber governance. The MHA established the Indian Cyber Crime Coordination Centre (I4C) to provide a platform where academics, industry, public, and government entities can work together for cyber prevention, detection, investigation, and prosecution. The I4C launched a program known as the Cyber Crime Volunteers Program to encourage interested citizens to fight cybercrime by bringing them together in a single platform. These volunteers will help the law enforcement agencies in identifying, reporting, and withdrawing illegal and unwanted content from websites (MHA, 2022).

Digital Threats and Cybersecurity Structures in India

India's national security is significantly influenced by cyber affairs. As technology progresses, both state and non-state actors have used cyberspace to acquire power and accomplish strategic objectives. While India is trying to expand its role in the digital world order, it perceives multiple cyber threats from both internal and external elements. At the external level, China and Pakistan, who have been engaged in a protracted conflict for decades, pose a cyber threat. To meet the challenge, the military cyber command, the DCA was established under the MoD in 2018. At the domestic level, it has been infested by violent movements including homegrown militancy in the North-East (NE) India, Jammu and Kashmir (J&K), Left Wing Extremism, terrorism in rest of India, organised crime, illegal networks, and other criminal activities where cyber operations are involved. Subsequently, to counter their exploitation in cyberspace, the Cyber and Information Security Division was created (PIB, 2018). Hence, India's cybersecurity approach is largely focused on addressing regional threats, particularly from China and Pakistan, while also tackling domestic cybercrime. It also intends to expand its influence in global cyber affairs, reflecting a balance of regional security concerns and growing involvement in international cybersecurity frameworks.

Threats and security in the real (non-cyber) world are studied objectively through internal and external dimensions with responsibility for these dimensions taken by dedicated state security forces of home affairs and military services, respectively. Similarly, security in cyberspace can also be examined from internal and external aspects along with their key responders from state police forces and armed forces. As cybercrime or cyberattacks occurs in an electronic medium with strategic, legal, scientific, economic, social, and ICT implications, there are other key institutions involved in cybersecurity affairs (beyond the police and military forces). Though the MoD and MHA normally act as the dedicated state enforcement agencies to challenge domestic and foreign cybercrimes, other civil agencies including MeitY, MEA, Ministry of Communication (MoC), Ministry of Science and Technology (MS&T), Ministry of Finance (MoF), Ministry of Information and Broadcasting (MI&B), Ministry of Law and Justice (MoL&J), along with the National Security Council Secretariat (NSCS) participate in state cybersecurity measures. Based on their activities, these agencies can be simply grouped into enforcement and non-enforcement cyber authorities of India. While the judicial system can also fit into the latter category, it is discussed separately in this section (Figure 3.2).

External Cyber Challenges

The geopolitical system in the region compels India to be proactive against strategic threats posed by neighbouring countries and other domestic criminal activities. In order to achieve their strategic and political goals, these elements of both state and non-state actors repeatedly disrupt India's key information infrastructures (CIIs) and ICT facilities. In addition, India also received threats from other concerning states *inter alia* North Korea and Bangladesh. If not for strategic or political purposes, these small powers involved in financial heists from banks, affect India's economy and digital ecosystem. Additionally, infamous cyberattacks that occurred in other regions of the world have a spillover impact that affects India's cyberspace (Stuxnet in Iran 2010, and Petya in Ukraine, 2017).

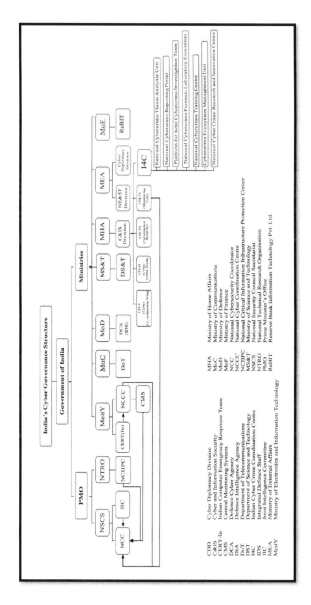

Figure 3.2 Cybersecurity Structure of India.

China's Digital Threat

China's rise as a global power represents the greatest threat to India, both in the physical world and in the realm of cyberspace. With a determination to become a "cyber superpower nation" by 2030, China has been trying to improve its ICT capabilities over the past two decades (IISS, 2021, p. 89). This has also been reflected in a series of national *white papers* released in 2011. Such an aggressive aspiration of China is perceived as a direct or indirect threat to India and its regional security structure. Most of the sophisticated cyberattacks on India are carried out by, or attributed to, China. The infamous attack on the power grid in Mumbai (Maharashtra) in October 2020 was attributed to China, though China officially denied the charges (Cunningham, 2021). Scholars believe that the attack was an asymmetric response to border tension between the two countries at Sikkim and Arunachal Pradesh in 2021 (Bommankanti, 2021). A significant Chinese cyber breach against Indian digital networks can be traced back to 2010 when the former hacked some of the latter's computer facilities of the Commonwealth Games in New Delhi. China was also allegedly involved in spying on the computer networks of important offices including military and non-military sectors. These Chinese aggressive actions are regarded as a form of cyberwarfare designed to achieve strategic goals against India. Considering it as a matter of sheer concern, 43 applications (apps) of Chinese origin including *PUBG Mobile*, *TikTok*, *Weibo*, *WeChat*, and *AliExpress* were proscribed in November 2020. Later, 267 apps were also suspended from operating in India (IndiaTV, 2020). Chinese telecom companies such as Huawei and ZTE are restricted in India as they are considered a "non-trusted source".

Pakistan's Cyber Threat

Over the last two decades or more, Pakistan has come to the fore for cyber incursions against India on different occasions. In the early 2000s, it did not have the potential capability to target networks of significant critical infrastructure, except conducting some website defacement and virus dessimination. However, being an ally of China, Pakistan can now conduct cyber surveillance with the assistance of the former (Das, 2020). The first cyber incursion against India took place in 1998 when a group of Pakistani hackers defaced the website of the Bhabha Atomic Research Centre (BARC). Further, many hacking groups including Death to India, Kill India, and G-Force Pakistan, declared an open challenge and provided instructions to attack Indian computers (Prasad, 2000). The Pakistan Cyber Army defaced the Central Bureau of Investigation (CBI) website and 270 other Indian websites in December 2010 (NDTV, 2010). Another mercenary group, Transparent Tribe, conducted *Operation Sidecopy* to steal strategic and sensitive data from CIIs by using remote access trojans (Das, 2020). In August 2012, a Pakistani originated terror threat spread through social media and caused natives of North East India (staying in Indian metropolitan areas including

Bangalore, Chennai, etc.) to flee their home states. The incident was considered cyberwarfare by many people including politicians in India. China may be able to assist Pakistan if it is unable to attack India's advanced targets on its own, and will do so at the right time. It is not only from China or Pakistan that India has suffered cyberattacks, but other countries too. The indirect effects of cyberattacks in other countries (Stuxnet, Petya, etc.) cause harm to India's digital assets.

Other External Threats

Although China and Pakistan have traditionally been seen as India's key rivals in cyberspace, other unstable nations like Bangladesh or North Korea pose a threat to India's cyber ecosystem. While the intention of the attacks was not for a political or strategic objectives, they were mostly conducted for economic benefits. In July 2016 suspected Bangladeshi or North Korean hackers tried to steal $170 million from the Union Bank of India and the modus operandi of the cyber incursion was said to be similar to the money heist of Bangladesh Central Bank that occurred earlier in February 2016 (Haran, 2017; Steinberg, 2017). Meanwhile, attacks in other countries such as Stuxnet (2010) in Iran and Petya in Ukraine (2017) affected India. Geographically, India is the third largest affected country (after Iran and Indonesia) from malware used in the Stuxnet incident (Nicolas Falliere, 2012) and it is also the seventh largest victim in the world (after Ukraine, US, Russia, France, UK, and Germany) of the Petya attack (Desk, 2017).

Internal Cyber Apprehensions

At the domestic level, India has been facing multiple threats associated with cyberspace. While the nation is dealing with militancy in several regions, threats to the state have also increased due to other organised crime including drug trafficking, cyber money laundering, weapons dealing, and child pornography, among others. It is obvious that non-state actors do not possess the digital infrastructure or resources that the state apparatus does. Nevertheless, there are indications that non-state actors may be able to readily exploit social media platforms or darknet resources (a part of the deep web) to achieve their goals.

Terrorism/Militancy

Terrorists exploiting cyber facilities in India became popular when groups such as Indian Mujahideen (IM), Islamic State of Iraq and Syria (ISIS), and their affiliates (David Coleman Headley, Burhan Wani) used cyberspace for terrorist activities. In the middle and later part of 2000s, any bomb blast that IM carried out was associated with hate mail prior to or after the incident. Headley used Google Earth map to identify the targets (hotels and railway stations) of the 26 November Mumbai terrorist attacks. Burhan Wani, the young commander of the Hizbul Mujahideen terrorist group was a popular media propogandist and poster boy of the group. He was a key architect of psychological warfare and campaigned for young people to join the group by using social media (*YouTube, Facebook*, etc.). His death in 2016 won the sympathy of believers and inspired many youths to join such groups, causing a long-term effect in the state (Rao, 2016; Pandya, 2020). Meanwhile, in July 2021, Umar Nisar Bhat, a member of ISIS (India chapter), was arrested with two associates in Anantnag District, J&K, for recruiting cadres by using the application, *Telegram* (Gupta M., 2021).

Drug Trafficking

India occupies a space between the world largest drug traders, the Golden Crescent (Pakistan, Afghanistan, and Iran) and the Golden Triangle (Myanmar, Thailand, and Laos). With the evolution of communication technologies, these illegal drugs are trafficked by using sophisticated technology such as *The Onion Router* (TOR). The Narcotics Control Bureau (NCB) of India for the first time exposed the marketing of such illegal substances in July 2016. It was acknowledged when the Director General of NCB, R.R. Bhatnagar expressed that the agency was able to detect for the first time illicit drug trafficking operating through the encrypted darknet using the unregulated currency bitcoin. The darknet is a complex underground internet network that operates with specific software, configurations, and authorisation, which are difficult to trace by common communications protocols and ports (PTI, 2016). While the practice has been continuing, there are also instances where law enforcement agencies are stopping such irregular trade conducted through cyberspace (Bhatia, 2021).

Digital Money Fraud and Laundering

India is extremely concerned about fraud and digital money laundering. These days, fraudsters frequently use stolen credit or debit card information to make purchases or withdraw money. Digital money fraud has increased from Rs. 2,537 crore with 2 million cases (2022–2023) to Rs. 4,245 crore in the first 10 months of April (2024) to January (2025) with 2.4 million incidents (Kumar, 2025). Meanwhile, cyber money laundering is a phenomenon in which original sources are concealed to transfer money illegally by using advanced technological solutions (Nahid Joveda, 2019). Concerned by this threat, the Union Finance Minister Nirmala Sitharaman in April 2022 expressed her worries that cryptocurrency shall be used in money laundering and terror financing (India Today, 2022). Meanwhile, the *Indiaforensic Consultancy Services*[17] reported that in the period between 2000 and 2010, approximately $1.9 million (Rs. 18.86 Lakh) has been involved in digital money laundering (Indiaforensic, 2021).

Arms Trafficking

Non-state actors in India are marketing illegal weapons through internet channels. Buying, selling, money transfer, etc., are conducted through cyber media, using the darknet as a new phenomenon. According to the National Crime Records Bureau (NCRB) report, *Crime in India-2019, the* number of arms seized in 2019 alone was 79,547, in which only 1,980 were licensed or factory made, and the other 77,567 were unlicensed, improvised, crude, or roughly made. Although it is believed that trading weaponry on digital platforms has been going on for some time, security agencies still struggle to stop it. This may be due to a lack of technological skills in security establishments. The Punjab Police, however, dismantled an arms trade network in April 2021 by apprehending three Madhya Pradesh-based arms dealers who sell weapons to Punjab and other states. While the police are not ruling out the involvement of the darknet, the use of *WhatsApp* to establish the intricate networks of the syndicate was exposed (ToI, 2021). Though it is hard to obtain the evidence, terrorist groups are apparently searching for new technologies and black markets to purchase arms and raise funds through these deep internet avenues.[18]

Child Pornography

India pays special attention to cybercrime against children and women. Additionally, with special attention paid to both, www.cybercrime.gov.in, a specialised platform for reporting cybercrime, was launched. According to an NCRB report, cybercrime against children has increased from 305 cases in 2019 to 1,102 in 2020. Similarly, in the same period, cybercrime against women has also increased from 8,379 and 10,405 (PIB, 2022). While the bureau released only the reported cases, there may be more such cases that are not registered probably because of social stigma. Across the globe, 60 per cent of cases of child pornography were committed by family acquaintances (or relatives) and 50 per cent of pornographic materials were filmed without the knowledge of the children (Babu, 2021). During the COVID-19 pandemic, the consumption of child pornography content in India jumped by 95 per cent (Sheth, 2020). To curb the menace, government institutes including the Ministry of Education, MeitY, and MHA took several initiatives. The *Protection of Children from Sexual Offences Act* was also implemented to protect children from crimes including those in the cyber realm (PIB, 2022).

India's Cybersecurity Setup

In response to the threats India perceives and to ensure that cyberspace functions smoothly, the Indian cybersecurity system has been structured with the involvement of enforcement and non-enforcement authorities including the state judicial system. While the enforcement (security) agencies will emphasise both defensive and offensive activities along with punishable actions against cybercrime actors, non-enforcement agencies will provide digital security policies and guidelines to stakeholders along with research and development assistance to the ICT sector. Meanwhile, the legal framework will support and provide state authorities with the power to control the domain through national laws and acts.

Cyber Legal/Judicial Body

The *IT Act 2000* (amended in 2008) served as the foundation for the cybersecurity architecture used (or adopted) by state authorities. Clause-I, Section 48, Chapter X (The Cyber Regulations Appellate Tribunal) of the act directed the Government of India (GoI) to establish one or more Cyber Regulations Appellate Tribunals to protect against cybercrime and punish those culprits involved in the activities. Subsequently, MeitY, following Section 87 of the Act that permits the GoI to make rules, commenced the *Cyber Regulations Appellate Tribunal (Procedure) Rules, 2000* on 17 October 2000 (MeitY, 2000). While the "role and responsibility" of the body is not clearly addressed, it emphasised the composition of the tribunal (Section 49), qualification of the presiding officer (50), terms of office (51), salary and allowance (52), recruitment (53), resignation and removal (54), orders of body (55), staff duty (56), appeal to the office (57), procedure and power (58), right to legal representation (59), limitation (60), civil court jurisdiction (61), appeal to High Court (62), compounding of contraventions (63), and recovery of penalty (64). The tribunal is headed by a presiding officer that is equivalent to a judge of High Court and not over the age of 65 (MeitY, 2000). While the ruling of the presiding officer will be the verdict of the case, an aggrieved petitioner (if not satisfied with the decision) can appeal to the High Court within 60 months. Although these tribunals still operate in some parts of India, the public has been critical of their poor performance (NDTV, 2016).

Cyber Enforcement Agencies

Cyber enforcement agencies are part of the Indian police and defence forces that are involved in defensive and offensive activities in the cyber realm with an objective to protect and defend India's digital ecosystem both internally and externally. While the MHA and its associated state police departments responsible for securing domestic cybersecurity affairs, the MoD monitors external cyber assaults and prepares for cyberwar. These are the two main ministries the state has designated to protect its digital space against domestic and foreign aggression, and their role is sensitive and complex too. However, their efforts have been supported by other technical agencies to fulfill their national objectives.

Ministry of Defence

The Union List (List-I) in the Seventh Schedule (Article 246) of the Constitution of India states that the military services (Army, Navy, and Airforce) are responsible for the defence of India in time of war and peace. Section 32 of the schedule addresses features related to the "posts and telegraphs, telephones, wireless, broadcasting and other like forms of communication", and this provision permits military services to operate in cyberspace (GoI, 2022). As military affairs advance into the domain of cyberspace, the concept of cyberwar became popular in the last decade. States began to introduce cyber commands to their military systems with offensive and defensive competencies. The integration of emerging technologies, such as AI (for military decision making), big data (intelligence gathering), and quantum computing (highly secure communication), in the defence sector has made the military system more complex. India, being an emerging power concerned with external cyber threats created the DCA. The DCA is a joint command with defensive and offensive capabilities and is responsible for building India's cyberpower capacity with the support of other state cybersecurity agencies (VIF, 2019). Multiple military doctrines such as the *Indian Army Doctrine-2004*, The *Joint Doctrine: Indian Armed Forces-2017*, and the *Land Warfare Doctrine-2018*, *Basic Doctrine of the Indian Air Force-2012*, and *Joint Doctrine for Cyberspace Operations-2024* address the relevance of preparing guidelines for cyberwarfare in the Indian defence system. Details of India's approach to cyberwarfare including its cyberwar doctrine are discussed in Chapter 4.

Ministry of Home Affairs

The State List (List-II) of the Seventh Schedule of the Indian constitution is responsible for the law and order (matters of policing and law) of the country without the involvement of military forces. While state police conduct enforcement activities (monitor, investigate, arrest, etc.), the MHA coordinates with all the states' police departments and supports them in maintaining peace and order. With the increase of cyber-enabled crimes, the ministry created the C&IS division with different units including the "Cybercrime Wing; Information Security Unit; Monitoring Unit; Coordination Wing; Indian Cyber Crime Coordination Centre or I4C" to deal with this issue (CIS, 2022). MHA released the *National Information Security Policy & Guidelines* in October 2014 and it addresses issues related to "network security, identity and access management, physical security, application security, data security, personnel security, threat management, incident management, cloud computing, social media and security auditing" (MHA, 2014). As a guideline to the safe use of computer devices and networks, another document on *Information Security Best Practices* (password security, safe access of devices) was issued by the I4C in June 2019 (MHA, 2019). Meanwhile, to set up an institutional mechanism, including forensic laboratories for handling cybercrime at the state and district level, the MHA issued a memorandum, *Advisory on Cyber Crime Prevention and Control* on 13 January 2018 to all Indian police departments. Subsequently, the State Cybercrime Coordination Cell, headed by an additional director general of police or inspector general, and District Cybercrime Cells, under the supervision of a deputy superintendent police or lower rank, were established in every state (MHA, 2018). The Gujarat Police Cybercrime Cell was also established based on the same advisory. Separately, it should not be forgotten that the Bureau of Police Research and Development (BPR&D) also plays an important role in cybersecurity by funding research projects in academic institutions and universities (BPR&D, 2019).

Non-enforcement Authorities

Non-enforcement cybersecurity authorities are government civil agencies that do not belong to the police or military. They belong to the Ministry of Civil Affairs related to the information and technology sector, telecommunication, e-financial services, science and development, digital diplomacy, and social media management. The following are government organisations with different responsibilities for the safety of India's digital space.

National Security Council Secretariat

The Cabinet Committee on Security[19] (CCS) is the highest body in India's security architecture and makes decisions for national security including cybersecurity directives in times of peace and war. This committee is supported by the NSCS, headed by the National Security Advisor (NSA) of India (not to be confused with the NSAs of other countries) who reports directly to the Indian prime minister. While the CCS acts as a political body, the NSCS serves as an executive group for national security. The *Cabinet Secretariat Resolution* dated 16 April 1999, in *Para b*, *Section 4*, highlights the significance of space and technology to the security council (GoI, Cabinet Secretariat Resolution No.281/29/6/98/TS 1999). Hence to deal with all national cybersecurity affairs, the position of National Cybersecurity Coordinator was created under the NSCS. The coordinator is the head of the National Cyber Coordination Centre (NCCC), an agency that monitors and conducts e-surveillance with the help of enforcement agencies. While it is affiliated with CERT-In, the Central Monitoring System (CMS) (MHA) functions alongside the NCCC (Aggarwal, 2019). The National Critical Information Infrastructure Protection Centre (NCIIPC) was established in 2014 to support the security and resilience of CIIs and also works closely with the NCCC.[20] Being a strategic institute, the NSCS was expected to release a *National Cybersecurity Strategy* in 2020 but it did not happen. However, Lt. Gen. Rajesh Pant, National Cybersecurity Coordinator, expressed that the strategy will cover all security aspects of the cyber ecosystem in India. It shall focus on creating a secure, resilient, vibrant, and trusted cyberspace along with data protection, capacity building, and cyber auditing (PTI, 2021). On 15 January 2020, the *National Cyber Security Strategy-2020* was released by the Data Security Council of India (DSCI), which functions under the National Association of Software and Service Companies (DSCI, 2020). The document discusses cyber strategy in three parts: promotion of cybersecurity, strengthening of structure and government institutions, and synergising the digital infrastructure.

Ministry of Electronics and Information Technology

The erstwhile Ministry of Communications and Information Technology was divided into the MeitY and Ministry of Communications (MoC) on 19 July 2016. Regarding their primary roles in cyberspace, the former focuses on formulating policies related to digital security, while the latter is responsible for ensuring secure cyber communication through reliable service providers. MeitY is the main ministry that is responsible for all cyber policy related matters of state, except matters related to licensing internet service providers. Besides 14 other separate divisions, MeitY has a dedicated division on cybersecurity known as the Cyber Security Division. This division deals with every security aspect of cyberspace related to the *National Cyber Security Policy 2013*, CISO guidelines and responsibilities, research and development in digital security, and training for government officials. The *IT Act 2000* and other laws related to data protection, data governance, and procurement of cybersecurity products are the responsibility of another division known as the Cyber Laws and E-Security Division. The ministry has 19 different organisations working on responsibilities from e-governance to cyber network monitoring (MeitY, 2022). The MeitY agency dedicated to cybersecurity (prevention and protection) is the Computer Emergency Response Team-India. As mandated by the *IT (Amendment) Act-2008*, CERT-In was established in 2004 to respond to computer incidents as and whenever they occur. As a national nodal agency, it collects, analyses, disseminates, forecasts and puts out alert information on cyber-related incidents; take emergency measures; coordinate cyber-incident responses; issue guidelines and advisories related to cybersecurity; conducts the state's data security practices; reports cases; and protects cyber incidents (MeitY, 2022). As the IT sector becomes more complex with the emergence of new technologies, the National Informatic Centre (NIC) (MeitY) established the Centre of Excellence for Blockchain Technology, the Centre of Excellence for Artificial Intelligence, and the Centre of Excellence for Data Analytics. These centres will work on issues related to blockchain, applying cognitive computing, and quality data analytical services (NIC, 2022).

Ministry of Communication

The Ministry of Communications' brainchild, the Department of Telecommunication (DoT), is in charge of the majority of the ministry's duties. According to the DoT *Annual Report-2021–2022*, the tele-density of India in November 2021 was 86.89 per cent (138.79 urban and 59.39 rural of the total population; DoT, 2022, p. 16). As internet networks expand, associated threats increase with every connection. In this context, the DoT plays a crucial role in ensuring the delivery of secure, resilient, and affordable communication services to protect users from these evolving risks. The Digital Communications Commission (earlier known as the Telecom Commission[21]) supports the functioning of the department in "policy, licensing, coordinating in matters related to telegraphy, telephone, wireless, data, facsimile, telematic services and other like forms of communications" (DoT, 2018). While it is supported by its six main units, the department introduced the *National Digital Communications Policy (NDCP)-2018* to lay out a policy framework that enables India to be a global leader in the telecommunication sector and ensure access to telecommunication systems to everyone in an affordable and equitable manner. It also highlights its desire to install broadband connections for every Indian and provide 4 million jobs in the digital sector by 2022 (DoT, 2018). To address emerging technologies, such as 5G, IoT, etc., the NDCP replaced the former *National Telecom Policy-2012*. The concerns of a 5G threat in India meant banned Chinese companies, *Huawei* and *ZTE*, could not introduce their service to the state. The DoT is very cautious in permitting foreign companies invest in India and buying equipment from overseas. Subsequently on 16 December 2020, the *National Security Directive on Telecom Sector* was implemented by the Indian authority. In the interest of national security and cyber safety, this ordinance made a new mandate that telecom apparatus could only be purchased by the public and private telecom service providers from trusted sources. The National Cybersecurity Coordinator in the National Security Council Secretariat (NSCS, PMO) took the responsibility to notify those responsible of trusted sources and products of reliable companies. Meanwhile, the National Telecommunications Institute for Policy Research, Innovation and Training organises high level programs on cybersecurity and other digital understanding.

Ministry of Finance

According to the Reserve Bank of India (RBI), digital transactions in India have increased at the rate of 33 per cent from 5,554 crore in the financial year 2020–2021 to 7,422 crore in 2021–2022 (Livemint, 2022). Meanwhile, the number of cases of money fraud (including internet, card, and loan) has also increased from 7,359 in 2020–2021 to 9,103 in 2021–2022 (Reporter, 2022). Excluding financial services, corporate business, and government payments, 40 per cent of the financial transactions in India are done through internet transactions (ETtech, 2022). As digital transactions and money fraud expand year by year, the MoF has been taking multiple steps to secure digital money operations through cyberspace. To secure its IT facilities and cybersecurity parameters, the RBI created Reserve

Bank Information Technology Pvt. Ltd. (ReBIT) in 2016. ReBIT will take the key responsibility to protect RBI facilities by detecting and responding to cyber threats using cutting-edge technology and services (RBI, 2022). Meanwhile, the Financial Intelligence Unit-India (FIU-In) along with its Financial Intelligence Network (FINnet) play an important role in preventing money laundering by collecting, collating, and analysing financial data. The *Comprehensive Cyber Security Framework for UCBs* was introduced in December 2019 to assess and grade the quality of urban corporative banks (UCBs). The *Technology Vision Document for Cyber Security for UCBs-2020–2023* was also released in September 2020 to address the strategic approach of banks on areas such as "governance oversight; utile technology investment; appropriate regulation and supervision; robust collaboration and developing necessary IT; and cybersecurity skills set". Also, to strengthen the digital payment and card payment system, the *Master Direction on Digital Payment Security Controls* was introduced for regulated banks in February 2021.

Ministry of External Affairs

The MEA contributes to cyber diplomacy and supports expanding India's position in global cybersecurity affairs. The MEA has a separate unit, known as the Cyber Diplomacy Division (CDD), to cooperate on digital threats, address multilateral and regional cyber risks, work on the stability of cyberspace, and support the UNGGE and UNOEWG. The division also promotes for an "open, free, secure, stable, peaceful, and accessible cyberspace enabling economic growth and innovation"[22] (MEA, 2020). Concerning the advancement of new technologies in the cyber realm, MEA created the New, Emerging and Strategic Technologies (NEST) division in 2020. NEST will constantly study and monitor development on emerging and strategic technologies that are relevant to India's national security and economic growth. It will observe and analyse information related to international frameworks and the behaviour (governance) of other countries on complex technologies. While it will analyse the legal implications of new technologies, NEST will research information on strategic technologies available at open sources and conduct meetings and seminars.[23] In its contribution to global cybersecurity, India has been an active member of the UNGGE since 2004. While India tries to expand its role in the international cybersecurity system, it encourages the formation of an "international cyber law" for a peaceful, secure, open and affordable access. It also supports the implementation of cyber sovereignty, forbidding states' use of non-state actors to carry out cybercriminal activities; reducing risk and protecting CIIs, confidence building, information sharing on cybersecurity laws and strategies amongst nation-states, and capacity building for less developed states (UNODA, 2019). With the help of the MeitY, the MEA is involved in bilateral and multilateral dialogues with other countries.

96 *State, Security, and Cyberwar*

Ministry of Science and Technology

The ministry, along with its key branch the Department of Science and Technology (DST), plays a critical role in India's cybersecurity system by contributing scientific research on various cyber-related applications and innovations. The DST launched a research program, Interdisciplinary Cyber Physical Systems[24] (ICPS), to promote the study and development of emerging aspects of cyber science. This program is based on the study of the interaction between the virtual domain and physical world. Cyberspace functions through "computation, communication and control that are discrete and logical" while the physical world acts on "natural and human-made systems governed by the laws of physics and operating in continuous time". The connection between these two is done by a computer-enabled communication system and this is known as the cyber physical system (CPS). The ICPS conducts different programs on data science, , cybersecurity, digital space, and epidemiology data and analytics (DST, 2019). The cybersecurity research program of the institute focuses *inter alia* on information security, data science, digital networks and services, quantum computing, and video and text analytics, with the support of Indian Institutes of Techonology (DST, 2022). The ICPS developed a Joint Network Centre that allows collaboration with scientists from other countries and joint research work in the field of cybersecurity. In 2020, DST along with the Ministry of Science and ICT of South Korea jointly called for research proposals from academics and scientists to work together on areas of AI and IoT with implications for agriculture, water energy, and transport systems. They will exchange researchers, conduct seminars, and publish research papers together as part of the program (DST, 2020). DST is also in charge of managing sharable Indian government data through the website data.gov.in, which was created under the *National Data Sharing and Accessibility Policy* 2012.

Ministry of Information and Broadcast

India is the second-largest internet user in the world with access to social media by a sizable number of its citizens. While the total number of social media users in India is 0.467 billion, 534.30 million are using *WhatsApp*, 503.37 million are using *Instagram*, 491.53 million are using *Facebook*, 374.40 million are using *Telegram*, and 324.39 users are using *Facebook Messenger* (India Social Media Statistics, 2022: Most Used Top Platforms, 2022). Social media is one of the sources to foment cybercrimes in India by practising misinformation, disinformation, spreading fake news, uploading illicit photographs of children and women, and defamatory comments. To support the control of this menace, the MI&B has established the New Media Wing (NMW) to effectively handle matters related to social and digital media along with public information and mass communication (MI&B, 2022). The NMW is headed by an the director general of the Electronic Media Monitoring Centre, which is associated with intelligence agencies in the country as well as information surveillance of electronic media. The agency conducts campaigns for the safe usage of digital media by the public and checks information circulated in social media. Meanwhile, the Broadcast Engineering Consultants India Limited, a public sector enterprise under the MI&B, is involved in monitoring cybercriminal activities for the Indian intelligence communities (Broadcast, 2021, p. 75). For the safe control of social media, the ministry follows the guideline of the *Information Technology (Intermediary Guidelines and Digital Media Ethics Code) Rules, 2021*, which was issued by MeitY in February 2021. In section three of the draft, it describes the due diligence to be followed by intermediaries and addresses any content that threatens the integrity of the nation, public order, causes offence, invades privacy, and harasses people (MeitY, 2021, 2022). Government organisations also use social media to advertise official events, new achievements, advertisement (recruitment), progress and developments. The *Framework & Guidelines for Use of Social Media for Government Organisations* was introduced by the MeitY in 2012 as a guideline for social media use by government organisations (Technology, Framework & Guidelines for Use of Social Media for Government Organisations, 2012).

Conclusion

The concept of state security is inherently ambiguous and constantly evolving (it is a non-static symbol). Its significance varies across different times and places, reflecting the changing priorities and challenges faced by states. Plague, which was once considered a major security threat, no more pose the same level of danger today; similarly poverty may consitutes a critical security concern in Sudan, but not necessarily in the US. Consequently, after the end of the Cold War, those concerned with traditional security shifted their focus to non-traditional security issues. With the distribution of the internet globally in the 1990s, cyberspace as a domain of communication emerged in the international system. Though it was initially created for communication, cyberspace was militarised and weaponised and became a part of the non-traditional security agenda. As there is no universal law of cyberspace, weak or strong states can take advantage of it to attain national objectives. In response to the threat, states and organisations have strengthened their cybersecurity systems by enacting new legislation, policies, structures, frameworks, and collaborations. Digital security is set to grow increasingly complex as emerging technologies such as artificial intelligence, big data, the internet of things, and quantum computing expand their applications. States will eventually have more challenges in securing both the virtual (data and information in digital networks) and physical (real-world cyber-enabled crimes) aspects.

Meanwhile, India, being an emerging nation, depends on ICT to support its economic growth, governance, security, society, and other sectors. It also perceives multiple threats from internal and external elements in the domain of cyberspace. Hence, India's cybersecurity framework is shaped by domestic cybercriminal activities, neighbourhood digital threats, and its aspiration to play a larger role in global cybersecurity affairs. Different agencies take multiple roles with new policies to challenge these digital threats from foreign states and non-state actors. India strengthened its IT laws by amending it to address all possible digital security systems in the country. It developed a new cyber military command (DCA) to address cyberwar and a digital security division (C&IS) to control cybercrime and fraud. It expanded its diplomatic role in the international cyber sphere through cyber diplomacy divisions and monitoring emerging technology regulations of other countries through NEST. The digital networks of the finance and economic sector have been secured through ReBIT. In the field of cyber research and development, India has been trying to improve by introducing new academic units and collaboration. As social media poses a potential threat to nations, regulation on new media has been formed and it is being monitored closely by concerned authorities. Meanwhile, the security council of the state is working to develop an overall strategy of cybersecurity. Though the state is continuously modernising its cybersecurity framework, its weakness has been exposed by frequent cyber incursions. Cybersecurity is an evolving concept that demands regular updates. India must stay ahead of emerging threats and align its security measures with the dynamic requirements of modern digital ecosystems.

Notes

1 A detailed discussion on cyberwar is in the next chapter, which is dedicated to state and cyber warfare.
2 While the meaning of cyber "terrorism" was not included in the Act, the definition of cyber "terrorist" is ambiguous. The "intent to damage other property, and integrity of the state" as an interpretation of a terrorist act, can also be carried out by any person, who may not fall under the definition of a terrorist.
3 Cybercrime costs include damage and destruction of data, stolen money, lost productivity, theft of intellectual property, theft of personal and financial data, embezzlement, fraud, post-attack disruption to the normal course of business, forensic investigation, restoration and deletion of hacked data and systems, and reputational harm.
4 The National Cyber Crime Reporting Portal (NCCRP) is a common public platform to register complaints about cybercrimes occurring in the nation. It functions under the Cyber and Information Security Division of MHA. The NCCRP is associated with the Crime and Criminal Tracking Network and System (CCTNS), which is an integrated system that connects Indian police units to enhance the efficiency and effectiveness of policing by having a common network for crime investigation and criminal detection (NCRB, 2022).
5 Here, Buzan's five levels of analyses are broken up into six, considering the analysis of India's cybersecurity policy and context. In his analysis, Buzan put national (India) and subnational (Kerala) into one unit, however, both are delved into separately in this section for better policy analysis.
6 However, it is still not clear whether the cybercrime monitoring desk has been established from information on the SAARC website or other secondary sources.

7 Details of the agreement are available in the referred document (SCO, 2009).
8 The Strategic Cybersecurity Headquarters of Japan implemented the *Basic Policy on Cybersecurity Capacity Building Support for Developing Countries* in 2021 to promote capacity building on cybersecurity in areas such as protection of CIIs, cybercrime measures, sharing ideas and confidence-building measures, and human resource development in divergent fields.
9 The NISC was earlier known as the National Information Security Centre. It took the key responsibility in coordinating government agencies and promoting partnerships amongst industry, academia, public and private sectors, etc.
10 The agencies are the Cybersecurity and Infrastructure Security Agency, Federal Bureau of Investigation, the US Cyber Command, Cyber National Mission Force, the United Kingdom's National Cyber Security Centre (NCSC-UK), and the National Security Agency (NSA).
11 The Israeli Security Agency (ISA) is the national organisation responsible for defending Israel and its institutions, governance against the threats of terror, espionage, political subversion, and the exposure of state secrets (ISA, 2022). It is also a leading intelligence, technological, and operational organisation in the intelligence community in Israel and worldwide (ISA, 2022).
12 This is the latest information quoted in the Gujarat IT/ITeS Policy (2022–2027), published on 7 February 2022 (DST, 2022).
13 Cybercrimes are defined as

> sophisticated crimes carried out with digital means for either monetary or non-monetary gains. In simple parlance, it can be defined as any misconduct using mobile phone, computer, laptop and/or internet to promote any kind of lure, fraud or causing harassment to other persons online. It includes financial fraud, use of abusive language, theft of password or digital data. The department has highlighted 19 types of cybercrimes including online debit card/credit card fraud, e-mail hacking, data theft, job fraud, online shopping fraud, social media related fraud, etc. (G. Police, 2022).

14 In an interview with an official from the Finance Department, it was said that it has been functioning in a confidential manner and hence there is no website available on the ICT unit (or role of CISO) of the department, 22 June 2022, Gandhinagar.
15 The Central University of Gujarat is chosen as the subject because its cybersecurity system is done at the local level under the supervision of an ICT head who acts as a CISO (which is more or less similar to a district office functioning at the substate level).
16 Information based on an interview with Mr Mayur, who earlier served as technical assistant in the ICT Department, CUG, on 6 June 2022.
17 Indiaforensic Consultancy Services, founded in 2005, is a Pune-based training and educational organisation engaged in fraud examination, security, risk management, and forensic accounting in India (Indiaforensic, 2021).
18 Telephone interview with Shri Sameer Patil, Fellow, Gateway House, Mumbai, 23 June 2021.
19 The CCS is headed by the prime minister of India and its members are the ministers of the MoD, MEA, MHA, and MoF.
20 The NCIIPC functions under the National Technical Research Organisation, a technical intelligence organisation that reports to the National Security Advisor of India (NCIIPC, 2022).
21 The Telecom Commission created in 1989 was re-designated as the Digital Communications Commission in 2018. See Department of Telecommunication, "Profile", 22 November 2018 at https://dot.gov.in/profile (Accessed 21 June 21 2021)

22 While the role of the CDD is not clearly disclosed in the MEA website, it was ascertained that the CDD conducted bilateral talks with different countries and expressed its responsibility as mentioned (MEA, 2020).
23 The official role of NEST is not available in the institutional published materials/sources, however, advertisements for recruitment of NEST scholars/employees disclosed directly or indirectly the responsibility of the division (MEA, 2020).
24 While the date of establishment of the ICPS was not revealed in the department's web sources, apparently it was launched in January 2017 as one of the advertisements on the call for proposals under the ICPS was released on 9 January 2017 (DST, 2017).

References

Acharya, A. (2021). Human security: East versus West. *International Journal*, 56(3), 442–460.

Achom, D., & Choudhury, R. (2024, September 2). 2 killed, 10 injured as "suspected Kuki insurgents" use drones to drop bombs in Manipur, say police. NDTV. https://www.ndtv.com/india-news/woman-killed-daughter-injured-in-firing-by-suspected-insurgents-in-manipur-6466188

Aggarwal, N. (2019, March 26). Lt Gen Rajesh Pant (retd) takes over charge from India's first cybersecurity chief Gulshan Rai: Sources. ET CIO. Retrieved June 18, 2022, from https://cio.economictimes.indiatimes.com/news/corporate-news/lt-gen-rajesh-pant-retd-takes-over-charge-from-indias-first-cybersecurity-chief-gulshan-rai-sources/68573039

Annan, K. (2005). In larger freedom: Towards development, security and human rights for all. New York: United Nations Publications.

Army, I. (2004). Indian Army doctrine. Shimla: Headquarters Army Training Command.

Army, I. (2018). *Land warfare doctrine*. Shimla: Army Training Command.

Ayoob, M. (1997). Defining security: A subaltern realist perspective. In M. C. & K. Krause (Eds.), Critical security studies: Concepts and cases (p. 121). Minneapolis: University of Minnesota Press.

Bajpai, K. (2003). The idea of human security. International Studies, 40(3), 195–228.

Baldwin, D. A. (1995). *Security studies and the end of cold war. World politics: A quarterly journal of international relations*. Cambridge: Cambridge University Press.

Babu, R. (2021, January 24). Sharp rise in child pornography cases worry experts. Retrieved from Hindustan Times : https://www.hindustantimes.com/india-news/sharp-rise-in-child-pornography-cases-worry-experts-101611457879318.html

Bhatia, A. (2021, June 26). NCB busts psychotropic drugs trafficking syndicate operating over darknet. Retrieved from https://www.indiatvnews.com/news/india/psychotropic-drugs-trafficking-syndicate-operating-over-darknet-busted-ncb-latest-news-714840

Bommankanti, K. (2021, March 10). Chinese cyber escalation against India's electricity grid amidst the boundary crisis. Retrieved from https://www.orfonline.org/expert-speak/chinese-cyber-escalatio-india-electricity-grid-boundary-crisis/

Booth, K. (1991). Security and emancipation. Review of International Studies, 17(4), 313–326.

Booth, K. (2007). *Theory of world security*. New York: Cambridge University Press.

BPR&D. (2019, April 22). Details of research proposals shortlisted in preliminary screening for consideration - Reg. Bureau of Police Research and Development. Retrieved June 18, 2022, from https://bprd.nic.in/WriteReadData/userfiles/file/201904220241580928985Shortlisted.pdf

Buzan, B., Wæver, O., & de Wilde, J. (1998). Security: A new framework for analysis. London: Lynnne Rienner Publisher.

Caballero-Anthony, M., & Desker, B. (2013). NTS framework. In M. Caballero-Anthony & B. Desker (Eds.), Non-traditional security in Asia: Issues, challenges and framework for action (p. 1). Singapore: ISEAS Publishing.

Cabinet Secretariat. (1999, April 16). *Cabinet secretariat resolution No. 281/29/6/98/TS*. Retrieved May 2, 2022, from https://ia800601.us.archive.org/13/items/in.gazette.e.1999.383/E_94_2013_050.pdf

Caldwell, D., & Williams, R. E. (2012). Seeking security in an insecure world (2nd ed.). Maryland: Rowman & Littlefield Publishers, Inc.

CIS. (2022, May 4). Cyber and Information Security (CIS) division. Retrieved June 12, 2022, from https://www.mha.gov.in/division_of_mha/cyber-and-information-security-cis-division

CISA. (2022, February 24). Iranian government-sponsored actors conduct cyber operations against global government and commercial networks. Retrieved June 8, 2022, from https://www.cisa.gov/uscert/ncas/alerts/aa22-055a

Colarik, A. M. (2006). Cyber terrorism: Political and economic implications. London: Idea Group Publishing.

Congressional. (2015, January 2015). Cybercrime: Conceptual issues for Congress and U.S. law enforcement. Retrieved July 2, 2022, from https://crsreports.congress.gov/product/pdf/R/R42547

Congressional Research Service. (2015, March 17). *Cyberwarfare and cyberterrorism: In brief*. Retrieved June 20, 2022, from https://crsreports.congress.gov/product/pdf/R/R43955

Congressional Research Service. (2021, December 10). *Use of force in cyberspace*. Retrieved June 20, 2022, from https://crsreports.congress.gov/product/pdf/IF/IF11995

CONWAY, M. (n.d.). Cyberterrorism: Media myth or clear and present danger? Retrieved June 21, 2022, from https://citeseerx.ist.psu.edu/viewdoc/download;jsessionid=EEAD7CB79BC3872EC14F2E7E7580F664?doi=10.1.1.570.3375&rep=rep1&type=pdf

CRS. (2017, August 03). North Korean cyber capabilities: In brief. Retrieved June 08, 2022, from https://crsreports.congress.gov/product/pdf/R/R44912

CUG. (2021, January 06). Final list of eligible candidates for the post of senior technical assistant–computer (OBC-I). Retrieved June 10, 2022, from https://beta.cug.ac.in/career/shortlist/nonteach/SenTechAss.pdf

Cunningham, F. (2021, April 29). Was China behind last October's power outage in India? Here's what we know. Retrieved from Washington Post: https://www.washingtonpost.com/politics/2021/04/29/was-china-behind-last-octobers-power-outage-india-heres-what-we-know/

Das, S. (2020, September 29). Cyber Warfare: China Is Helping Pakistani Hackers Launch Cyber Attacks on India. Retrieved from https://www.news18.com/news/tech/cyber-warfare-china-is-helping-pakistani-hackers-launch-cyber-attacks-on-india-2916023.html

Department of Finance. (2013). About finance department, government of Gujarat. Finance Department, Government of Gujarat. Retrieved June 09, 2022, from https://financedepartment.gujarat.gov.in/aboutus.html

Department of Science and Technology, Government of Gujarat. (2022, February 07). IT/ITeS policy (2022–27). Gujarat State Government. Retrieved June 06, 2022, from https://gil.gujarat.gov.in/Media/DocumentUpload/IT%20POLICY-FInal-2022.pdf

Department of Science and Technology, Government of Gujarat. (2022, June 06). Introduction. DST Gujarat. Retrieved June 06, 2022, from https://dst.gujarat.gov.in/introduction.htm

Desk, 2017, Press Trust of India. (2017, June 29). India worst hit by Petya in APAC, 7th globally: Symantec. The Economic Times. https://economictimes.indiatimes.com/tech/internet/india-worst-hit-by-petya-in-apac-7th-globally-symantec/articleshow/59367013.cms

DoD. (2018). Cyber strategy. U.S. Department of Defense. Retrieved June 05, 2022, from https://media.defense.gov/2018/Sep/18/2002041658/-1/-1/1/CYBER_STRATEGY_SUMMARY_FINAL.PDF

DoI. (2022, June 05). Overview of the department, Directorate of Information. Directorate of Information. Retrieved June 05, 2022, from https://gujaratinformation.gujarat.gov.in/overview-of-the-department-2

DoT. (2018, October 31). Functioning of DoT. Department of Telecommunications, Government of India. Retrieved June 14, 2022, from https://dot.gov.in/objectives

DoT. (2022, May 15). Annual report 2020–2021. Department of Telecommunications, Government of India. Retrieved June 12, 2022, from https://dot.gov.in/sites/default/files/Final%20Eng%20AR%20Min%20of%20Tele%20for%20Net%2009-02-22.pdf

DSCI. (2020, January 15). National cyber security strategy 2020. DSCI. Retrieved June 17, 2022, from https://www.dsci.in/sites/default/files/documents/resource_centre/National%20Cyber%20Security%20Strategy%202020%20DSCI%20submission.pdf

DST. (2006, November 01). IT policy 2006–2011. Gujarat Informatics Limited. Retrieved July 7, 2022, from https://gil.gujarat.gov.in/assets/img/data/it_policy_2006-2011.pdf

DST. (2017, January 9). Detailed call for proposals (CFP) under ICPS programme. Department of Science and Technology. Retrieved June 17, 2022, from https://dst.gov.in/callforproposals/detailed-call-proposals-cfp-under-icps-programme

DST. (2019, October 13). Interdisciplinary cyber physical system (Home). Department of Science and Technology. Retrieved June 16, 2022, from https://dst.gov.in/interdisciplinary-cyber-physical-systems-icps-division

DST. (2020, March 23). India-Korea joint programme of cooperation in science and technology. Department of Science and Technology. Retrieved June 17, 2022, from https://dst.gov.in/sites/default/files/Call%20for%20JNC_DST_MSIT_Final.pdf

DST. (2022). *Annual report 2020-21*. Ministry of Science and Technology, Department of Science and Technology. New Delhi: DST.

E-Governance Division. (2018, April 10). Annual maintenance contract for computers and peripherals, servers and network equipment and internet cabling work in the Ministry. Ministry of External Affairs. Retrieved June 08, 2022, from http://mea.gov.in/Portal/Tender/3646_1/1_AMCTenderMEA-1.pdf

ETGovernment. (2021, November 5). Public Affairs Index rankings 2021: Kerala adjudged best governed state. ETGovernment. Retrieved June 4, 2022, from https://government.economictimes.indiatimes.com/news/governance /public-affairs-index-rankings-2021-kerala-adjudged-best-governed-state/87535893 . Retrieved June 04, 2022, from https://government.economictimes.indiatimes.com/news/governance/public-affairs-index-rankings-2021-kerala-adjudged-best-governed-state/87535893#:~:text=Kerala%20has%20been%20ranked%20as,and%20sustainability%2C%20the%20CM%20added.

ETtech. (2022, June 03). India's digital payments market will triple to $10 trillion by 2026: PhonePe-BCG study. ETtech. Retrieved June 15, 2022, from https://economictimes.indiatimes.com/tech/technology/indias-digital-payments-market-will-triple-to-10-trillion-by-2026-phonepe-bcg-study/articleshow/91963637.cms

Federation, R. (2008, December 12). Information security doctrine. International Telecommunication Union. Retrieved June 5, 2022, from https://www.itu.int/en

/ITU -D/Cybersecurity/Documents/National_Strategies_Repository/Russia _2000 .pdf
GoI. (1999). Cabinet secretariat resolution (No.281/29/6/98/TS). New Delhi: Government of India.
GoI. (2022). *The constitution of India. 2022.* Government of India, New Delhi.
Government of Canada. (2022). Canadian centre for cyber security. Retrieved June 08, 2022, from https://cyber.gc.ca/en
Government of Canada. (2022). Communications security establishment. Retrieved June 08, 2022, from https://www.cse-cst.gc.ca/en
Government of Canada. (2022). Cyber security. Retrieved June 08, 2022, from https://www.canada.ca/en/services/defence /cybersecurity.html
Government of Himachal. (2017). *National cyber security strategy 2016–2021.* Retrieved June 7, 2022, from https://assets.publishing.service.gov.uk/government /uploads/system/uploads/attachment_data/file/567242/national_cyber_security _strategy_2016.pdf
Gujarat Police. (2022). *About us.* Retrieved June 06, 2022, from https:// gujaratcybercrime.org/eng/#accordion18
Gupta, M. (2021, July 19). ISIS J&K Chief Used His Media Outlet, Ground Soldiers to Spread Terror in India: Report. Retrieved from https://www.news18.com/news /india/isis-jk-chief-used-his-media-outlet-ground-soldiers-to-spread-terror-in-india -report-3981962.html
Hameiri, S. (2013). The politics and governance of non-traditional security. International Studies Quarterly, 57(3), 462–473.
Hanna, A. (2019, October 25). The Invisible U.S.-Iran Cyber War. Retrieved June 8, 2022, from https://iranprimer.usip.org/blog/2019/oct/25/invisible-us-iran-cyber -war
Haq, M. U. (1995). Reflections on human development. New York: Oxford University Press.
Haran, V. (2017, April 14). Attack Against Indian Bank Closely Resembled Bangladesh Bank Hack. BankInfoSecurity. https://www.bankinfosecurity.com/ attack-against-indian-bank-resembled-bangladesh-bank-hack-a-9842
Herring, K. B. (1994). Keyguide to information sources in strategic studies. London: Mansell Publishing Limited.
IDS. (2017). Joint Doctrine Indian Armed Forces. New Delhi: Integrated Defence Staff.
IISS. (2021). Cyber Capabilities and National Power: A Net Assessment. London: IISS.
INCD. (2020, January 20). Israel national cyber directorate. Government of Israel. Retrieved June 8, 2022, from https://www.gov.il/en/departments/about/ newabout
India Social Media Statistics 2022 | Most Used Top Platforms. (2022, August 07). The global statistics. Retrieved June 15, 2022, from https://www.theglobalstatistics .com/india-social-media-statistics/
Indiaforensic. (2021). About us. Retrieved from India Forensic: https://indiaforensic .com/category/about-us/
IndiaTV. (2020, November 19). Complete list of 267 Chinese apps banned in India: PUBG Mobile, TikTok, AliExpress and more. Retrieved from https://www .indiatvnews.com/technology/news-list-of-all-chinese-apps-banned-in-india-2020 -667131
India Today. (2022, April 19). Cryptocurrencies could be used for money laundering, terror financing: Nirmala Sitharaman. https://www.indiatoday.in/business/story/ nirmala-sitharaman-money-laundering-terror-financing-cryptocurrency-concerns -1939113-2022-04-19

ISA. (2022). Core values of the Israel Security Agency. Israel Security Agency. Retrieved June 8, 2022, from https://www.shabak.gov.il/english/about/Pages/values.aspx

ISA. (2022). Information technology (ISA). Israel Security Agency. Retrieved June 8, 2022, from https://www.shabak.gov.il/english/cybertechnology/Pages/technology.aspx

ISA. (2022). Technology and cyber division. Israel Security Agency. Retrieved June 8, 2022, from https://www.shabak.gov.il/english/cybertechnology/Pages/cyber.aspx

ISMG. (2021, March 2021). Keynote session: Enterprise security in an adaptive era. ISMG. Retrieved from https://events.ismg.io/event/virtual-cybersecurity-summit-india-and-saarc-2021/

Janczewski, L. J., & Colarik, A. M. (2007). Cyber warfare and cyber terrorism. London: Information Science Reference.

Kakar, H. (2021, 23 November). *Evolving concepts of national security*. Retrieved May 01, 2022, from https://www.thestatesman.com/opinion/evolving-concepts-national-security-1503026282.html

Keohane, R. O., & Nye, J. S. (1977). Power and interdependence: World politics in transition. Boston, MA: Little, Brown and Company.

Kerala Government. (2017). IT Policy 2017. ICFOSS. Retrieved June 4, 2022, from https://icfoss.in/doc/IT_Policy_2017/ITPolicy_english.pdf

Kerala Police Cyberdome. (2020, June 22). Cyber crime police station. Retrieved June 05, 2024, from https://keralapolice.gov.in/page/cyber-crime-police-station

Kerala Police Cyberdome. (2022). *About Cyberdom*. Retrieved June 05, 2022, from https://cyberdome.kerala.gov.in/about.html

Kerala Police Cyberdome. (2022). *Cyberdom vision statement*. Retrieved June 05, 2022, from https://cyberdome.kerala.gov.in/vision.html

Kumar, R. (2018). Security threats to e-business among SAARC nations – A preliminary study. International Journal of Engineering Research in Computer Science and Engineering, 5(1), 5–7.

Kumar, H. (2025, March 20). Digital financial frauds touch Rs 4,245 crore in the Apr-Jan period of FY25. Business Standard. https://www.business-standard.com/finance/news/digital-financial-frauds-touch-rs-4-245-crore-in-the-apr-jan-period-of-fy25-125032001214_1.html

Libicki, M. C. (2009). *Cyberdeterrence and cyberwar*. Santa Monica: RAND Corporation.

Lippmann, W. (1917 (originally published in 1937)). The good society: With an introduction by Gary Dean Best. London: Routledge.

Lippmann, W. (1943). U.S. foreign policy: Shield of the republic. Boston: Little Brown and Company.

Livemint. (2022, March 23). India made 7,422 cr digital payments in FY22 at 33% growth rate: MeitY. Livemint. Retrieved June 15, 2022, from https://www.livemint.com/technology/tech-news/india-made-7-422-cr-digital-payments-in-fy22-at-33-growth-rate-meity-11648038672792.html

Malik, S. (2015). Framing a discipline. In P. Hough, S. Malik, A. Moran, & B. Pilbeam (Eds.), International security studies: Theory and practice (pp. 3–11). London: Routledge.

McNamara, R. (1968). *The essence of security*. London: Hodder and Stoughton.

MEA. (2020, December 17). 6th India-EU cyber dialogue. Ministry of External Affairs. Retrieved June 16, 2022, from https://www.mea.gov.in/press-releases.htm?dtl/33308/6th_IndiaEU_Cyber_Dialogue

MEA. (2020, May 22). Advertisement for engagement as NEST fellows in the ministry of external affairs on contract basis. Ministry of External Affairs (Administration

Division). Retrieved June 17, 2022, from https://www.mea.gov.in/Images/amb1/NEST_Advertisement.pdf

MEA. (2022, August 01). EG & IT [E-governance & information technology] division. Ministry of External Affairs. Retrieved June 8, 2022, from https://www.mea.gov.in/divisions.htm

MeitY. (2000, October 17). Notification of rules for cyber regulations appellate tribunal. Ministry of Electronics and Information Technology. Retrieved June 12, 2022, from https://www.meity.gov.in/content/notification-rules-cyber-regulations-appellate-tribunal

MeitY. (2008). *IT (Amendment) act 2000.* New Delhi: Ministry of Electronics and Information Technology.

MeitY. (2013, July 2). https://www.meity.gov.in/writereaddata/files/National%20Cyber%20Security%20Policy%20%281%29%20%281%29.pdf

MeitY. (2021, February 25). Information technology (intermediary guidelines and digital media ethics code) rules, 2021. Ministry of Electronics and Information Technology. Retrieved June 15, 2022, from https://mib.gov.in/sites/default/files/Digital%20Media%20Ethics%20Code%20Rules%20%20Notification%20%281%29.pdf

MeitY. (2022, April 04). *MeitY organisations.* Retrieved June 14, 2022, from https://www.meity.gov.in/content/meity-organisations

MeitY. (2022, August 11). *Computer emergency response team.* Retrieved August 11, 2022, from https://cert-in.org.in

MHA. (2014, October 9). *National information security policy and guidelines.* Retrieved June 12, 2022, from https://www.surveyofindia.gov.in/documents/NATIONAL%20INFORMATION%20SECURITY%20POLICY%20AND%20GUIDELINES.pdf

MHA. (2018, December 3). *A handbook for adolescents/students on cyber safety.* Retrieved June 10, 2022, from Ministry of Home Affairs: https://www.mha.gov.in/sites/default/files/CyberSafety_English_Web_03122018.pdf

MHA. (2018, January 13). *Advisory on cyber crime prevention and control.* Retrieved June 13, 2022, from Ministry of Home Affairs : https://www.mha.gov.in/sites/default/files/CIS_AdvisoryCyberCrime_14112019_0.pdf

MHA. (2019, August 30). *User manual for reporting cyber crimes (except child pornography, rape/gang rape and obscene content related cybercrimes).* National Cyber Crime Reporting Portal. Retrieved June 10, 2022, from https://cybercrime.gov.in/Webform/Citizen_Manual.aspx

MHA. (2019, June 25). Information security best practices. Ministry of Home Affairs. Retrieved June 12, 2022, from https://www.mha.gov.in/sites/default/files/Documents_InformationSecurity_25062019.pdf

MHA. (2022). *National cyber crime reporting portal.* Retrieved June 12, 2022, from https://cybercrime.gov.in/Webform/cyber_volunteers_concept.aspx

MHA. (2022). What is unlawful content. National Cyber Crime Reporting Portal. Retrieved June 10, 2022, from https://cybercrime.gov.in/Webform/about_unlawful_content.aspx

MI&B. (2022). *About Us: New media wing.* Retrieved June 15, 2022, from http://nmw.gov.in/AboutUs.aspx

Ministry of Foreign Affairs, People's Republic of China. (2020, September 8). Global initiative on data security. Retrieved June 4, 2022, from https://www.fmprc.gov.cn/mfa_eng/wjb_663304/zzjg_663340/jks_665232/kjlc_665236/qtwt_665250/202010/t20201029_599871.html

Ministry of Information and Broadcasting. (2021). *Annual report 2020–21.* New Delhi: Ministry of Information and Broadcast.

Ministry of Internal Affairs and Communications, Japan. (2022). ICT in Japan. Retrieved June 7, 2022, from https://www.soumu.go.jp/main_sosiki/joho_tsusin/eng/ictinjapan/index.html

MoD. (2024, June 18). CDS gen anil chauhan releases joint doctrine for cyberspace operations. Press Information Bureau, Government of India. Retrieved from https://pib.gov.in/indexd.aspx?reg=3&lang=1

Morgan, S. (2020, November 13). *Cybercrime to cost the world $10.5 trillion annually By 2025*. Retrieved July 1, 2022, from https://cybersecurityventures.com/cybercrime-damages-6-trillion-by-2021/

Myers, N. (2020). *ODU model united nation society*. Retrieved July 22, 2022, from https://www.odu.edu/content/dam/odu/offices/mun/docs/1st-cyber-attacks-un-day.pdf

Nahid Joveda, M. T. (2019). Cyber Laundering: A Threat to Banking Industries in Bangladesh: In Quest of Effective Legal Framework and Cyber Security of Financial Information. International Journal of Economics and Finance, 11(10), 54.

National Cyber Crime Reporting Portal. (2022). *Learn about cyber crime*. Retrieved June 03, 2022, from https://cybercrime.gov.in/Webform/CrimeCatDes.aspx

National Cyber Directorate. (2017, September). Israel national cyber security strategy. Cyber@Haifa. Retrieved June 08, 2022, from https://cyber.haifa.ac.il/images/pdf/cyber_english_A5_final.pdf

National Information Technology Development. (2012, April 01). Framework & guidelines for use of social media for government organisations. Retrieved June 12, 2022, from https://www.meity.gov.in/writereaddata/files/Approved%20Social%20Media%20Framework%20and%20Guidelines%20_2_.pdf

National Information Technology Development. (2013). National cyber security policy, 2013. New Delhi: Ministry of Communication and Information Technology.

NATO. (2014, September 05). *Wales summit declaration*. Retrieved July 4, 2022, from https://www.nato.int/cps/en/natohq/official_texts_112964.htm#cyber

NATO. (2016, July 08). *Cyber defence pledge*. Retrieved July 04, 2022, from https://www.nato.int/cps/en/natohq/official_texts_133177.htm

NATO. (2018, July 11). *Brussels summit declaration*. Retrieved June 4, 2022, from https://www.nato.int/cps/en/natohq/official_texts_156624.htm

NATO. (2022). *NATO's cyber security centre*. Retrieved June 4, 2022, from https://www.ncia.nato.int/what-we-do/cyber-security.html

NCIIPC. (2022, August 12). *About Us, national critical information infrastructure protection centre*. Retrieved June 17, 2022, from https://nciipc.gov.in

NCRB. (2022, July 29). *About crime and criminal tracking network & systems (CCTNS)*. Retrieved June 14, 2022, from https://ncrb.gov.in/en/crime -and-criminal-tracking-network-systems-cctns

NDTV. (2010, December 4). Retrieved from Hacked by 'Pakistan cyber army', CBI website still not restored: https://www.ndtv.com/india-news/hacked-by-pakistan-cyber-army-cbi-website-still-not-restored-441100

NDTV. (2016, December 14). *India's cyber appellate tribunal barely functioning*. Retrieved June 12, 2022, from https://www.youtube.com/watch?v=zaOY0w88oBw

New York City Agency Services. (2022). *About the agency*. Retrieved June 05, 2022, from https://its.ny.gov/about-agency

NIC. (2022, August 11). *National informatics center*. Retrieved August 11, 2022, from https://www.nic.in

Nicolas Falliere, L. O. (2012). W32.Stuxnet Dossier, Installation and Propagation. California: Symantec.

Norton. (2021). *What is cybercrimes?*. Retrieved June 02, 2022, from https://us.norton.com/internetsecurity-how-to-how-to-recognize-and-protect-yourself-from-cybercrime.html#

NYPD. (2022). *Detectives*. Retrieved June 04, 2022, from https://www1.nyc.gov/site/nypd/bureaus/investigative/detectives.page

OITS. (2022a). NYS chief information security office. New York State ITS. Retrieved June 5, 2022, from https://its.ny.gov/welcome-nys-chief-information-security-office

OITS. (2022b). Statewide policies. New York State ITS. Retrieved June 5, 2022, from https://its.ny.gov/tables/technologypolicyindex

Pandya, A. (2020). The Threat of Transnational Terrorist Groups in Kashmir. Perspectives on Terrorism, 13–25.

PIB. (2018, February 07). *Creation of CTCR and CIS divisions in MHA*. Retrieved June 04, 2022, from https://pib.gov.in/Pressreleaseshare.aspx?PRID=1519500

PIB. (2021, October 28). Ministry of Electronics & IT organises week-long CISO deep dive training program from 25th to 30th October organised under Cyber Surakshit Bharat initiative, the program will help in creating a cyber resilient IT setup in India. Retrieved June 08, 2022, from https://pib.gov.in/newsite/PrintRelease.aspx?relid=226039

PIB. (2022, March 16). Online cyber grooming of women and young children. Government of India. https://pib.gov.in/PressReleaseIframePage.aspx?PRID=1806602

Prasad, R. V. (2000, December 19). India must be established an information security system to counter cyber threats from China and Pakistan. The Hindustan Times.

PTI. (2016, July 17). *In a first, drug trafficking reported in India through Darknet, Bitcoin*. Retrieved from https://www.hindustantimes.com/india-news/in-a-first-narcotics-trade-detected-via-darknet-bitcoin-in-india/story-5n5MDRe9gqhPAnRMQ9oouJ.html

PTI. (2021, July 3). *Government to unveil national cyber security strategy soon: National cyber security coordinator*. Retrieved June 17, 2022, from https://www.thehindu.com/business/government-to-unveil-national-cyber-security-strategy-soon-national-cyber-security-coordinator/article35119538.ece

Rao, P. (2016, July 16). Online Radicalisation: The Example of Burhan Wani. Retrieved from https://idsa.in/issuebrief/online-radicalisation-burhan-wani_prao_160716

RBI. (2022). *About ReBIT*. Retrieved June 15, 2022, from https://ReBIT.org.in

Reporter Business. (2022, May 27). *RBI annual report: FY22 saw more bank frauds but value decreased by half*. Retrieved June 15, 2022, from https://www.business-standard.com/article/finance/rbi-annual-report-fy22-saw-more-bank-frauds-but-value-decreased-by-half-122052700468_1.html

Ritchie, H., Mathieu, E., Roser, M., & Ortiz-Ospina, E. (2022). *The internet's history has just begun*. Retrieved May 5, 2022, from https://ourworldindata.org/internet

SAARC. (2020, July 16). *Information and poverty alleviation*. Retrieved June 04, 2022, from https://www.saarc-sec.org/index.php/areas-of-cooperation/information-poverty-alleviation

SAARC. (2021, March 22). *SAARC charter*. SAARC. Retrieved from https://www.saarc-sec.org/index.php/about-saarc/saarc-charter

SAARC. (2021, March 23). Information and poverty alleviation. Retrieved from https://www.saarc-sec.org/index.php/areas-of-cooperation/information-poverty-alleviation

SAARC. (2022). About South Asian association for regional cooperation. Retrieved June 04, 2022, from https://www.saarc-sec.org/index.php/about-saarc/about-saarc

Schneier, B. (2013, August). *Cyberconflicts and national security*. Retrieved June 2020, 2022, from https://www.un.org/en/chronicle/article/cyberconflicts-and-national-security

SCO. (2009). *Agreement on cooperation in ensuring international information security between the member states of the Shanghai Cooperation Organization.* Beijing: SCO.

SCO. (2018, January 26). *SCO calls for safe functioning and development of internet.* Retrieved June 10, 2022, from http://eng.sectsco.org/news/20180126/377347.html

SCO. (2019, May 2017). *SCO RATS technical experts meet in Beijing.* Retrieved June 10, 2022, from http://eng.sectsco.org/news/20170519/271457.html

SCO. (2022). The Shanghai cooperation organisation. Retrieved June 10, 2022, from http://eng.sectsco.org/about_sco/

Sheth, H. (2020, April 14). India lockdown: Online child pornography consumption spikes by in India, says ICPF. Retrieved from The Hindu: https://www.thehindubusinessline.com/info-tech/india-lockdown-online-child-pornography-consumption-spikes-by-in-india-says-icpf/article31337221.ece

Steinberg, J., & Parussini, G. (2017, April 10). Was North Korea behind the hacking of a bank in India? The Wall Street Journal. https://www.wsj.com/articles/was-north-korea-behind-the-hacking-of-a-bank-in-india-1491814202

Stuxnet (2010) and Petya (2017) incidents..."This structure places the year in parentheses immediately after each cyber incident,following standard academic conventions.

Talihärm, A.-M. (2013, August). *Onwards cyberpeace: Managing cyberwar through international cooperation.* Retrieved June 20, 2022, from https://www.un.org/en/chronicle/article/towards-cyberpeace-managing-cyberwar-through-international-cooperation

Tarry, S. (1999). 'Deepening' and 'widening': An analysis of security definitions in the 1990s. *Journal of Military and Strategic Studies,* 2(1), 1–13.

TCS. (2022). Cyber security & risk mitigation services for future-ready businesses. Retrieved June 10, 2021, from https://www.tcs.com/services/cyber-security-future-ready-enterprise

TCS. (2022). *Service, tata consultancy service.* Retrieved June 10, 2022, from https://www.tcs.com

Terrorism, U. N. (2022, June 20). *Cybersecurity.* Retrieved June 20, 2022, from https://www.un.org/counterterrorism/cybersecurity

Today, I. (2021, June 29). *India raises Jammu air base attack at UN, says use of drones for terrorism needs serious attention.* Retrieved June 20, 2022, from https://www.indiatoday.in/india/story/india-jammu-air-base-attack-un-drones-terrorism-attention-1820611-2021-06-29

TRAI. (2022, August 27). The Indian telecom services performance indicators: January – March 2021. Retrieved June 05, 2022, from https://trai.gov.in/sites/default/files/QPIR_27082021.pdf

UN. (2015, February 26). *ICT strategy endorsed.* Retrieved June 04, 2022, from https://www.un.org/webcast/pdfs/ICTtownhall-feb2015.pdf

UN. (2022). *Developments in the field of information and telecommunications in the context of international security.* Retrieved June 04, 2022, from https://www.un.org/disarmament/ict-security/

UNCCT. (2022, June 20). *UN office of counter terrorism.* Retrieved June 20, 2022, from https://www.un.org/counterterrorism/cct/programme-projects/cybersecurity

UNGA. (2014, October 10). *Information and communications technology in the United Nations.* Retrieved June 04, 2022, from https://documents-dds-ny.un.org/doc/UNDOC/GEN/N14/565/39/PDF/N1456539.pdf?OpenElement

UNIDR. (2019). *Cyber policy portal: North Atlantic treaty organization.* Retrieved June 04, 2022, from https://cyberpolicyportal.org/organizations/north-atlantic-treaty-organization-nato

UNODA. (2019, July). *Developments in the field of information and telecommunications in the context of international security*. Retrieved June 17, 2022, from https://front.un-arm.org/wp-content/uploads/2019/07/Information-Security-Fact-Sheet-July-2019.pdf

UNODC. (2022). *Ad hoc committee to elaborate a comprehensive international convention on countering the use of information and communications technologies for criminal purposes*. Retrieved June 02, 2022, from https://www.unodc.org/unodc/en/cybercrime/ad_hoc_committee/home

UNODC. (2022). *Cybercrime*. Retrieved June 02, 2022, from https://www.unodc.org/unodc/en/cybercrime/index.html

UNODC. (2022). *Meetings intergovernmental expert group (IEG) on cybercrime*. Retrieved June 02, 2022, from https://www.unodc.org/unodc/en/cybercrime/egm-on-cybercrime/meetings.html

UNODC. (n.d.). *Global programme on cybercrime*. Retrieved June 02, 2022, from https://www.unodc.org/unodc/en/cybercrime/global-programme-cybercrime.html

USCRS. (2015). *Cyberwarfare and Cyberterrorism*: In Brief. Retrieved March 27, 2015, from https://crsreports.congress.gov/product/pdf/R/R43955

Vaughan-Williams, C. P. (2010). *Critical security studies: An introduction*. London: Routledge.

VIF. (2019, March). *Credible cyber deterrence in armed forces of India*. Vivekananda International Foundation. Retrieved June 13, 2022, from https://www.vifindia.org/sites/default/files/Credible-Cyber-Deterrence-in-Armed-Forces-of-India_0.pdf

Walt, S. M. (1991). *The* renaissance of security studies. International Studies Quarterly, 35(2), 211–2319.

Waltz, K. N. (1979). Theory of international politics. Reading, MA: Addison-Wesley.

Wolfers, A. (1952). 'National security' as an ambiguous symbol. Political Science Quarterly, 67, 481–502.

4 Interstate War and Cyberwarfare

Introduction

The fourth industrial revolution (Industry 4.0), driven by advancements in information technology, has significantly transformed the political, economic, and strategic (military) dynamics of society. This technological shift has positioned the information sector as a critical element of the global security framework, influencing how states approach wars in the international system. In the past two decades, as a component of information technology, cyberspace has been used by the state, armed forces, and security services to acquire national dominance and strategic goals. The domain has been completely militarised, and cyber commands with offensive and defensive capabilities are integrated into the state military system. After land, sea, air, and space, the cyberspace medium has eventually developed into a theatre of interstate conflict and is now regarded as the fifth domain of warfare. However, unlike traditional forms of warfare, there is no international law of armed conflict for cyberspace. This predicament has made the international community struggle in regulating digital conflict in the global anarchic system. Unable to find a practical answer, the UN created the UN Group of Government Experts (UNGGE) and the UN Open Ended Working Group (UNOEWG) to create guidelines for responsible state behaviour in cyberspace. Meanwhile, the NATO Cooperative Cyber Defence Centre of Excellence published the *Tallin Manual* (2009) and *Tallin Manual 2.0* (2013) on 'International Law Applicable to Cyber Operations', describing how international law could be applied to cyberwarfare. Both the manuals are non-binding documents similar to a kind of book written by an author to understand a specific subject.[1]

Taking advantage of the unregulated nature of cyberspace, potential states seek opportunities to interrupt the sovereignty of other's digital space by stealing sensitive data and harming critical information infrastructures. This scenario fuels a security dilemma among nations, triggering a cyber arms race and a "new cold war" in the digital world order. The intensifying competition increases the number of cyber powers, shaping a multipolar digital world. This could potentially escalate into a global cyber conflict, akin to the world wars of the early 20th century (Mearsheimer). Meanwhile, the nature of this warfare is cheap, vague, and unruly, creating more complexities in the states' functioning. Small powers that are not capable of challenging great powers with regular military deployment choose the cyber domain as a means to attack their opponent (Iran or North Korea against the Western world), because it is unregulated and affordable and they can avoid investigation and trial. Hence, weaker nations easily compete with the great powers in the domain of cyberspace.

Actors involved in cyber conflicts are often ambiguous, as both state and non-state entities actively participate. Beyond a state's official military forces, non-state actors, such as paid mercenaries, nationalist hackers, or even independent groups, can engage in digital warfare. This lack of clear distinction complicates the identification of participants and accountability in cyber conflicts. As per Mary Kaldor's "new war" theory, cyberwar could be a type of novel war where the actors involved are blurred, the war economy is ambiguous as who sanctions for it, and the battleground is unpredictable. Unlike traditional war (physical and kinetic), cyberwar is uncertain and it is not easy to detect where an attack comes from and by whom. As it is difficult to attribute the attacker's origin or footprint, it is not so difficult for any involved party to escape criminal charges (war crimes). Meanwhile, states do not follow the norms of the reason for going a war (*jus ad bellum*) or conduct of the cyber-armed conflict (*jus in bello*). The "means and methods"[2] of cyberwarfare remain unclear, as the tools and systems used in these conflicts often lack identifiable signatures of state governments or private industries. This anonymity complicates attribution, making it challenging to determine the origin of attacks and hold perpetrators accountable. Considering all these grey areas and the ambiguous nature of warfare in cyberspace, states will persist in interfering or attacking one another based on their technical capabilities. This is likely to continue until universal international norms and principles are established to regulate cyberwar.

As one of the world's leading economies, India aspires to establish itself as a global power while simultaneously building a secure cyber ecosystem. However, its progress has been facing significant challenges from internal and external threats, spanning both physical and digital domains. The internal dimension is criminal activities carried out by an individual or a group of spoilers (militants or terrorists) for personal, monetary, or ideological objectives. They include crimes that are conducted within a circle of cyber networks (online money heist), as well as cyber-enabled crimes with physical implication (selling and buying of guns and drugs through the dark web). Though it has national security implication, these are offences orchestrated mostly by non-state actors at the non-strategic level where state forces or government agents are unlikely to be involved. However, in the external dimension, the sovereignty of India has been challenged by foreign aggressors such as China or Pakistan through cyberspace for political and strategic achievements. These arrangements are done at the strategic level, and hence the involvement of state actors is pragmatic in such cases. While the internal or non-strategic threats (cybercrimes) are handled by homeland security establishments, the external or strategic threats (cyberwarfare) are the responsibility of the military armed forces. To challenge the internal menace, India strengthened its homeland security by establishing the Cyber and Information Security (C&IS) Division under the Ministry of Home Affairs (MHA). Subsequently, to defend against digital aggression from an external force, the Defence Cyber Agency (DCA) was introduced under the Ministry of Defence (MoD) and started operating with a new doctrine of cyber warfare. While various military doctrines highlight the risks of future digital conflicts, the recently released *Joint Doctrine for Cyberspace Operations-2024* provides comprehensive guidelines on cyber warfare. As India's first dedicated cyberwar doctrine, it outlines strategies for cyberspace operations, though it remains classified and unavailable to the public.

Before delving deeper into the discussion on cyberwarfare, it is essential to understand some fundamental typologies of cyberwar. These typologies are derived from the characteristics of wars experienced in the physical world, providing a conceptual framework for analysing cyber conflicts. The following types of warfare are distinguished from each other as suggested in Table 4.1

Theories of War and Cyberwarfare

While there is no universally accepted theory of cyberwarfare, it is evident that state-sponsored cyberattacks are increasingly employed to achieve

Table 4.1 Typologies of Cyberwar

SL No.	Type	Definition
1	Interstate cyberwar	Digital war between two sovereign states (e.g., India and China)
2	Intrastate cyberwar	Digital war within states (if the Karnataka and Tamil Nadu Cauvery conflict involves the cyber realm)
3	Extra-state cyberwar	Digital conflict between state and non-state actors outside the state itself (US over Al-Qaeda)
4	Declared cyberwar	One side made a formal declaration of cyberwar
5	Undeclared cyberwar	No formal declaration announced for a cyberwar
6	Total cyberwar	Use of all national cyber-related resources for a complete victory
7	Limited cyberwar	Limited resources used for a war of a specific objective
8	Conventional cyberwar	Fought by professional cyber armies
9	Guerrilla cyberwar	Cyberwar that involves organised non-state actors
10	Conquest	Fight for conquest of cyber territories or control of specific networks or a country's network system
11	Liberation	Fight with the help of outsiders to free subjugated cyber networks (US helped the UK to escape Russian cyber ransome)

Source: Developed based on the typologies of interstate war (Pilbeam, 2015).

political or strategic objectives, effectively shaping the concept of cyberwarfare. In his seminal work, *On War*, Clausewitz emphasises that theory cannot provide rigid formulas or fixed solutions for complex problems. Instead, he asserts that theory should help the mind comprehend the vast array of phenomena and their relationships. By doing so, it prepares individuals to act effectively and adapt to the demands of higher decision-making and action without being confined by predetermined principles or paths (Clausewitz, 1832, 2007, p. 223). In other words, Colin Gray rephrased this as "theory is not a direct guide to action, but rather educates the mind so that some useful order can be imposed on an apparently disorderly universe" (Gray, 1996). Likewise, following discussions on the theory of cyberwar or cyberwarfare[3] is not a guide to action (for any state or a group) but to teach minds a useful order in cyberwar implementations. Cyberwar can be discussed in three aspects. First, by considering the classical theory of regular war (old war or new war concepts) propounded by strategic thinkers or theorists such as Sun Tzu, Thucydides, Kautilya, Machiavelli, Jomini, and Clausewitz who focus on military and interstate war affairs. The second perspective can be analysed through the lens of irregular warfare by drawing connections to key thinkers like Mao Zedong, Che Guevara, and B.H. Liddell Hart (countering "cyber guerrillas"). The third aspect draws on theories related to domains of war and power (land, sea, air, and space) introduced by notable thinkers such as Halford Mackinder, Alfred Thayer Mahan, Giulio Douhet, and Colin Gray. These domains are analysed in connection with cyberspace as a new strategic domain. Just as power is projected physically in traditional domains, cyberspace offers an intangible yet critical battlefield where influence and control can be asserted. Meanwhile, the concept of conventional war and its components including an arms race, security dilemma, deterrence, doctrines, along with weapon systems and command structures in connection with cyberwar are examined in this chapter. The doctrine and command structure of India's approach to cyberwar will also be explored separately.

Regular War and Cyberwarfare

Many strategic thinkers, starting from the ancient war scholar Sun Tzu to contemporary new war theorist Mary Kaldor, observed war from various perspectives and developed different theories and principles of it. Their insights on war studies provide assistance in developing and theorising cyberwar. Accordingly, this section refers to ancient war theorists, Sun Tzu, Thucydides, and Kautilya; and modern period war scholars such as Machiavelli, Jomini, Clausewitz, and contemporary war analyst Mary Kaldor. This section is an analysis based on their writings, particularly the books and treaties they introduced, and what they would have to say about cyberwarfare if some of them were living today. Indeed, they would change their views based on the revolution taking place in modern society. However, the following is a comparative study that underscores the historical theories of these thinkers and continue to hold significant relevance and applicability to the realm of contemporary cyberwar. Their foundational principles, designed for traditional conflicts, seamlessly adapt to the digital domain, providing a valuable framework to address modern technological and strategic challenges.

Sun Tzu and the Art of Cyberwar

The Chinese military treatise (book), *The Art of War*, written by Sun Tzu (544–499 BCE) is the oldest and most widely quoted literature in war studies. Though it was developed based on ancient traditional war principles, there are areas that still can be aligned with modern cyberwar strategies. Out of the 13 chapters dealing with various aspects of conflict in the book, the most suitable discussions on cyberwar include planning, combat, strategy, and spying that are addressed in Chapters I, II, III, and XIII. In the plan of warfare, Tzu says that interstate wars are based on deception, and hence a country should be seen as what it is not; when it is capable, it should be seen incapable; and when it is inactive, it should be projected as active. He further advised that an attack against the enemy should be carried out when they are unprepared and not expected (surprise attack). As there is no benefit for a state from a prolonged conflict, war should be quick and fast. He famously counsels to attack an enemy by adopting strong strategies and said, "know your enemy and know yourself, you will not fear the result of a hundred battles" (Para. 18, Chapter III).

In the domain of cyberspace, small powers such as North Korea, which seem incapable, projected themselves as potential threats and challenged great powers such as the US by attacking its "government, Department of Defense, and Defense Industrial Base" (CISA, 2023). On the contrary, larger powers attack smaller states while denying their involvement (e.g., US Stuxnet attack against Iran in 2010). A country usually avoids officially declaring cyberwar. It always happens covertly, and the majority of the attacks take place when states are unprepared resulting in zero-day effects. Cyberwarfare, according to Sun Tzu's strategic principles, should be swift and decisive to prevent prolonged engagements that could allow adversaries to trace and counterattack—emphasising a "hit and disappear/run" tactic. In the context of modern cyberwar strategies, he might favour zero-day attacks, such as the Morris Worm incident (1988), over prolonged operations like advanced persistent threats (APTs). To achieve cyber superpower status, states should not only assess their own digital capabilities but also understand others. If country A initiates an attack on country B, and country B absorbs the first strike only to retaliate massively, the survival of country A hinges on its ability to defend against or mitigate the response. To avoid such catastrophic risks, country A must not only understand its own capabilities but also have a comprehensive awareness of country B's military and strategic potential, as advised by Sun Tzu in *The Art of War*. For instance,

Iran (A) will always assess the US's (B) digital capabilities before it launches a cyberattack against the country. In an interesting development, Hamas's inability to anticipate Israel's response capabilities led to a significant countermeasure. Following a cyberattack by Hamas, Israel retaliated not just in cyberspace but also kinetically, targeting Hamas's cyber operations facility with an airstrike in May 2019.

For Sun Tzu, espionage is a vital element of warfare, as he emphasises that "knowledge of the enemy's dispositions can only be obtained from other men". During his era, spying primarily relied on human intelligence (HUMINT). If he were alive today, given the technological advancement, he would have incorporated cyber intelligence into *The Art of War* as a modern counterpart to traditional espionage. He identified five types of spies: local, inward, converted, doomed, and surviving spies (Giles, 2009, p. 54). They can be effectively applied to cyber espionage, offering a clear framework for understanding how cyber operations can be executed against an adversary's digital infrastructure. A hypothetical example of Russia using cyber means to spy on Ukraine is mentioned here within the context of the ongoing conflict between the two since February 2022 (Table 4.2).

Thucydides and the Causes of Cyberwar

Thucydides (460–400 BCE), an Athenian general, is widely recognised as a scholar, historian, and strategist whose work contributes to the foundational study of international relations and security studies. Some critics argue that he cannot be considered a true war theorist like Sun Tzu or Clausewitz, as his hypothesis lacks a systematic theory on the causation of war (Nation, 2008). However, his insights on the "causes of war", discussed in Section 23, Book I of his renowned treatise, *The Peloponnesian War*, have been referred to by numerous scholars as a foundation to the study of war and conflict. He explains that the cause of the Peloponnesian war was due to the expansion of Athenians' power, which made the Spartans insecure and afraid (Hammond, 2009, p. 13). This adage is particularly relevant to the contemporary theory of the "security dilemma", which fuelled the arms race during the Cold War (and beyond) between the two superpowers (or great powers), destabilising the international system and heightening the risk of war. The arms race between the US and Soviet Union during the Cold War, or Russia's reason to invade Ukraine in 2022, is a result of fear (insecurity) instilled by the growing power of opponents.

In the realm of cyberspace, Russia's digital assaults in Estonia (2007) and Georgia (2008) created widespread insecurity amongst NATO countries, ultimately prompting the establishment of the Cooperative Cyber Defence Centre of Excellence in 2008. Similarly, the joint US-Israeli cyberattack on Iran's nuclear facilities (Stuxnet, 2010) provoked Iran into developing its Cyber Defense Command in the same year. These events create a growing security dilemma in the cyber realm where nations increasingly feel the need

Table 4.2 Cyber Espionage in Physical and Logical Layers

Sl No.	Physical layer	Logical layer
1	Local cyber spies in the physical layer refer to those informants, utilising digital services, residing in an adversary's state to gather intelligence from local blogs, social media, government websites, etc. Example: Russia employing its local supporters in Ukraine to monitor open-source intelligence from Ukraine-based websites, e-resources, and other digital platforms, subsequently reporting the information to Russian handlers.	Local cyber spies in the logical layer could be local software embedded in an adversary's computer system that can monitor and extract relevant information by detecting specific keywords from government websites, blogs, and social media. Example: local software in Ukraine's military computer system transmits selective information to Russia's intelligence agency.
2	Inward cyber spies refer to making use of technical officials of the enemy nation for one's own interest. Example: a technical officer employed in Ukraine's military office secretly sharing classified or sensitive information with Russian intelligence counterparts for a specific purpose or personal benefits.	"Pre-existing software" in an enemy's system, controlled or manipulated by another country for a strategic purpose. Example: software embedded in Ukraine's military digital networks that could be exploited by Russian cyber operatives to extract sensitive information (Hezbollah's pager or Pegasus spyware controlled by Israel).
3	Converted cyber spies are compromised enemy digital operatives that are redirected to work for one's own strategic advantage. Example: a Pakistani cyber spy caught or compromised by Indian sleuths, later making him work for the Indian government.	Converted cyber spies in a virtual world could be malware that was working for an enemy state but now working for one's country. Example: spyware initially deployed by Pakistan to steal sensitive information from Indian military computers could be identified and intercepted by Indian cyber operatives. Instead of neutralising the malware, the operatives could convert it into an Indian asset, modifying it to feed Pakistan false or misleading information.
4	Doomed cyber spies, or failed cyber spies, ready to sacrifice and authorised to be burned for the national interest/objective. Example: an Iranian cyber spy caught in the US, ready to be imprisoned in jail for life or ready to sacrifice his life in the interest of his nation.	Malware, spyware, or a botnet, sacrificed to deceive targets and distract from the real attack, to create confusion or spread false information. Example: Iranian spyware, compromised by US operatives, may be neutralised or intentionally "burnt off" by Iranian authorities if it is deemed unrecoverable or poses a security risk.
5	Surviving spies are those who successfully complete their mission and return with valuable intelligence from the enemy's digital infrastructure. Example: a Russian cyber operative belonging to any of the previous spy categories, who infiltrates Ukraine's systems, gathers critical intelligence, and safely transmits the data back to Russia.	Surviving cyber spies in the logical world are like the Advanced Persistent Threats (APTs) designed to remain undetected for a long time, and continuously gather intelligence, surviving enemy surveillance. Example: Russia using "Amadey Spyware" to monitor devices used by frontline Ukrainian military units.

to defend or survive against potential cyber adversaries. This phenomenon led to the establishment of the dynamics of the "cyber Cold War", fostering a cyber arms race for countries to heavily invest in research and development of sophisticated cyber arsenal. The rapid advancement of offensive and defensive cyber capabilities encourages further instability amongst nations, escalating risks to digital conflict. As states were concerned about the cost of such war, they began to establish dedicated cyber commands in their military system. This cyber command takes the responsibility of defending cyberspace, countering potential cyberattacks, and conducting digital operations for national strategic objectives. In addition, states began to form cyber alliances by having bilateral and multilateral collaborations (UNOEWG), acknowledging cooperation in cyberspace is imperative for collective defence. The rise of such alliances indicates a new era of digital diplomacy in the international system, where cyberwarfare capabilities are key components of national power.

Kautilya and Cyberwar

Kautilya, also popularly known as Chanakya and Vishnugupta (375–283 BCE), is widely discussed for his renowned treaties, *Arthashastra*, in military and administrative studies. While Sun Tzu's *The Art of War is* dedicated to warfare, *Arthashastra* is a treatise on state governance, politics and economic and military strategy (Kautilya, 1915). However, out of the 13 parts in the book, Part X (Relating to War) has six different short chapters on war that directly or indirectly can be linked to cyberwarfare. The first chapter discusses the encampment of soldiers that could in a cyberwar context be the raising of a digital operation room in the military formation. The second chapter advocates for the marching of soldiers and protection of the army from an attack, which relates to how a cyber army should prepare to launch an attack and defend its digital networks. The next section refers to striking an enemy's critical assets when they are in trouble (vulnerable) and in an unfavourable position. It is followed by Kautilya's counsel on battlefield-based activities of the infantry, cavalry, chariots, and elephants, where in a cyberwar case, that would be the deployment of digital war weapons such as DoS/DoSS attack programs, malicious software implants, exploiting vulnerabilities, and IP packet manipulation against enemy's devices (Tyagi, 2015, p. 92).

Like soldiers are trained to fight on "desert tracts, forests, valleys, plains, ditches, heights, rivers, mountains, marshy lands, lakes, etc.", cyber armies could be prepared to deploy for specific network attacks on different machines or sectors. The fourth chapter deals with combat zones related to the wing, flank, and front as a cyber army would follow an operation procedure in attack time. The sixth chapter is a continuation of the fifth and explains the array of the army against the enemy and advises that a "wise man can kill even those who are in the womb" than a single target by one arrow. This is applicable to one cyberattack that has a cascading effect on other digital devices. This indicates that a smart cyberattacker should aim to eliminate not only current threats but also potential future threats, striking at the root causes (heart) even before they are fully developed (e.g., the US-Israel orchestrated Stuxnet attack, before Iran's nuclear reactor was fully matured or became functional). Meanwhile, Chapter XII deals with the "institution of spies" and activities of secret services as key elements of statecraft (Kautilya, 1915, pp. 27–30). In the modern cyberwar context, similar practices are adopted through cyber commands and specialised cyber espionage units, such as Israel's Unit 8200 and Russia's Unit 29155. Unit 8200 is an elite Israeli cyber-intelligence force involved in developing advanced surveillance tools and conducting sophisticated digital operations such as the pager attack on Hezbollah in September 2024 (NDTV, 2024). Unit 29155, a covert cyber and espionage team functioning under Russia's military intelligence (GRU) has been involved in potential cyberattacks against Ukraine and NATO allies (CISA, 2024).

Machiavelli and the Art of Cyberwar

Like other war theorists, Niccolò Machiavelli (1469–1527 CE) was not a soldier but a civil servant (he last served as the Second Chancery of Florence). He published the *Art of War* (1521) during his lifetime besides his other works, *Discourses on Livy* (1531) and *The Prince* (1932), which were published posthumously. The book was written based on his conversation with Fabrizio Colonna, a professional *condottiere* (mercenary) captain and a war advisor to the king. The *Art of War* laid a foundation to the theory of civil-military relations (politics and military) in war studies. It also promotes the use of technology in military and war affairs. Book VII in the *Art of War* details the use of gunpowder not only to break the walls of fortresses into pieces but also mountains (Christopher, 2003, p. 478). Machiavelli articulates that the military reformation and new approaches in warfare are the most urgent and essential prerequisites of the time. He also highlights how paid militia are commissioned to fight a war (Gilbert, 1986).

In the field of cyberwarfare, cyber mercenaries are hired by handlers (state or non-state) to achieve political or strategic objectives. The emergence of new technology in the field of cyberspace has made the military system more sophisticated and cyberwar more destructive. Unlike physical war, the direction for waging a cyberwar may not be necessarily in the authority of political community. As the principle of digital war itself is vague, the decision for such a war can be made at the institutional level. Meanwhile, Machiavelli's other book, *The Prince*, advises that a prince should never leave war from his mind and conduct war gaming or exercises in peacetime than wartime (Mansfield, 1998, p. 59).[4] Similarly, contemporary leaders' worldwide view of cyberwarfare is as a vital component of state policy. As a result, military and law enforcement agencies actively conduct exercises, training, and operations during both peacetime and wartime to counter cyber aggressions.

Jomini and the Art of Cyberwar

Antoine-Henri Jomini (1779–1869 CE), was a banker turned military strategist, born in Switzerland, who served France and the Russian military. He worked until 1813 as a staff officer for the French military General Ney (who was a trusted associate of Napoleon), and observed the principle of war very closely from a military perspective. He left France at the age of 34 as a brigadier general and began to serve the Russian army from 1813 to 1869 until his last breath (as a full general). He kept writing and improving his theories and ideas on military and war affairs before he died (Shy, 1986). One of his influential books, *Art of War*[5] is considered as the magnum opus on war studies of the 19th century and is referred still today by war scholars. It has seven chapters on statesmanship, military policy, strategy, tactics, combined operations, logistics, and troop formation. While all the chapters may apply to cyberwarfare, the first three chapters suit it the most. In the first chapter, Jomini explains the main reason to go for war is to reclaim rights and expand the influence and power of the state against another as Hamas and Hezbollah fights for rights, while Israel advances for power. He was the first author to precisely write on the offensive and defensive dimensions of warfare to achieve a national objective by using armed forces (offensive) and political diplomatic means (defensive) (Jomini, 1830, 2008, p. 3). He further explains in the second chapter that military policy is different from a strategy or a tactic, and it encompasses military knowledge, theatre understanding, passion of the people, moral of the army, and recruitment process, which contribute to the success of an interstate war. The third chapter elaborates on strategy and how it differs from tactics.

In the international system, the reason for states to engage in cyberwar is to earn power and expand their influence in cyber affairs. In cyberwar, apart from the strategy and tactics, the people's patriotism, technical know-how of cutting-edge technology, and recruitment of digitally advanced professional attributes are needed to win digital wars. Cyberattacks are also seen carried out by nationalist non-state actors (Pakistan Cyber Army) against the enemy state (for instance, India). While *strategy* is based on the selection of war theatre, target detection, objective identification, manoeuvring of forces; *tactic* pertains to battle position, orders of battle, collision of army, and surprise attacks. Strategy comes before war activity and tactics are during war activity. He also laid the foundation of developing doctrines in military institutions. Likewise, the development of cyberwar doctrine, identification of targets based on the national objective (strategy), and use of sophisticated malware (tactic) during operations to eliminate a footprint (or avoid from tracing by the opponent) are key elements to cyberwarfare.

Clausewitz on Cyberwar

Carl von Clausewitz (1780–1831 CE), a major general in the Prussian military, is far more renowned than Jomini in the realm of war literature. He is regarded as the most influential theorist of war, and his seminal work, *On War*, published posthumously in 1832 by his devoted and affluent wife, continues to be widely referenced by modern military scholars.[6] Peter Paret claims that Clausewitz's main contribution was the thorough analysis of war, which is more relevant to contemporary, nuclear (or cyber) era warfare than his generation (Paret, 1986). The volume has eight "books" discussing the theory and nature of war, strategy, engagement, forces, defence (defensive), attack (offensive), and planning. He explains war is a duel between two soldiers on a large scale aiming to disarm or win over each other. It is an act to compel the enemy to do what the state wants. It is also a continuation of policy to achieve a political objective by using other means. He further elaborated that a war doctrine is a manual of action for armed forces and it is different from strategy and tactics (Clausewitz, 1832, 2007). According to Clausewitz, "*tactic* is the theory of using battle for the purpose of war, *strategy* as the theory of the use of armed forces in battle" (Paret, 1986, p. 190). Meanwhile, he proposed that war is driven by a "trinity" consisting of hatred (by the public), violence (by soldiers), and enmity (by the state or governance), which represents enduring grievances over time. His writing reflected the Prussian concept of *Auftragstaktik*,[7] which is truly applicable in the contemporary cyberwar system.

Clausewitz's theory of war holds significant relevance and applicability in the evolving domain of cyberwarfare. Cyberwar includes various activities ranging from state's policy (strategy) to an operative's action (tactic). Unlike traditional warfare, cyberwar does not require large-scale duels, instead, a small number of skilled operatives can effectively engage and make a significant impact in cyber conflict. Cyberwar is an ongoing process, strategically conducted as a state policy to achieve political or digital objectives. According to Clausewitz, cyberwar doctrine should be distinctly formulated and kept separate from cyberwar strategies and tactics to ensure clarity in purpose and execution. In his view, cyberwar doctrine should serve as a comprehensive guide for the operations to be carried out by cyber forces, similar to how India's *Joint Doctrine for Cyberspace Operations* (2024) provides a structured framework for cyber operations. Subsequently, tactics would be a theory of using cyber operations for the purpose of winning digital skirmishes, and strategy should be the planning of using cyber forces in the operation to achieve victory. Cyberwar occurs because of prolonged grievances, hatred, and enmity against the enemy (Iran/North Korea against US/West). Meanwhile, the concept of *Auftragstaktik* is adopted in digital war in which a military institute can launch a war against the enemy without political approval in the interest of national politics. Similarly, a technical unit or a leading officer of the unit in a military institution can take a decision to carry out a cyber operation without the approval of his superior if the goal is in favour of the latter.

Mary Kaldor and the New Cyberwar

Notably, the theory of regular war, or "old war", has been challenged by academics such as Mary Kaldor, who argues that the traditional concept of warfare has evolved and been supplanted by what she terms "new war". She makes an effort to explain that the term *new war* refers to a "privatised and informal" conflict that evolved during or after the Cold War and whose participants, objectives, tactics, and sources of funding are distinct from those of conventional warfare (Kaldor, 2013). It is linked to other different types of war such as conventional warfare, counter insurgency, civil war, degenerate warfare (Shaw), remnants of war (John Miller), and hybrid war (Frank Hoffman). In the framework of new wars, the boundaries between private and public entities, state and non-state actors, as well as formal and informal organisations, have become increasingly blurred.[8] Modern warfare features a diverse range of participants, including paramilitary units, local warlords, militants, civil armed volunteers, criminal gangs, police forces, mercenary groups, regular armies, and even breakaway factions of state forces. Unlike old wars, traditionally driven by geopolitical considerations, new wars are centred on issues of identity, ethnicity, individual rights, religion, land control, and regime change. Old wars were characterised by decisive battles conducted primarily through state-military means, while new wars often see territories captured through political manoeuvring using methods like protests, demands, negotiations, propaganda, and subversion rather than extensive combat operations. The funding models of warfare have also evolved. While old wars were largely state-funded, new wars draw from a variety of sources, including private donations, illicit trade, foreign aid, and decentralised financial networks. This shift reflects the complex and multifaceted nature of contemporary conflicts, where traditional distinctions and approaches no longer suffice.[9]

Mary Kaldor recognised that the advent of information technology is as significant as the invention of tanks and aeroplanes for war fighting. Quoting Chris Hables Gray, she discussed that new war can also refer to virtual wars and wars in cyberspace (Kaldor, 2012, p. 22). While the goal of cyberwar is ambiguous unlike old wars, its objective can vary from personal hatred (Clausewitz's trinity) to national achievement. As North Korean and Iran attack the US for reasons of hatred, Israel strikes Hamas for political and strategic purpose. The actors for this type of conflict are government and non-government entities or a group of mercenaries, terrorists, or even a nationalists. State actors typically refrain from claiming responsibility for cyberattacks to protect their international image and avoid political fallout. In contrast, non-state actors often take credit for such attacks, as they are less concerned with maintaining a public image and instead view it as a source of pride or a means to further their cause. The method of this warfare is defacing or disrupting the enemy's information system by using malicious means (malware, virus, etc.). Similar to new war, cyberwar is not waged in decisive battles but rather for short-term goals and monetary gain, often funded through diverse sources.

Irregular War and Cyberwarfare

In the study of warfare, it is essential to consider not only interstate or regular conflicts, but also civil wars and political movements organised by non-state actors, as these forms of conflict play a significant role in modern warfare dynamics. Since there is no international law governing cyberwarfare and state actors typically do not claim responsibility for digital strikes, these engagements can be classified as irregular warfare (IW),[10] often carried out (represented by) by non-state actors. This aspect can be addressed in two ways. The first aspect involves civilians using cyberspace as a tool to overthrow regimes, as seen during the Arab Spring, while the second pertains to covert cyber partisans (digital armed groups) working secretly against states or other actors to achieve political objectives. This section will primarily focus on the latter, examining the cyber activities of non-state actors within the virtual world. Non-state actors and the public can play a crucial role in cyberwarfare, notably through the use of social media in events like the Arab Spring, where cyber-enabled mass movements or campaigns were sparked. The study of "cyber guerrilla" tactics, drawing from the ideas of key proponents such as Mao Zedong, Che Guevara, and Liddell Hart (particularly in the context of counter-insurgency approaches[11]), should be explored in tandem with IW as a political strategy.

Mao and Guerrilla Cyberwarfare

In his book *On Guerrilla Warfare*, Mao Zedong (1893–1976 CE) describes the characteristics of conflict and discusses the strategy, tactics, and logistics of revolutionary movements led by non-state actors. He characterised such movement as a political armed movement by a group of militias with support from general masses to achieve a political objective or overthrow the state administration. This goal is achieved by "organizing the public, unified internally to "establish bases, equip forces, recollect national strength, destroy enemy's strength, and regain lost territories" (Corps, 1989, p. 43) with appropriate organisation, strategy, and tactics. The organisation should be formed from a diverse mix of individuals, including disillusioned regular army personnel, deserters from the enemy ranks, local militias, bandit groups, and other disgruntled segments of society (Ibid, p. 71). The fundamental strategy of guerrilla warfare is predominantly based on alertness, mobility, and attack, which would be adjusted based on the opponent's situation, terrain, weather, communication, and strength. Meanwhile, the tactics should be based on decentralised, quick and fast mobile operations (hit and run) and there is no decisive battle in a guerrilla war (Ibid, pp. 52, 96) unlike regular warfare where armies of both sides stand face to face and fight (Clausewitz's large duel concept). Mao advised his cadres not to harm or disturb anyone's property, except for combatants' or state authority's, emphasising that the movement or militias (fish) depended on the support of the populace (the water) to survive. This principle highlights the importance of maintaining the support and trust of the local population, as their backing is essential for the success and sustainability of the insurgency or movement.

Due to the crucial role that non-state actors play in cyberwar, it has been observed that weaker forces can compete with stronger ones in the network system. According to the "People's War" theory, anyone with computer skills can join the struggle in cyberspace and launch a massive attack involving hundreds of millions of people. This was observed in the mass online movement of the Arab Spring, though it was not exactly an attack on cyber networks but using it to achieve a political goal (Ford, 2010, p. 63). Meanwhile, Jelle and colleagues in their book *Cyber Guerrilla*, explain that "cyber guerrilla warfare" is a war that is waged as asymmetric warfare in a specific situation against a conventional army not only in times of struggle, political crisis and unrest, or conflict, but also in times of peace in the form of protest like cyber civil disobedience (Van Haaster, 2016, p. 2). The objective of the war is to collect (reconnaissance), control, deny, disrupt, or destroy adversary's information systems for a strategic objective.

The cyber guerrilla functions within an organisation framework with proper strategy and tactics to achieve political or non-political objectives. These groups often operate in a grey zone of cyber conflict, acting as nationalist entities targeting domestic or foreign adversaries. For instance, the Transparent Tribe, or APT-36 (an unofficial cyber group in Pakistan) or the Indian Cyber Force, Iranian Cyber Army, Bangladesh Grey Hat Hackers, Chinese Red Hacker Alliance, Syrian Electronic Army, and Anonymous Suda operate "illegally" in the same manner. The strategy (methods) of cyber guerrillas is specific, attainable, and realistic with a long-term plan to achieve the goal. In their strategy, the exit route after conducting an operation (attacking enemy's computer) is important as they should not compromise their identity. Tactics are done at the disposal of the attacker depending on the target environment and available resources. Tactics are deployed at the operational level with APTs and a cyber kill chain[12] system. In cyberwarfare, there is no decisive battle and it primarily relies on hit-and-run tactics. In this context, a state information facility could be targeted by cyber guerrillas, who strike swiftly and then retreat without leaving a clear trail for the enemy. While these attacks may be traceable based on the technological capabilities of the victim, the anonymity of the attackers often complicates attribution, making it difficult for the targeted state to identify the source with certainty. While cyber guerrilla tactics are flexible and stealthy, their target should be restricted to state and combatant information facilities, not to civil properties, as it practices in the principle of insurgency or people's war.

Che Guevara and Guerrilla Cyberwar

In addition to Mao, Che Guevara (1928–1967 CE) extensively discussed guerrilla warfare in his 1961 monograph *Guerrilla Warfare*. He identifies three specific aspects of war principles: cadre (band or fighter), organisation, and holding power after winning the movement. The principles of guerrilla warfare are based on the essence, strategy, tactic, terrain system (favourable and non-favourable), and urban combat of the cadres. These principles are to be closely connected with guerrilla bands (fighters) and they should function as a social reformer as well as a combatant. The organisation of the guerrilla fighters functions with various divisions including logistic (food and civil supplies), civil bodies (overground supporters), women's wing (combat and non-combat work), health (hospitals), sabotage (enemy's infrastructure), war industry (workshop, armory), propaganda (media, e.g., Rebel Radio 1958), intelligence (reconnaissance), training (armed exercise) and indoctrination (recruitment), and an organigram (chain of command) of the guerrilla army (Guevara, 2006). Che's central idea in *Guerrilla Warfare* is that a popular, irregular force can defeat a regular, conventional army through tactics that exploit the weaknesses of the enemy. Harry Villegas,[13] in a forwarding note of *Guerrilla Warfare* (2006), expressed that at the tactical level, there are seven golden rules[14] to win a war against the state (some of which are applicable to cyberwarfare). These include, not to engage a fight one would not win; hit-and-run tactics to be used continuously; enemy to be the supplier of war weapons; any movement should be clandestine; the element of surprise in military action; create new columns to win; and in general, maintain strategic defence, and balance between guerrilla and enemy action, along with complete destruction of enemy (Ibid, p. 5).

Compared with Che's guerrilla band (or bandit), Jelle describes a cyber guerrilla group as a group of likeminded hackers who aim to be popularised and enlarge their potential, competing with larger authorities to achieve an objective (Van Haaster, 2016, p. 2). For a cyber "band", its core strategy lies in challenging larger adversaries with the goal of disrupting the enemy's information systems. While victory in cyberwar is difficult to quantify, a smaller group or actor achieves success when it incapacitates the critical information infrastructures (CIIs) of a larger opponent. Unlike traditional warfare, where victory is typically defined by the occupation of territory or population, in cyber warfare, success is measured by the ability of an actor (whether state or non-state) to influence or control the actions of the enemy within the cyberspace domain. This can be done by exploiting vulnerabilities, paralysing key systems, or forcing the adversary to act according to the attacker's objectives. For instance, a Bangladeshi cyber group could declare victory by compromising state financial systems and forcing the government to pay a ransom to regain control of the breached networks. This action compels the authorities to transfer funds to the attackers, marking a strategic success for the weaker entity.[15]

While Che's strategy and tactic of cyber guerrillas are more or less similar to what Mao has explained (as discussed), the seven golden tactical rules of guerrilla war that cyberwar adopts to achieve success, shall be worthy of study. Unlike traditional war, cyberwar is irregularly fought and to win, non-state actors challenge superior authorities to achieve desired goals (economic, political, strategic). Attackers that plan to attack in the digital realm always try to get away and remove any trace of their involvement. It's interesting to note that cybercriminals frequently employ technology that was developed by governments or related sectors, whether it's malware to attack adversaries or firewalls to defend themselves. Any hacker movements are hidden, and attacks are a surprise in nature with a zero-days effect. Meanwhile, non-state actors' concerned for their strategic defence calculate the potential of their adversaries to annihilate them.

Liddell Hart and Cyber Non-state Actors

Liddell Hart (1895–1970 CE), a British military officer and a war theorist, became popular in the 1920s through his writings on the mechanised army or warfare (Alexander, 1986, p. 602), which are referred to by many war scholars and military strategists. Introducing the intensive role of science and technology in military affairs, his book, *The Revolution in Warfare* (1956), explains the two sides of war, the instrument and technique on one aspect, and the character on another. While his writing on guerrilla war, what he also termed as "camouflage war", is rooted in "counter" insurgency doctrine, his strategy and tactics are applicable to both regular forces (state actors) and irregular forces (non-state elements). Regarding guerrilla tactics, he emphasises that no nuclear weapon can effectively deter guerrillas, nor can weapons of mass destruction be deployed to counter them.[16] The old maxim of *if you want peace, understand war* has shifted to *if you want peace, understand "guerrilla and subversive form of war"* (Hart, 1954, 1967, p. 361). To control non-state actors, he advises state militaries to develop new strategies and adopt tactics to fight like guerrillas. Defining tactics as an application of strategy, and strategy as grand strategy, he provided eight maxims of war strategy. These include adjustment of end by means; the objective to be always kept mindful; choose the least expected course; exploit the line of least resistance; operate in a way that offers different options; plan to be adaptable to the circumstances; do not throw your weight when the enemy is guarded; and do not repeat an attack in the same form (Hart, 1956, pp. 335–356).

In the context of cyberwarfare, the eight maxims propounded by Liddell are applicable not only to state forces but also to non-state actors. As they do not take on more than they can handle, smaller groups conduct cyber incursions (means) based on their limited resources for specific objectives. For instance, a cyber nationalist group such as the Iran Cyber Security Group Hackers may not be able to attack the sensitive infrastructure of the US's nuclear system but can deface or disrupt government websites as a specific achievement within their limited capability. Internet money heists, online recruitment by terrorist groups, and cyber-enabled drone attacks, amongst others, are strategies of warfare by non-state actors to achieve their adjustable ends. While attackers will keep their objective in mind with alternate options, they shall choose different IP addresses or gateways to attack a network. They will choose the weakest link or the neglected path (less resistant) to penetrate government cyber domains. Attackers will choose a single action that will provide multiple impacts or objectives, just as *Petya* ransomware affects multiple countries although the target was Ukraine. Any plan may failed in operation, so the actors shall be flexible to adapt to any situation. Non-state actors will not throw their weight if the state's (or enemy's) network system is shielded with unbreakable firewalls. Hence, non-state actors attempting to hack a state's satellite system could be rarely possible. Once an attempt to attack has failed, successive effort on the same line should be avoided. For instance, terrorists will refrain from retrying malware attacks that have already failed once and exposed to government systems. Instead, they will seek a new avenue to attack their adversary's facilities. While non-state actors may not possess cyberwar capabilities equivalent to those of state authorities, disruption of public digital networks will still occur because it is one of their ongoing goals, albeit at a low intensity. Meanwhile, no nuclear weapons or weapons of mass destruction can deter cyber non-state actors.

Domains of Warfare and Military Power

Cyberspace is widely regarded as the fifth domain of warfare, following land, sea, air, and space. War and military power are two sides of the same coin. War can only be won when states possess sufficient power across political, military, economic, and social dimensions. Having power will make the enemy act in accordance with one's will, limiting their opponent's choices and enforcing or resisting change as needed to secure victory. In the context of digital conflict, understanding the evolving concept of cyberwar[17] requires associating it with the theory of military power applications in other domains—such as land, sea, air, and space—through the foundational texts of established theorists and subsequent analyses by their followers. Conventional battles are normally fought on the domain of land, sea, and air. While battle in space is forbidden by international laws, it still supports the military system in navigation, communication, and reconnaissance through satellites in times of war and peace. However, cyberspace as a strategic weapon and an enabler supports conventional war, and as a domain also provides a virtual ground for battles. This section will discuss cyberspace as a domain of warfare (battle platform) not as a tool to support conventional conflict. This section will examine cyberspace primarily as a domain of warfare, emphasising its role as a battleground rather than merely a tool for supporting conventional conflicts (adjunct role).

As cyberspace evolves, it no longer remains merely a domain originally created for communication purposes but it has transcended now into a domain of warfare. States increasingly strive to establish themselves as cyber powers by formulating new policies, crafting strategies, and creating dedicated military cyber commands and doctrines. Similarly, theorists have begun analysing the power dynamics of this domain, much like those of land, sea, air, and space. For instance, Mackinder and Spykman explore the ideas of "land power" by introducing their popular theories of Heartland and Rimland, respectively. Similarly, A.T. Mahan's work on sea power and, as well as the air power theories of Douhet, Mitchell, and Trenchard, have shaped strategic thoughts. Although space has not yet become a direct battleground, the concept of space power has been analysed by scholars including Colin Gray, John Shaw, and Brian Fredriksson. Lately, disciplinary specialists such as Joseph Nye and Stuart H. Starr have initiated discussions on "cyberpower" theory. However, because of the rapidly evolving nature of technology and the shifting characteristics of cyberspace, scholars continue to face challenges in developing comprehensive theories of cyber power or cyberwarfare, leaving the field as a work in progress.

Land Power and Cyberwar

States often seek to enhance their land-fighting capabilities, not solely by improving military tools but by asserting control over strategically significant locations at local, regional, and global levels. While occupying such pivotal areas can yield economic advantages, their primary value lies in serving military objectives, enabling states to achieve their broader national goals. Consequently, strategic thinkers have propounded significant theories or advisories to modify the traditional method of war thinking. One of them was renowned geographer Halford J. Mackinder (1861–1947 CE), who is still cited by numerous military scholars for his contributions to land warfare. In his symbolic article "The Geographical Pivot of History" first published by *The Geographical Journal* in April 1904, he highlights the concept of "land power" (heartland)[18] theory. Explaining the correlation between the natural environment and political institutions, he explains the strategic significance of Eurasia, calling it a heartland or a pivot area. He affirms that the introduction of the steam engine and Suez canal in the 19th century enhanced sea power as well as land power. Railways chiefly feed the commercial activities of the sea, and it contributes to the "land power" system of Eurasia (Mackinder, 1904, p. 434). Three sides of Eurasia, east, south, and west of the heartland, are marginal crescents[19] of the land accessible to the Pacific and Indian oceans (Ibid, p. 31). His idea proposed that the development of land power in this area could acquire continental power, which would lead to world domination. This concept (idea) was enlarged in his book *Democratic Ideals and Reality* published in 1919 by citing his often quoted dictum, "*Who rules East Europe commands the Heartland; Who rules the Heartland commands the World-Island; Who rules the World-Island commands the World*" (Mackinder, 1919, p. 186). Meanwhile, another political geographer Nicholas John Spykman (1893–1943 CE) propounded the theory of rimland, where he says land power is relevant to sea power. He renamed Mackinder's inner crescent as "Rimland", which has opportunities to access the heartland in the north and the ocean in the south. Hence, he proposed the dictum "*Who controls the Rimland rules Eurasia; Who rules Eurasia controls the destinies of the world*". He further expressed that "geography is the most fundamental factor in foreign policy of states because it is the most permanent" (Spykman, 1942, p. 41).

If cyberspace is regarded as a domain of warfare akin to land, sea, air, or space—which are traditionally tied to geography—one might question whether cyberspace qualifies as a part of geography or exists as a purely abstract, non-physical entity. Unlike the tangible dimensions of geography, cyberspace is an intangible, borderless realm that operates without a fixed geographical structure. Yet, it functions dynamically, shaping states' foreign policies and influencing global power dynamics. The idea of a "geographical map" for cyberspace is intriguing. Although it lacks physical boundaries, cyberspace does possess a form of functional geography, defined by data flows, network infrastructures, server locations, and the digital territories controlled by states or corporations. If cyberspace were to be regarded as part of geography, the concept of a "Cyber Eurasia" in the digital world emerges as a possibility. Much like its physical counterpart, Cyber Eurasia could represent a strategic digital region of influence, essential for controlling global cyber power dynamics. Those who dominate Cyber Eurasia could potentially hold sway over the destinies of the cyber world, echoing the geopolitical significance of the heartland in traditional geopolitics.

However, for hackers or cyberattackers, technical "pivot areas" can exist and controlling them can allow dominance over entire systems. In cyberspace, these pivot areas could be critical points within a key information system. At the local level, for example, control over the Supervisory Control and Data Acquisition (SCADA) systems of a power plant, dam, or traffic system can allow one to dominate the entire grid. A case in point is the 12 October 2020 malware attack on a power grid that caused a blackout in Mumbai and surrounding areas. At the state level, cyberattacks on countries like Estonia and Georgia serve as significant references. On the global stage, while attacks like Stuxnet and Petya were targeted at specific countries, their effects cascaded worldwide, even if they couldn't be classified as global attacks. A direct global attack remains challenging to execute in practice, as Clausewitz's concept of "total war" is theoretically possible but not feasible in modern warfare. However, it is possible that whoever controls the world's internet system can rule the world's information system, which provides the power to dominate global cyberspace.

Sea Power and Cyberwarfare

As Mackinder and Spykman are popular for their land power theories, Alfred T. Mahan is widely recognised for his concepts of sea power. In his book *The Influence of Sea Power upon History, 1660–1783* (1980), Mahan provides numerous historical examples to explain the significant role of the sea in times of war and peace and the blue economy, emphasising the importance of "sea commerce". Traveling and conducting trade by sea have always been more cost-effective and efficient than by land. While troops can move freely across the sea to their desired locations, losing control of the sea during wartime can severely impact both military objectives and economic interests (Kennedy, 1988). Interestingly, in the first chapter, "Discussion of the Elements of Sea Power" of his book, Mahan discusses six key determinants of sea power. The success and failure of a nation to become a true sea power rely on these six elements. They are "geographical position, physical conformation, extent of territory, number of population, national character, and character of government" (Mahan, 1987, p. 103). These elements can be examined directly or indirectly in the context of cyberwarfare.

As cyberspace is considered borderless, "geographical position" may not affect digital warfare much. Countries in the far east can attack countries in the far west as long as the network directly or indirectly connects them (e.g., North Korea and the US). However, the geopolitical system and the history of the countries can lead to cyberwar between neighbours (India against China and Pakistan). While "physical confirmation" is the advantage of a state that has coastal facilities, likewise, countries that are closer to their allies have support from each other in times of cyberwar and cyber peace (NATO countries). The "extent of the territory" in cyberspace can refer to the state's cyber resource capabilities, its extendibility, and ability to access or penetrate the information systems of other countries. The "number of population" matters in cyberwarfare as states with more skilled cyber soldiers are likely to gain advantage in digital warfare. "National character" refers to states' interest in exploiting cyberspace to achieve a national strategic objective in both times of war and peace. Meanwhile the "character of government" pertains to a state's central policies and implementations for digital commercial matters and cyberwar activities.

Air Power and Cyberwarfare

The world order is critically dependent on air power. Without aviation, the atom bomb could not have been used and the Second World War might have dragged on much longer, causing even greater destruction to humanity. The power of air was theoretically analysed by three air-power advocates, Douhet,

Mitchell, and Trenchard. Giulio Douhet (1869–1930 CE), in his seminal work *The Command of the Air* (*Il dominio dell'aria*), first published in 1921 in Italian, elaborates on the significance of air power in warfare. Recognising it as a revolutionary form of combat, he advocated for the establishment of an independent air force within military structures.[20] Douhet discussed various aspects of aerial warfare, including the strategic importance of aerial battles, the roles of auxiliary, combat, and reconnaissance aircraft, and the balance between defensive and offensive air operations. He also emphasised the need for meticulous planning and organisational frameworks, the execution of aerial bombings, and the moral, intellectual, and material dimensions of aviation in modern warfare. Aircraft are offensive instruments of war with great potential to maim and mar the enemy. By using all means, including "explosives, incendiary, and poison gas", the target of the airstrike should be the industrial and commercial facilities, significant buildings, transportation centres, and even some selected populated area (Douhet, 2019, 1921, p. 18). The controversial advocacy for bombing civilians compelled Douhet to testify in a court-martial, where he clarified that the strategy was intended to "bend the enemy's will" and should not be misinterpreted (Ibid, pp. 53, 250). An air attack against a defenceless city population would create fear in everyone in the enemy state, which will force the government to end the war and bring peace at an early stage. Another prominent air-power strategist, Brigadier General William Billy Mitchell (1879–1936 CE) of the US Army shared some ideas about bombing civilians but advocated for moderation in its application. He argued that even a few gas bombs would compel the population to flee the city, disrupting factory operations and halting production critical to the war effort. The extensive bombing of London during 1940 to 1941, despite causing significant fear and disruption, resulted in relatively minor destruction to the city as a whole. Mitchell emphasised that to cripple the enemy's power and war-making capability, strategic targets such as factories, communication networks, food production facilities, farmlands, fuel and oil supply chains, as well as industrial and residential areas, should be prioritised.[21] Meanwhile, Hugh Trenchard (1873–1956 CE), though not as prolific in publishing as Douhet or Mitchell, made a significant contribution to British military service by establishing the Royal Air Force (RAF) as an independent branch, separate from the army and navy. Rising to the rank of Marshal of the RAF, Trenchard focused on resolving key disputes between the army and navy over the nature of aerial bombardment, particularly regarding long-range bombing operations. He advocated for clear distinctions in responsibilities, proposing that each branch of the armed forces maintain its own aviation schools with unique principles tailored to their respective missions.

The concept of air power, as promulgated by the aforementioned theorists, highlights that "airspace" is a distinct domain of warfare, meriting an independent service such as the air force, rather than being subordinated to the army or navy. This notion interestingly raises the question of whether cyberspace, as a separate domain, similarly necessitates an independent service (e.g., an Indian Cyber Force), akin to the traditional branches of the military.[22] Though a cyber command system has already been established under the joint forces, there is a possibility that it may evolve into a separate force in the future, especially as digital space becomes as significant as other domains of warfare. Air power is seen from two perspectives, one is battle in the air, where aircraft fight against aircraft in the air, and the other is attacking ground facilities. Similarly, in the cyberwar context too, battle can take place between two enemies within the network system (logical based). The other would be attacking ground facilities through the internet, damaging or disrupting critical assets (physical attacks). Based on the air-power theory, targetable facilities in cyberwar could be public online facilities (social media, communication systems, e-governance, health sector, etc.), attacked not necessarily to hurt civilians but to pressure the authorities (war authorities) into avoiding or ending the war. Civilian network facilities (civil logistics including foods and clothing) that support the military system can also be attacked to affect the military functioning in the time of war. Other core targets should be key military network and communication systems, along with other sectors including transportation, energy, industries, and factories.

Space Power and Cyberwarfare

Colin S. Gray (1943–2020 CE) remains one of the most frequently cited scholars on space power, particularly following the publication of his influential article, "The Influence of Space Power upon History," in *Comparative Strategy* in 1996. This work paved the way for other scholars, such as John E. Shaw, who authored "The Influence of Space Power upon History, 1944–1988," published in *Air Power History* in 1999. Another notable contribution came from Brian E. Fredriksson, whose book, *Globalness: Towards a Space Power Theory*, published in 2006, added significant depth to the discourse on space power theory. In his article, John E. Shaw briefly discusses the characteristics of space weapons, such as intercontinental ballistic missiles, and examines the space race through its various phases, particularly between the United States and the Soviet Union. He highlights the first practical use of space in warfare during the 1991 Persian Gulf War and explores the future prospects of space forces as an integral part of military strategy (Shaw, 1999). Brian E. Fredriksson discusses the theory of space power, examining it as a critical instrument of both military and national power. Referring to Smith, he argues that the militarisation of space is inevitable, emphasising that space power serves as a coercive force capable of shaping global power dynamics and national security strategies (Fredriksson, 2006, p. 45).

Colin Gray's paper delves deeply into the concept of space power, becoming a widely referenced work among scholars and practitioners. His insights contributed significantly to the discourse on space power and its strategic implications, influencing policy and strategy. Notably, Gray's work is often credited with shaping the rationale that led to the establishment of the US

Space Force under the Department of the Air Force in 2020 (Klein, 2021). Gray, in this article, explains space power as "the ability to use space for military, civil, or commercial purpose while denying the ability of enemy to do the same" (Gray, 1996, p. 299). He suggested that states (especially the US) should establish a space force equipped with weapons, if not to fight in space, but to support land, sea, and air powers through space facilities (information supply, navigation, reconnaissance, surveillance, early warning of missile attack, etc.). As air and sea power are an adjunct (contributor) to land power,[23] space power will be an adjunct to the triad. As weaponisation is denied in space,[24] space power will play an adjunct role to war on Earth. Space power may not be able to directly sink a submarine or destroy an aircraft, but it empowers combat capabilities to carry out actions indirectly by passing information to the troops (as seen in the 1991 Operation Desert Storm air campaign). Space power begins and ends with information (intelligence) from satellites, contributing potential to military operations in other domains. Colin further extended his space power studies by integrating the latest technologies of "cyberspace" along with the potentials of land, sea, and air for 21st-century modern warfare, in his book *Modern Strategy*, released in 1999 (Gray, 1999, p. 271).

Cyber power can similarly be analysed through the lens of space power theorists. Just as air-power advocates and later space power strategists emphasised the need for independent forces to address their respective domains, the establishment of a separate cyber force, equipped with advanced and relevant cyber weapons, may become essential for a state aiming to assert itself as a dominant power in the digital domain. This force will work with non-combatant (support system) and combatant (fighting) roles in times of peace and war. In the non-combat role, the cyber force may not be necessarily prepared to destroy a tank, sink a carrier, take down an aircraft, or blow up a satellite directly, but it will serve as an "adjunct" enabling the troops to do so. The cyber force will provide vital intelligence, monitoring and surveillance, strategic reconnaissance, navigation, data analysis, AI decision-making, and many other services related to emerging technologies for the security forces. As a combat force, it will conduct offensive operations to harm the land, sea, air, and space systems with logical (within cyberspace) and physical (beyond cyberspace) implications. Unlike space power, cyber power does not began and end with information. It has more other powerful characteristics than simply generating and passing valuable information to troops and their leaders. Not only can it share or disseminate vital intelligence input to the combatants, but it can disrupt the enemy's military and non-military critical information infrastructure. Details will be addressed in the following section.

Cyber Power and Digital Warfare

Like other war environments (domains), military cyber power has been discussed by several scholars including Joseph Nye, Colin Gray, Franklin D.

Kramer, Daniel T. Kuehl, Stuart H. Starr, and Martin C. Libicki. Military cyber capability is still evolving, and the theory of cyberpower remains in its infancy, with its conceptualisation only beginning around 2006[25] (Starr, 2009, p. 43). Consequently, current and future policymakers along with other stakeholders are likely to face significant challenges in addressing the structural aspects (security, research, governance, organisation) and geographical dimensions (network operation, deterrence, doctrines, leadership, education, cooperation) of cyberspace. Among other elements of cyberspace, Kramer explains that "*cyberpower* has the ability to use cyberspace to create advantages and influence events in all the other operational environments and across the instruments of power" (Kramer, 2009). The generation of state military power through digital space, or the transformation of cyberspace into cyber power, is a daunting task fraught with significant challenges and complexities. These hurdles begin with the fundamental need to develop a cohesive vocabulary for the cyber realm and to define the terminologies associated with its elements and operations (Kuehl, 2009). Meanwhile, cyber power acts as a force enabler like air power that influences ground power by bombing enemy troops or supplying goods from the sky. Network centric capabilities do impact military missions (Libicki, 2009). Cyber power is merely the use of digital based information that exists or is available in the "infosphere" to achieve a political objective. The infosphere is a data based information environment or a domain, a place in space and time where information exists and flows. Cyber power is pervasive and an enabler of land, sea, air, and space powers. Cyber power is a complementary instrument to other powers and at the same time a stealthy tool of military affairs (Sheldon, 2016, p. 296). In the Indian context, the *Joint Doctrine: Indian Armed Forces-2017* explains cyber power as "the ability to use cyberspace freely and securely to gain an advantage over the adversary while denying the same to him in various operational environments, and by applying the instruments of National Power" (IDS, 2017, p. 25).

Among the various scholars who have written on cyber power, Joseph Nye's approach stands out for its unique perspective, as he examines cyber power through both soft and hard power lenses. In the chapter "Diffusion and Cyberpower" from his book, *The Future of Power*, Nye highlights the critical role cyber power plays in shaping world politics. The power of computers has doubled in every 18 months for the last four decades. There was only one website in 1990 and 1.88 billion in August 2021 (Armstrong, 2021). While information has always played a crucial role in military power dynamics, smaller actors find themselves better positioned to exercise both hard and soft power within the realm of cyberspace. Joseph Nye explores the hard and soft power dimensions of cyberspace, addressing their intra- and extra-digital implications across the physical and virtual layers of the cyber environment, as illustrated in Table 4.3. While multiple actors, ranging from teenage prodigies to government professional experts, can serve as resources

Table 4.3 Physical and Virtual Dimension of Cyber Power

Target of cyber power		
Instruments	Intra cyberspace	Extra cyberspace
Information layer	Hard: DoS or malware attacks Soft: adhere to new norms and standards	Hard: SCADA disruption Soft: political campaign to influence voters (fake news, disinformation, misinformation)
Physical layer	Hard: government control over companies that are functioning within a geographical area Soft: instruments to enable human rights activists to promote agendas of state interest	Hard: server blown up by bombs or cut cables by state or non-state elements Soft: protests to name and shame service providers for the misuse of cyberspace (internet)

Source: Joseph Nye, "The Future of Power", 2011.

for cyber power, Joseph Nye further explains that cyber power can be analysed through three distinct dimensions.

1. A state (A) persuades another state (B) to do what B would otherwise never do willingly. State or non-state actors inserting spyware into enemy systems to monitor them (hard power and offensive in nature) to hijack information that B will never share with A. Another example could be a terrorist using the internet to capture youths' attention to join its movement (soft power with offensive nature), that the youth otherwise would never join voluntarily.
2. A controls the agenda of B and prevents B from pursuing its own strategies or choices. For example, state A may deliberately slow down the internet speed for the public in state B during a crisis to prevent the circulation of anti-national videos. This could also extend to state authorities compelling specific companies to reject certain viewpoints, exemplifying hard power with an offensive nature. Similarly, state policies on filtering unwanted videos from being uploaded to social platforms and mass surveillance conducted by intelligence agencies represent soft power in a defensive mode, aimed at monitoring and preempting potential threats.
3. The third facet involves state A shaping state B's preferences. For instance, a state may issue laws and guidelines for internet service providers, imposing penalties for non-compliance or warnings to deter individuals from engaging in cybercrimes. This represents hard power with a deterrence factor, as individuals are likely to avoid committing such offences to evade punishment. Additionally, the state may promote public awareness of cyber norms to discourage actors from engaging in undesirable activities, such as discussing anti-national issues on social

media or circulating child pornography. This form of public awareness reflects the use of soft power to influence behaviour and uphold societal standards (Nye, 2011).

Meanwhile, Colin S. Gray, after his influential publication on space power concepts in the mid 1990s, attempted to theorise the strategic perceptions of cyber power by publishing a monograph, *Making Strategic Sense Of Cyber Power: Why The Sky Is Not Falling*, published by the Strategic Studies Institute, US Army War College in 2013. If the power of other domains can be strategically conceptualised, cyber power can similarly be analysed and applied from a military perspective. Hence, he defines cyberpower as "the ability to do something strategically useful in cyberspace". Due to its non-physical characteristics, cyberspace differs from other domains of warfare, such as land, sea, air, or space. However, it serves as a critical force multiplier, enhancing joint military missions during both peace and war. However, cyberspace acts as a useful force enabler to joint military missions during peace or war. Meanwhile, the concept of cyberwar has to be differentiated from cyberwarfare. While cyberwarfare can be defined as actions taken by state or non-state actors to penetrate, disrupt, or damage computer systems, cyberwar refers to a conflict conducted entirely through cyber operations between belligerents (Gray, 2013, pp. 55–56). Therefore, labelling a cyber activity as an act of war or warfare can have significant and potentially harmful consequences, as such classifications are subject to the judgement and decisions of rational actors. Colin argues that, due to the absence of physical assault, cyberwar cannot result in the occupation of a physical territory. Similarly, Thomas Rid asserts that cyberwar does not directly harm human beings or shed blood, although it can indirectly affect the machines upon which humans rely. Although cyberspace can be used as a military weapon, its non-kinetic nature raises an interesting question: should "cyber arms" (digital abilities) be considered a legitimate source of weaponry, given that they lack the kinetic force to directly harm or strike an object? The following discussion will address this question.

Interstate War and Cyberwarfare Tenets

The integration of cyber technology into military affairs has led to the emergence of cyber warfare. Indeed, cyberwar is a product of the "revolution in military cyber affairs". Although the definitions of cyberwar and cyberwarfare are not universally agreed upon and vary according to the concerns of states and organisations, a plausible concept is briefly presented in this section. While there is no universal law governing cyberwar in the international system, many states have developed their own cyberwar doctrines. This section discusses some potential parameters of interstate cyberlaws, referencing the popular volume of the *Tallinn Manual 2.0*. Additionally, it examines military concepts such as humanitarian laws, the security dilemma, arm races, deterrence, war doctrines, balance of power, cyber truce, and digital disarmament, within the context of international cyber affairs, to aid in future policy development. Along with the many security concepts that emerged during the Cold War in international politics, this section focuses on select perspectives relevant to current cybersecurity concerns.

Revolution in Cyber Military Affairs

Cyberspace could be considered as the part of the revolution in military affairs, a concept that emerged in the 1980s. In the past, technology has brought fundamental changes in military affairs from rifles and telegraphs of the 19th century to ballistic missiles and satellite communication systems of the 20th century (Buzan, 1987). Similarly, digital networks become military technology in the later part of the 20th century. As its applications are widely used in defence systems, it became a crucial tool for achieving military goals in the 21st century. As nuclear weapons were once popular in the Cold War era, cyber technology has become a powerful weapon in the post-Cold War international system. Strategists argue that the nation that controls the global information system (the cyber world) will also hold significant power over the global security system. The revolution in military (cyber) affairs, or RM(C)A, can be understood as the changes that are taking place in the cyber technological (hardware, software, etc.) and non-technological (policy, strategy, doctrine, etc.) realm to achieve military objectives or combat effectiveness for national security. These include changes or improvements in the digital aspect of military philosophy, national vision, organisation, new digital technology, operational innovation, doctrines, organisational adoption, strategy (everchanging tactics), and national will. India, aspiring to establish itself as a global leader, has been striving to enhance its military cyber capabilities over the past two decades.

Meanwhile, Barry Buzan suggested that the technological revolution affects five military capabilities, "firepower, protection, mobility, communication, and intelligence" (Buzan, 1987, p. 19). It indeed applies to cyber technology as well. *Fire power*: in the current world order, it is commonly acknowledged that cyber tools have been developed as a lethal weapon (fire power) by state and non-state actors to pursue their military objectives. *Protection*: enhancing cybersecurity, or the protection of the cyber ecosystem, has emerged as the top priority for military systems of the global community. *Mobility*: to facilitate faster file transfer and movement, the speed of cyber networks has increased from 2G to 5/6G, which is highly useful for military operations. The ledger technology and blockchain system are integrated into the defence industry to monitor and secure strict data transactions. *Communication*: military communication networks have been significantly enhanced through advancements in digital technology. Notably, countries, including India, have developed innovative quantum communication systems to ensure the highest

level of cryptographic security for satellite communications and military networks. In 2022, the Indian Space Research Organisation[26] played a key role in advancing this technology for India's defence infrastructure (ISRO, 2023).
Intelligence: AI or deep machine learning systems support generating military intelligence and the decision-making process. Many believe this is likely to be the future of the military system.

Cyberwarfare versus Cyberwar

While the terms "cyberwar" and "cyberwarfare" are often used interchangeably in discussions of cyber conflict, the concepts require further clarification and precise definition. As several "cyber scholars" including Colin Gray affirm that while the differentiation between cyberwar and cyberwarfare is necessary, there are complications subject to the understanding of states, institutions, and individuals. Warfare is the "conduct of war". While theories of warfare are useful, they are not as durable as the theory of war. Clausewitz's study was specifically "on war", but not on warfare. Meanwhile, Sun Tzu's work encompasses both war and warfare, offering a strategic perspective that is often regarded as more concise compared to Clausewitz's writings (Blomme, 2015). "Cyberwar" is the conduct of, or preparation for, a military action based on information-related principles to interfere with or destroy communication systems while using military tactics to pursue a political objective (Lachow, 2009, p. 441).

While there is no universally accepted definition, the UN Interregional Crime and Justice Research Institute defines cyberwarfare as any action undertaken by a nation-state to infiltrate the computer networks of another state with the intent to cause harm. Broadly, it includes acts of cyber hooliganism, cyber vandalism, or cyberterrorism, and other threats including espionage, security breaches, sabotage, and attacks on SCADA (UNICRI, 2023). It can also be described as digital engagement equivalent to an armed attack that occurs between one state and another, or the use of forces in the digital world that can lead to a military response with proportionate use of kinetic force (CRS, 2015). While cyberwar is limited to the cyber battleground or from keyboard to another keyboard, cyberwarfare is not limited and exists from the planning of war to the achievement of a goal or even post war. Cyberwarfare can be considered as the means and methods of cyberwar. While the means of cyberwarfare comprise digital weapons, resources, and their associated electronic systems and machinery, the methods of cyberwarfare include digital tactics, techniques, strategy, procedure, skillsets where hostilities are orchestrated (Schmitt, 2017, p. 452).

International Law of Cyberwarfare

Every domain of warfare, air, sea, land, and space, operates under legal jurisdictions and established principles governed by international laws,[27] treaties, and conventions during both peace and war. In contrast, cyberspace lacks a universally accepted law, convention, or treaty agreed upon by UN member states. However, the UNGGE established in 2004, and the first Open Ended Working Group developed in 2018, have been actively working to bring cyberspace under international regulation. Their efforts include developing norms for the conduct of interstate cyber operations, particularly in hostile environments. As states' involvement in cyber operations increases, the *UNGGE Report-2013*, which is also a unique document on cyberwarfare, emphasised that the "international law and in particular the UN Charter" should apply to digital space. It asserted that states must adhere to norms, rules, and principles in all cyber-related activities. The report also stressed that state sovereignty extends to cyberspace, requiring states to respect each other's cyber ecosystems (UN, 2013).

Though it is non-binding, the *Tallin Manual 2.0* (second edition) released in 2017 covers the international law to govern cyber warfare. The document has been widely referred to by many stakeholders and became a supportive text in framing cyberwar doctrines and operational guidelines. It also embraces the areas of states sovereignty, responsibility, and laws of war domains (air, space, and sea). As Article 51 of the UN Charter allows the "use of force" for self-defence, the possibility of using the military in cyber operations was discussed in Rule 71 of the *Tallin Manual 2.0*. Because digital war is fought in virtual spaces, it will be challenging to apply the principles of *jus ad bellum* (the conditions under which states can resort to war or use of force) and *jus in bello* (conduct of the war). A simple cyber operation does not typically qualify as the use of military force. However, if such an operation is conducted by a state's armed forces, intelligence agency, or private contractor, it may fall under different considerations. Rule 73 of the *Tallinn Manual 2.0* stipulates that, under Article 51 of the UN Charter, a state may respond with kinetic force to a "considerable" cyberattack when exercising its right to self-defence.

State force may be used in response to a cyberattack when it results in significant damage, such as the explosion of a national nuclear facility, disruption of air traffic, failure of a water dam, a plane crash, or the collapse of a power grid, events that lead to loss of human lives. Such incidents set up the possibility of a primitive strike (kinetic) in defence against a cyberattack. For instance, if state A evaluates or confirms a cyberthreat from state B that can cause human casualties, then A is eligible to employ a physical first strike against B. This was demonstrated on 5 May 2019, when the Israeli Defense Forces conducted an airstrike targeting a Hamas cyber operations building. The strike was carried out in retaliation for cyberattacks by Hamas that aimed to "damage the quality of life of Israeli civilians". As a result of that kinetic attack, both the parties reached a ceasefire agreement in less than 24 hours. The incident illustrates the possibility of cyberwarfare going beyond the domain of the virtual world. This incident not only raises questions about the proportionality of responses in cyberwarfare but also highlights the risk of digital conflicts escalating into physical confrontations. In the meanwhile, several forms of reprisals are used in cyber operations. Through sanctions and indictments, the US responded to North Korea's cyber assaults on Sony in 2014 and the *WannaCry* ransomware attack in 2017 (Borghard, 2019). Whether or not these events constitute cyberwar or merely electronic disturbances, the involvement of states compels us to approach them as such. And this aspect led to a study on the reasons why states engage in cyberwar, its causes, and response to it.

Cybersecurity Dilemma

All scholars of security studies and international relations agree that the security dilemma has long been recognised as a significant factor in the causes of war (Jervis, 2011). While the term "security dilemma" can be traced back to Thucydides' *Peloponnesian War*, it was first formally coined by John H. Herz, in 1950 (Herz, 1950) as a product of the Cold War when the world was viewed through the prism of a bipolar system. At the end of the Cold War, the remaining sole superpower, the United States, was expected to guide the world toward reducing the security dilemma through arms control and disarmament. However, its exercise of unilateral power, such as the invasions of Afghanistan and Iraq, heightened insecurity among other nations, including Russia and China, thereby exacerbating the security dilemma (Booth, 2008, p. ix). The security dilemma refers to a situation in which the increase of one state's military capabilities leads to the insecurity of other states. According to Ken Booth, "the idea that unresolvable uncertainties arising out of the 'other minds problem', and the ambiguous symbolism of weaponry, tends to produce strategic competition between states" (Booth, 2007, p. 404). While it has been one of the reasons for states going into war, there are different other factors such as people's behaviour (Waltz, 1959, p. 16); desire for territorial gain or expansion of power (Evera, 1998); economic advantage (US against Iraq); revenge (US against Afghanistan); religion (ISIS against the West); and nationalism (Kashmir against India). However, there is no war that was fought without people and weapons (product of humans), hence people's evil and offensive behaviour are the main reasons to start a war (Waltz, 2001, 1959, p. 30). According to Friedrich Nietzsche, madness is an exception in individuals, but for groups, it becomes the rule. Since no individual wages war alone, it is carried out collectively by "factions, tribes, nations, states, and perhaps even 'civilization'" (Garnett, 2019) with the involvement of new weapons and emerging technologies such as cyberspace.

Cyberwar is real and there are reasons for the conduct of cyber operations in the international system. Cyber operations or digital attacks in the form of war or crimes have been conducted by state and non-state actors for political benefits or strategic objectives. However, in the context of interstate cyberwarfare (not cybercrime), its underlying causes are similar to those of physical warfare. Cybersecurity dilemmas and the emergence of a multipolar system in the cyber world order could be the main causes of a cyberwar. Others would include a state's desire to dominate the digital domain, access strategic data and information, gain financial advantage, revenge against an enemy, religion and hate campaign, and cyber nationalism. Competition and mistrust among the great cyber powers (US, China, and Russia) produces fears and escalates spirals of threats that can lead to a digital war. States' growing investment in the research and development of military digital technologies, along with the establishment of cyber commands within their military systems, further intensifies the security dilemma among nations. Meanwhile, the dilemma is further exacerbated by the multipolar nature of cyberspace where numerous players, both major and minor powers, along with non-state actors, actively participate. Cyberwarfare tools are accessible, unregulated, and allow for anonymity, making them available to a wide range of actors. Sensitive weapons that a powerful state can produce or possess can also be easily acquired by smaller powers or non-state groups. Furthermore, states' greed and desire to expand their power can undermine the sovereignty of other states. Cyber activities such as illegal mass surveillance, data theft, and attacks on state information infrastructures for economic or strategic purposes hold the potential to ignite conflict between aggressor and victim states. For instance, if Pakistan, motivated by financial reasons, attacks the Indian banking system, this could potentially initiate a cyberwar depending on how India chooses to retaliate against such aggression. Notable incidents such as the Sony attack in 2014 and the Hamas cyber operations in 2019 were clear acts of retaliation against their opponents. Similarly, the recruitment of Hizbul Mujahideen (HM) militants in Kashmir through social media poses a significant digital challenge to security agencies. Meanwhile, Islamic fundamentalist campaigns on digital platforms could provoke hostility among Hindu nationalists, potentially escalating into digital conflicts between the two communities. However, these atrocities and conflicts are ultimately the creations of human minds, not machines themselves. Thus, it is the human operator or the mind behind the machine that is responsible for any digital wars. Digital rules and regulations should prioritise controlling the actions of individuals, as it is human intent, not the technology, that drives misuse and potential digital conflicts, thus addressing the cybersecurity dilemma where the actions of one state or actor can escalate insecurity and provoke retaliatory responses.

Cyber Arms Race

In Benjamin Franklin's famous words, "failing to prepare is preparing to fail". Consequently, states focus on strengthening their arsenal to avoid losing wars, which often leads to an arm race. An arms race is a result of states preparing for war by increasing its weapons to protect themselves from the threat of defeat. It is also a product of the security dilemma, which arises when state A fears state B's (or others') military build-up, prompting A to enhance its own military preparations in response. An arms race can be defined as a situation in which two or more countries engage in competition to increase the quantity or improve the quality of their war materials and military personnel (Smith, 1980, p. 254). Barry Buzan, by referring to the definition of an arms race from Huntington (1958), Bull (1961), Gray (1971), and Steiner (1973), concludes that "arms racing is an abnormally intense condition in relations between states reflecting either or both of active political rivalry, and mutual fear of the others military potential" (Buzan, 1987, p. 69). Meanwhile, Colin Gray explains that in an arms race, two or more parties consider themselves adversaries and try to improve or increase their own arsenals at a rapid rate. They structure their military posture with an attention to the past, present, and anticipated politico-military system of the other parties. Countries involved in an arms race seek to balance their military power with their opponents' and monitor its opponent's martial activities. According to Colin Gray, any form of arms race would be ruled or directed by four conditions. First, there would be two or more states that are aware of their antagonism and threats perceived from each other. Second, each participating state should position its armed forces with effective combat facilities and deterrent capabilities. Third, participants' competition would be based on the quantity of troops, materials and weapons, along with the quality of personnel, weaponry system, armed institutions, military doctrines, and deployments of armed forces. Fourth, rapid quality enhancement and quantity increments would be the last feature of an arms race (Gray, 1971, pp. 39–41). Meanwhile, an arms race is associated with the term "maintenance of military *status quo*" where a state preserves its military position for itself, or in relation to others. It can lead to an escalation or reduction of the arms race between the two countries or more (Buzan, 1987, p.73). Or, it can also be a situation where the military status is kept in a constant state, neither escalating nor reducing (static military budget or a fixed gross domestic product for annual defence expenditure).

A cyber arms race can be considered as competition between two or more countries looking to enhance its quantity and quality of cyber warfare capabilities, including technological resources and skilled personnel, within the international system. According to Colin's perspective, when considering cyberspace as a weapon or an enabler for military forces, a cyber arms race can be characterised by several key elements. First, it involves at least two or more participants engaging in competition. Second, the digital weapons of each competitor must possess both combat capabilities and deterrent capacity against their adversaries. Third, the competition extends to the quantity of cyber experts ("cyber wizards") and the digital weapons they deploy, supported by the quality of war commands (institutions), leadership, digital doctrines, and weapons development facilities. Lastly, a fundamental principle of a cyber arms race is the rapid improvement in both the quality and quantity of cyber-related systems. Considering these features, the cyber arms race can be discussed across two key dimensions, defensive and offensive mechanisms.

Defensive mechanisms focus on a state's preparation to safeguard its digital ecosystem by improving the quality and quantity of protective measures such as antivirus software, firewalls, password management systems, and robust cybersecurity guidelines and policies. Offensive mechanisms emphasise the development and enhancement of cyber weaponry, including spyware, malware, viruses, trojan viruses, and ransomware. A state may choose to maintain its *status quo* by abstaining from active participation in the cyber arms race, even while possessing sufficient defensive capabilities to shield its digital infrastructure and offensive potential to target adversarial cyber facilities when necessary.

Cyber Deterrence

Although the term "deterrence" was already in use, its articulation as a military strategy and a theory within security studies emerged prominently during the first wave of the Cold War (1950s), shaped by academics such as Bernard Brodie, Arnold Wolfers, and Jacob Viner. In the second wave (1960s) of the Cold War, the concept gained further prominence and specific elaborations through the works of scholars like Brodie, Thomas Schelling, Glenn Snyder, and Albert Wohlstetter (Jervis, 1979). However, Thomas Schelling has been the most influential scholar and is often regarded as the inventor of classical deterrence theory (Zagare, 2008, p. 54) by explaining deterrence as an act "to prevent from action by fear of consequences". Though primarily associated with military strategy, the concept also finds application in criminal law to deter criminal activities (Schelling, 2008, 1966, p. 71).

For Joseph Nye "deterrence means dissuading someone from doing something by making them believe that the costs to them will exceed their expected benefit" (Nye, 2017, p. 45). Deterrence differs from "compellence" in its approach and objectives. Deterrence involves non-hostile stage-setting by declaration and incurring obligation along with "waiting" to respond to an enemy's action. However, compellence involves initiating an irreversible action that can only be avoided and become harmless if the adversary refrains from further escalation or confrontation (Schelling, 2008, p. 71). Barry Buzan emphasised that technology is a significant intervening variable in deterrence, alongside factors such as politics and geography, within the realm of international politics. Technology, particularly nuclear technology, has played a pivotal role in shaping deterrence since the Cold War. The logic of deterrence can be viewed from two perspectives: the defensive, which focuses on denial of action, and the offensive, which is rooted in deterrence by retaliation. The immense destructive capability of nuclear weapons and their delivery systems ensures "easy" deterrence, reinforcing the primacy of deterrence theory in strategic thinking by fostering stability through the threat of mutually assured destruction (Buzan, 1987, p. 178).

Can cyber weapons, like nuclear arms, instill fear in an adversary to deter hostile actions? The answer depends on the opponent's behaviour. However, cyber technology can complement nuclear systems but cannot replace nuclear threats. The threat posed by a nuclear warhead or weapon is incomparable to that of even the most advanced malware. Nuclear deterrence operates in the physical, kinetic realm, whereas cyber deterrence (if implemented) exists primarily in the digital domain—though it can extend beyond—depending on a state's policy framework. Threats and retaliations are unlikely in cyberspace when the attacker's identity remains uncertain. This makes it impossible to view cyber deterrence through the lens of Cold War deterrence, where the origin of a nuclear strike is straightforward to trace for retribution. In the cyber domain, the challenge of attribution complicates the ability to threaten or retaliate against an aggressor effectively. However, according to Joseph Nye, deterrence or dissuasion could possibly be achieved in cyberspace through four major means: threat of punishment, denial by defence, entanglement, and norms (Nye, 2017, p. 54).

1. *Deterrence by punishment*: while threat of punishment would be difficult to implement without attributing the aggressor (to enable retaliation), integrating cyber strategy with a kinetic response could offer a more reliable approach to cyber deterrence. For instance, Iran might risk a US cyber retaliation similar to the Stuxnet attack within cyberspace but would be far less willing to provoke a kinetic assault from a great power like the US.
2. *Deterrence by denial*: a strong cyber defence or resilient systems can diminish the adversary's incentives to target critical information infrastructures, ensuring that both cyber and non-cyber military retaliation remain viable options. For example, North Korea or Iran would likely reconsider attacking US information facilities if the likelihood of success is uncertain or prone to failure. An aggressor will carefully evaluate the probability of success before committing time and resources to cyberwarfare.
3. *Dissuasion through entanglement*: in addition to the classical concepts of punishment and denial, dissuasion can also be achieved through "entanglement". Entanglement refers to the interdependence between various actors, where an uncalculated attack could impose significant costs on both the attacker and the target. This perception can deter actors by making them realise that a single hostile action may result in greater losses than the benefits they seek. For instance, a Chinese cyberattack on the US's online trading system could backfire, causing harm to Chinese businesses closely tied to US companies, effectively resulting in self-inflicted retaliation.
4. *Dissuasion by norms*: if a country adheres to established norms, rules, and moral values, dissuasion through these mechanisms can be effective in the international system. Normative considerations can impose reputational costs on an actor, potentially damaging its national image far more than the benefits gained from an attack. For example, nuclear-armed states

refrain from using nuclear weapons against non-nuclear states due to norms and taboos (as seen with the US in Vietnam or China regarding Taiwan). Similarly, the prohibition on the use of chemical and biological weapons by states is rooted in international conventions and treaties. The principle of "no first use" of cyber weapons could also be effective if actors follow established norms. Hypothetically, if both the US or Israel and states like Iran adhere to these norms, they may be deterred from attacking each other's critical information infrastructures, particularly considering the relative weakness of the latter. In this scenario, cyber norms could impose significant risks to an aggressor, even if the victim chooses not to retaliate.

Cyberwar Doctrines

For centuries, no significant war, whether in the air, on the sea, or on land, has been fought without the application of a military doctrine. The word "doctrine" is derived from the Latin word *doctrina*, which means teaching. The literal meaning of doctrine therefore is "what is taught" to those who are learning or being trained in military strategy and tactics. Military doctrine is a set of principles that guide the actions of military forces, outlining how different branches of the armed forces such as the army, navy, and air force should operate to achieve specific objectives. It provides a framework for planning and executing military operations, ensuring coherence and coordination across various forces to effectively achieve strategic goals (Sloan, 2012, pp. 243–244). According to Posen, military strategies can be categorised into three basic operations or doctrines: offensive, defensive, and deterrence. While the offensive doctrine aims to disarm the enemy or destroy their forces, the defensive doctrine denies the aggressor the objective it seeks to achieve. "Deterrent doctrines" aim to punish the aggressor by getting them to believe that the risk would be costlier then benefits (Posen, 1984, p. 14). Doctrines should not be confused with tactics and strategy, though the trio are related. Tactics refer to the study of how battles are fought, while military doctrine addresses the question of "how" battles should be conducted. In contrast, strategy involves determining "which" wars should be fought (Posen, 1984, p. 245). Doctrines permit countries to achieve victory in a short period with fewer recourses during war. While a national strategy can afford to compromise or maintain diplomatic adjustment, military doctrine can neither be easily compromised or altered. Doctrines can be revised after each failure, but standard operating procedures will always continue to govern their application. Technology plays a critical role in shaping military doctrines (Sloan, 2012, p. 252). However, Posen questions the true value of technology, pointing to cases such as Britain and France having tanks at the end of World War I but failing to leverage them effectively in offensive warfare (Rosecrance, 1987, p. 171). A similar situation occurred with India's costly decision not to use its available military aircraft during the 1962 war with China, as Prime Minister Nehru feared that doing so would escalate the conflict, despite China lacking significant air power to retaliate. Ultimately, when military doctrines are ineffective, no amount of technological advantage can prevent failure.

Military doctrine is a key pillar of national security providing the framework for how wars are fought and won. Similarly, a cyberwar doctrine (CWD) is a critical component of military strategy in the modern era. Cyberwar doctrine can be defined as a set of military principles or standards developed based on the state's interest and past experience to guide and govern a conflict that takes place in cyberspace (Colarik, 2012, p. 34). According to a McAfee report on cyberwarfare capabilities released in 2013, out of 44 countries, 11 countries implemented a cyber warfare doctrine, 25 states developed a cyber warfare strategy, 31 nations conducted cyberwarfare training, and 29 countries conducted cyberwarfare exercises or simulations frequently (Relia, 2015, pp. 46–48). As Posen's military doctrines prescribe, the doctrines of cyberwarfare can also be categorised into three types: offensive, defensive, and deterrence.

1. *Cyber offensive doctrines* aim to disturb the enemy's network facilities with an impact beyond the information layer that could also lead to the opponents disarming or surrendering. Technologically, how powerful the offensive weapons are would be determined by their capability to disrupt the network, deny a service, degrade system performance, destroy critical components of a system, and completely exploit or take over a system (Relia, 2015, p. 170).
2. *Cyber defensive doctrine* focuses on denying the enemy's ability to achieve its objective without harming them. The aim is to neutralise or mitigate any attempted attacks by an aggressor through a combination of diplomatic efforts and robust "cyber shield" capabilities. The effectiveness of the defensive doctrine is largely determined by the strength and reliability of protective measures such as firewalls, antivirus systems, intrusion detection mechanisms, and other cybersecurity technologies.
3. *Cyber deterrent doctrines* could be defined as efforts to dissuade an aggressor from launching cyberattacks by convincing the enemy that the risk would be more costly than the benefits it expects. While measuring the credibility of retaliation in cyberspace is inherently challenging, the effectiveness of deterrence often depends on the perceived capability and resolve to respond. Lesser powers are more likely to adhere to the principles of cyber deterrence, as great powers possess the ability to punish them not only through cyber retaliation but also through kinetic means.

Cyber technologies are integral to modern military command and control systems, spanning across sea, air, land, and space (particularly in satellite communications). Therefore, cyberwar doctrines must integrate seamlessly with the command structures of each domain, functioning as a support system to enhance operational effectiveness. In countries like India, the military doctrines of various forces have recognised the significance of cyberwarfare and its interconnection with each service branch. Reflecting this recognition, on 18 June 2024, India introduced the *Joint Doctrine for Cyberspace Operations*, emphasising the integration of cyber capabilities across all military domains (further details are discussed in the Indian warfare section later in this chapter).

Cyber Weapons and Strategic Objectives

Cyber weapons, whether defensive (antivirus) or offensive (malware), are ambiguous in nature. There is no differentiation between software codes used as a cyber weapon for military or non-military operations. The weapon that the military (or state actor) used can also be available in the hands of a civilian (or non-state actor). In a standard state policy, a government licence may be required to purchase a gun or a weapon, but this may not be the case when buying easily available software (malware or an antivirus) in the market. Subsequently, there are no basic principles that a weapon produced by a vendor should only be meant for military purpose, as Lockheed Martin defence products cannot be procured by civilians. There is no doubt that state armed forces are conducting sophisticated cyber weaponry programs with hefty investment, the same can also be possibly achieved by potential non-state outfits (private software industries) with deadly objectives. Nonetheless, this section will delve into the concept of military or states' interest (not the civilian or non-state capability) in the militarisation and weaponisation of cyberspace for their strategic objectives. The aspect of imminent threat posed by cyber weapons and its ability to cause mass "disruption" (if not destruction) within and beyond the realm of digital space will be discussed. Meanwhile, the fundamental reason for states seeking to obtain cyber weapons will be discussed in comparison with nuclear weapons.

The Militarisation and Weaponisation of Cyberspace

The integration of cyberspace into warfare and the growing establishment of cyber commands within state military systems have contributed significantly to the militarisation of cyberspace in the contemporary world order. Following the 2010 Stuxnet incident, a 2012 survey conducted by the UN revealed that out of 193 states, 47 had incorporated cyberwarfare programs into their military strategies, planning, and organisation, while 67 countries were focused solely on civilian cyber programs (UNIDR, 2013, p. 1). Referring to Article IV of the *Treaty on Principles Governing the Activities of States in the Exploration and Use of Outer Space, including the Moon (1966)*, the militarisation of cyberspace (considered as a domain similar to space, air, land, and sea) can be defined as the "establishment of military bases, installations, and fortifications, testing of any type of weapons, and the conduct of military maneuver[s]" within the virtual platform. However, military research activities in cyberspace are permitted, provided they are conducted for peaceful purposes (UN, 2002, p. 4). While the model of controlling space is feasible because it exists as a geographical and physical domain, Gomez defines the militarisation of cyberspace as the adoption of this virtual domain by the military for offensive and defensive purposes (Gomez, 2016, p. 43). The main objective of the militarisation is to counter the existential threat posed by state and non-state actors in cyberspace, as the world became more and more dependent on technology. The militarisation of this domain is a result of its anarchic system, lawlessness, asymmetrical nature, attribution deniability, and offensive advantage. States that are a victim of cyberattacks have a greater chance of being involved in militarisation. Cyber-power nations will gain more advantages than other participants in the cyber-militarised world (Gomez, 2016). In the absence of international cyber laws and with the continuous evolution of technology, the scope and manner of militarisation in cyberspace could expand further.

Meanwhile, the weaponisation of cyberspace can be defined as the use of cyber technology as a weapon to hurt or harm living or non-living beings within the realm of the digital domain and beyond, extending to the physical layer. Since the Stone Age, weapons have been employed as instruments to inflict harm or damage upon a target. While weapons have been used for hunting animals and harming humans, they range widely in form and function, from nuclear warheads to the martial arts skills of an individual (McBurney, 2012, p. 6). Cyber weapons are non-physical unlike nuclear weapons or others such as biological or chemical weapons of mass destruction. Though not a weapon of mass destruction (WMD), it can be considered as a weapon of mass "disruption" that has the ability to cripple critical information facilities with physical implications. While operating in the virtual realm, cyber weapons can have impact that extends beyond cyberspace, causing physical damage to information infrastructures or harm to humans. Cyber weapons, according to Thomas Rid and Peter McBurney are "a subset of conventional weapons which is generally a computer code used or designed to be used, with an aim of threatening or causing physical, functional, or mental harm to structures, systems, or living beings" (McBurney, 2012, p. 7). Meanwhile, Rule 103 of the *Tallin Manual 2.0* defines cyber weapons as a means of cyberwarfare that are "used, designed, or intended to be used to cause injury to, or death of, persons or damage to, or destruction of, objects" (Schmitt, 2017, p. 452). Cyber weapons are normally considered as software programs that are used to conduct cyber operations in defensive and offensive environments. Firewalls and antivirus software are defensive weapons, whereas malware, viruses, spyware, ransomware, and logic bomb are offensive weapons.

As the threat posed by emerging technologies escalates, cyber weapons have continuously improved in quality and increased in number.

Cyber Arms as Weapons of Mass "Disruption"

A cyberattack does not cause physical destruction or break computers, networks, or information facilities like a nuclear explosion, nor does it detonate like a conventional bomb. A cyberattack simply disrupts the normal functioning of systems within the virtual realm or, in some cases, beyond. However, cyber weapons cannot be classified as or equated with non-conventional weapons of mass destruction, such as nuclear, biological, chemical, or radiological materials. However, concerning the sophistication of cyber arms and its potential impacts, states and experts have been examining its merit in regard to it as a weapon of mass destruction. For an armament to be called a WMD, it has to qualify the UN defined standards set by the UN General Assembly through its 1977 resolution *A/RES/32/84-B*. It pronounced WMDs as 'atomic explosive weapons, radioactive material weapons, lethal chemical and biological weapons, and any weapons developed in the future which might have characteristics comparable in destructive effect to those of the atomic bomb or other weapons mentioned above". Subsequently, WMDs should have the capability to kill millions of people, endanger the natural environment, and alter the livelihood of future generations by its devastating effects. It not only could cause death, but injure humans by releasing chemicals with short- or long-term effects. A WMD should possess the potential to spread disease causing an organism (e.g., a virus) to kill or maim humans, animals, and plants. WMDs include delivery system such as missiles that can carry and deliver nuclear explosives and chemical or biological agents to be used in armed conflict or hostile activities (UNRCPD, 2022).

For a cyber weapon to be classified as a WMD, it must meet the criteria established by the UN. Cyber weapons may not directly kill people but can serve as enablers to cause mass casualties. Similar to how missiles play a role in delivering WMDs from one location to another, cyber weapons can be used to trigger catastrophic events, such as causing aircraft or train collisions, opening water dams or chemical chambers, or compromising nuclear facilities—actions that have the potential to result in significant loss of life. However, such events remain hypothetical to this day, unlike the devastation witnessed in Hiroshima and Nagasaki, which demonstrated the tangible and catastrophic dangers of the atomic (nuclear) bomb. No international cyber convention or prohibition treaty has been signed to regulate cyber weapons, unlike the agreements in place for other WMDs. More accurately, while cyber weapons may not cause "destruction", they can inflict significant "disruption" to critical facilities embedded in a state's digital network systems. Such disruptions have occurred, as seen in the cases of Estonia and Georgia, where over 85,000 computers were affected (Buresh, 2021, p. 16). It is mostly the catastrophic effects of the Estonia, Georgia, and Iran Stuxnet attacks that are widely referred in the study of cyber weaponry systems or cyberwarfare. Scholars such as Rid and McBurney (2012) argue that cyberwar remains a metaphor, as no dedicated cyber offence has yet occurred that meets the established criteria for qualifying as "cyberwar".

A cyber weapon is a weaponised software tool, ranging from low-potential digital tools, such as simple viruses, to highly sophisticated and disruptive malware. Even the use of political propaganda, though not technically weaponised software, should not be excluded from this spectrum of cyber capabilities. Meanwhile, states and their supporters continue to expand the scope of cyber weaponry and the concept of warfare within the cyber domain. Some even consider it as a potential weapon of mass destruction. Benjamin Hatch highlights the catastrophic effects of cyber threats, emphasising their capability to cause massive casualties or widespread destruction (Hatch, 2018). Cyber weapons are poised to play a critical role in future military operations. Referring the UN 1977 resolution *A/RES/32/84-B*, cyber weapon can be described as the "arm[s] of [the] future" that are already in use today and likely to be employed for increasingly offensive strikes in the future, regardless of whether their impact is comparable to that of atomic bombs. Therefore, the existence of cyber weapons is real (Libicki, 2007, p. 271) and the danger they pose is imminent. While conventions and treaties on the reduction of cyber arms shall be hard to achieve in the absence of international cyber laws, the behaviour of states and maintaining transparency on cyberspace could help in controlling or regulating cyber arms. Additionally, until there is a clear demarcation on which technology or software is meant for military or civilian use, regulating cyber weapons will remain a significant challenge.

Why States want a Cyber Weapon

The frequency of cyber operations targeting state facilities has increased alongside the development and proliferation of sophisticated cyber arms. The absence of a universal definition for cyber weapons and the ease with which they can be obscured, make it difficult to determine which countries are engaged in specific digital weapons programs. Furthermore, unlike its detailed data on military hardware, the Stockholm Peace Research Institute does not maintain records on cyber arms trade, the cyber arms industry, or cyber military expenditure. However, the assimilation of cyber and AI applications into military weapons such as drones, combat aircraft, missiles, and other systems is increasingly rapidly. Reports indicate that at least 140 countries are actively engaged in developing sophisticated cyber arsenals (Paganini, 2012). While the market size of cyber weapons is uncertain, major key weapons companies include FireEye Inc., Broadcom, Northrop Grumman, Boeing, Cisco Systems, McAfee L.L.C., and Lockheed Martin

Corporation in the US, Kaspersky Lab (Russia), BAE Systems (UK), Airbus SAS (Netherlands), and Avast Software (Czechia). Other countries including China, India, South Korea, and Germany are also involved in developing powerful cyber weapons for defensive and offensive purposes (Insights, n.d.). The rapid development and increase in cyber arms and states' aspirations to become cyber powers raises the question of why countries pursue cyber weapons. Kenneth Waltz posed a similar question regarding nuclear weapons and outlined reasons why nations seek them (Waltz, 1981). These reasons include imitation of others, fear and mistrust of allies, rivalry and competition for regional power, imbalance of conventional power, cost-effectiveness and relative safety, offensive purposes, and the desire to enhance status. While these motivations also apply to the pursuit of cyber weapons, additional factors unique to cyberspace, such as its lawless nature and the difficulties of attribution, further drive countries to acquire cyber capabilities.

First, any new military technology or weapon, whether an atomic bomb or a space satellite introduced by a major power is likely to be replicated by others in an effort to defend against or counter its capabilities. Similarly, after the establishment of a cyber command and its associated agencies within the US military system, other countries, including Russia, China, India, and others, have followed suit in creating their own cyber commands and associated institutions. Second, the UK's fear and mistrust of its ally, the US, led it to pursue nuclear weapons. Similarly, countries may seek to acquire cyber weapons out of concern that if collaboration with allies were to break down, those allies would not be able to protect the vital cyber infrastructure of the country in question. Third, countries like China, India, and Pakistan, which lacked nuclear allies, pursued nuclear weapons due to regional rivalry dynamics. Similarly, states may strengthen their cyber capabilities in response to their non-alignment with major cyber powers and to bolster their position in regional rivalries. Fourth, a country may pursue cyber weapons when challenging a formidable adversary possessing significant conventional military strength (e.g., Iran against the US). Cyber capabilities provide a means to level the playing field and challenge a stronger opponent. Fifth, cyber weapons are relatively inexpensive and secure to maintain or stockpile. A nation may choose to invest heavily in cyber capabilities as a cost-effective alternative to the substantial financial commitments required for conventional or non-conventional weapons. Sixth, states develop cyber weapons for offensive purposes, stealing data, extorting money, and assaulting vital information infrastructures (North Korea). Seventh, countries develop digital armaments to gain international attention (North Korea earned international attention with the 2014 Sony attack). Most importantly (besides these seven ideas propounded by Kenneth Waltz), the lawless nature of cyberspace in the international system and the difficulties in attributing or tracing the origin of a digital attack made countries develop cyber weapons as a secret strategic instrument for national security.

India's Approach to Cyberwarfare

India's approach to cyberwarfare will be shaped by a combination of factors, including its geopolitical context, strategic objectives, economic strength, technological capabilities, political determination, and assessment of security threats. India, as a rapidly growing economy, faces a range of challenges both internally and externally, in the physical world and the digital realm. Externally, India continually faces cyber-related threats originating from adversaries like China and Pakistan, which have significant implications for its national security and digital infrastructure. Internally, India grapples with challenges such as militancy in the northeast and Jammu and Kashmir, left-wing extremism, and Islamic terrorism, all of which have increasingly exploited cyberspace to leverage their agendas. In other words, threats that were previously confined to the physical domain, such as those from China, Pakistan, insurgency, and terrorism, are now assimilated within cyberspace, adding new layers of complexity to the state's security agenda. While internal cybersecurity issues are managed by MHA and Intelligence Bureau (IB), the external aspect is handled by MoD and its associates such as Research and Analysis Wing (R&AW) and the National Technical Research Organisation (NTRO). The military plays a vital role in safeguarding India's cyber ecosystem, both within and beyond the digital realm, by employing defensive and offensive strategies. Recognising the inevitability of cyberwar, India established its military cyber unit, the DCA, within its defence framework to address these challenges. This cyberwar command is further bolstered by the development of military cyber operation doctrines, designed to align with and support the objectives of cyberwarfare. Considering its future digital challenges, this section will explore India's strategy for cyberwarfare, focusing on its perceptions of cyber conflicts, doctrinal frameworks, and command structure.

India and Cyberwarfare

India recognises the use of cyber technologies as a tool in both combat and non-combat situations. While cyber codes act as a military weapon, cyberspace behaves as a battleground for strategic operations. Over the past few years, India began to focus on military cyber doctrines, command, and control systems. India's cyber military affairs can be seen from two perspectives, one concerning warfare (offensive and defensive) and the other focusing on a non-war or scientific approach (research and development). While both aspects are inter-related, this study primarily focuses on the warfare dimension.

Since the arrival of the internet in India, the military offices have utilised the application of cyberspace for regular communication such as emailing. However, the precise timeline of when cyber technology was first utilised as a military weapon or when Indian soldiers became involved in cyber warfare is not well documented, though it is believed to have begun in the late 1990s.[28] The first war India fought after the widespread availability of the internet in the country was the 1999 Kargil conflict with Pakistan. The involvement of "cyber soldiers" from both sides trying to sabotage the computer systems of each country may not be ruled out. Cyber incursion by Pakistan even during peacetime was observed in the previous year when it attacked the Bhabha Atomic Research Centre (BARC) network facilities in 1998. One year after the Kargil incident, in 2000, the first *IT Act* of India was introduced. In the successive years, the significance of cyberwarfare was highlighted in the Indian military official documents such as the *Indian Army Doctrine 2004* by addressing "cyberwarfare" as a part of information warfare. The document further explains cyberwarfare as "techniques to destroy, degrade, exploit or compromise the enemy's computer-based systems" (Command, 2004, p. 21). Based on this definition, whether by state or non-state actors, any disruption against India's computer system by using the techniques mentioned above could be considered as a form of cyberwar.

Although not formally declared, cyber skirmishes between India and Pakistan have persisted for two decades or more. This can be categorised as a cyber war, as both parties utilised cyber technology to disrupt each other's infrastructure with the involvement of state elements to achieve political or strategic objectives. Pakistan has been involved in attacks on Indian cyber network facilities since the late 1990s. The first recorded attack of its kind was the defacement of the BARC website in 1998. Subsequently, a series of digital assaults were launched against India, including the defacement of the Central Bureau of Investigation (CBI) website and 270 other Indian websites in 2010, among other incidents (NDTV, 2010). In March 2022, hackers allegedly affiliated with the Pakistani government created fake websites mimicking those of the Indian military and government to distribute malware and target Indian users. Earlier in February 2022, by using social engineering and USB-based worms, a Pakistani group deployed a remote access trojan virus to conduct espionage against Indian military and diplomatic targets (CSIS, 2022). Not only Pakistan, but China has also emerged as a significant rival in India's military cyber affairs. In a strategic attack on India's critical infrastructure in October 2020, the Mumbai power grid experienced a major outage, with suspicions pointing towards Chinese involvement in the incident (Cunningham, 2021). Many Indians believe it was an alternative response to the tensions raised in the border areas of the Line of Actual Control (LAC) (Bommankanti, 2021). Meanwhile, India has taken measures to counter Chinese influence in its digital space by banning 43 Chinese applications, including popular ones like *PUBG Mobile*, *TikTok*, *Weibo*, *WeChat*, and *AliExpress*. In total, 267 Chinese apps have been prohibited from operating in the country so far (IndiaTV, 2020). Chinese telecom companies like Huawei and ZTE have also been restricted from providing 5G services in India, reflecting concerns over national security and the potential risks associated with critical infrastructure. As a result of increasing cyber-related uncertainties and threats, India developed a dedicated cyberwar doctrine in 2024 to address emerging challenges and secure its digital infrastructure effectively.

India's Cyberwar Doctrine

On 18 June 2024, for the first time, the *Joint Doctrine for Cyberspace Operations* (JDCO), a dedicated cyberwar doctrine (CWD) of India was introduced . The document was formally released by the Chief of Defence staff, General Anil Chauhan during the Chiefs of Staff Committee meeting held on the same day in New Delhi. While the detailed contents of the JDCO remained confidential, it was revealed that the doctrine lays emphasis on understanding military dimensions of cyberspace operations. It provides conceptual guidance of planning and conducting cyber operations to commanders, staff, and practitioners. The doctrine aims to enhance awareness among warfighters at all levels about the strategic action of digital space (PIB, 2024).

India's cyberwar doctrines should be rooted in its geopolitical dynamics, strategic objectives, threat perceptions, military capabilities, technological prowess, political will, and operational practices in cyberspace. A CWD can be described as a set of principles by which the military forces guide their cyber activities in support of national objectives. It can also be viewed as a formal expression of cyber knowledge and thought that the armed forces accept as relevant at a given time. This insight includes understanding the nature of current and emerging digital conflicts, strategies for preparing forces to address these challenges, and approaches for successfully engaging in them. While the CWD is authoritative, it requires judgement in application.[29] Although a dedicated CWD or JDCO has been recently developed in India, its necessity was recognised much earlier in foundational military documents such as the *Indian Army Doctrine-2004*, *Joint Doctrine Indian Armed Forces-2017*, *Land Warfare Doctrine-2008*, *Basic Doctrine of the Indian Air Force-2012*, and *Indian Maritime Security Strategy-2015*. Meanwhile, the *Cyber Doctrine*, distinct from concepts of cyberwar or cyber warfare, was reportedly prepared as a classified official document by the Flag Officer Doctrines and Concepts office of the Indian Navy in July 2013.[30] With or without a formal doctrinal framework, the Indian Armed Forces have commenced cyber operations through the DCA, which became functional in 2019. The DCA is tasked with addressing cybersecurity threats posed by external aggressors and responding through both defensive and offensive measures during times of peace or war. Its operational effectiveness is further reinforced by the recently formulated cyberwar doctrine (JDCO).

The origin of the cyberwar doctrine can also be linked with the implementation of the Indian *IT Act-2000*, which was amended in 2008 after the 26 November 2008 Mumbai terrorist attack. The Indian military[31] was directly or indirectly involved in a counter-terrorism campaign. The *IT (Amendment)*

Act 2008 was designed to address only defensive measures, excluding provisions for offensive capabilities that the armed forces might employ. The development of the Defence Information Assurance Agency (DIARA) under the Headquarters of Integrated Defence Staff (IDS) brought cyber operations into the Indian military system. DIARA was the nodal agency of the three services (Army, Navy, and Air Force) that functioned at the national level to effectively deal with all cybersecurity aspects of defence institutes (IDS, 2017, p. 49). Eventually, the Defence-Computer Emergency Response Team (D-CERT) was developed under the IDS to coordinate the cyber-related activities of the three services. DIARA and D-CERT have apparently been merged to form the DCA, with the term "agency" adopted from DIARA to emphasise a unified and streamlined cyber defence structure.

Meanwhile, other military doctrines such as the *Indian Army Doctrine-2004*, *Joint Doctrine: Indian Armed Forces-2017*, *Land Warfare Doctrine-2018*, *Basic Doctrine of the Indian Air Force-2012*, and *Indian Maritime Security Strategy-2015*[32] address the significance of cyberwarfare to protect and achieve the national interest. While the 2004 document laid the foundation for integrating cyberwarfare into official military discussions by providing its definition, subsequent documents have further elaborated on the framework and structure of cyberwarfare strategies. The 2017 joint doctrine explains the importance of cyberspace for national security and expressed India's willingness to become a "cyber power" nation (IDS, 2017, p. 25). Meanwhile, the 2018 doctrine of land warfare acknowledges cyberwarfare as a key factor to win the battle against future conflicts, it also encourages all forces to retain the capability to fight through a disruptive cyberwarfare environment. The doctrine also discusses the objective to develop cyber deterrence, and mechanisms to eliminate threats, along with the operational preparedness for both defensive and offensive engagements (Army, 2018, pp. 10, 13). The 2012 *Indian Air Force* doctrine also addresses the "conduct of offensive cyber warfare to achieve national objectives". It also acknowledges the crucial role of cyberwarfare capabilities in future military conflict. The nation's ultimate dominance in cyberwarfare can be achieved along with the collaboration of other agencies of the civil sector, but not by armed forces alone (Force, 2012, p. 132). Although the *Indian Maritime Doctrine-2009* does not address cyberwarfare, the *Indian Maritime Security Strategy-2015* briefly highlights the importance of operations in cyberspace and leveraging the domain to acquire critical information, while emphasising the Indian Navy's commitment to prioritising cybersecurity.

Prior to the development and release of the JDCO, earlier military doctrines were ill-suited to address the realities of modern cyberwarfare, as conventional elements such as weapons, terrain, laws, targets, and damage held limited relevance in the cyber domain (Samuel, 2021, p. 8). Consequently, a dedicated CWD was deemed essential to tackle emerging unconventional challenges effectively. Although not publicly disclosed, the formulation of the new JDCO or CWD required consideration of five fundamental pillars:

political and strategic objectives, legal and constitutional aspects, military objectives and targets, resource capabilities, and military cooperation. The *strategic objective* should be based on India's overall cyber-power projection and its influential capabilities in the geopolitical system. The objective should be specific, attainable, realistic, and time bound. The *legal aspect* should refer to the Indian constitutional values and judicial parameters such as *jus ad bellum* and *jus in bello*, morals, ethics, duty, and legal acts of war. *Military goals* with both offensive and defensive options along with first- and second-strike capability, agility, speed, and deterrence by punishment or denial must be considered. Meanwhile, *resource capabilities*, including manpower, logistic, skills, and talents of the military establishments should be reflected in the doctrine. Lastly, *military cooperation*, including information-sharing, cyberwar simulation exercises, and collaboration among the three services, civil agencies, and foreign allies during peace, crisis, and war, is a critical aspect that must not be overlooked.

Cyber Command Structure

Following the release of the *Land Warfare Doctrine* in 2018, the DCA, established the same year, began its operationalisation in 2019. This doctrine emerged as a pivotal military document, offering critical insights into India's approach to cyber warfare prior to the release of the JDCO. The DCA was a product of the Naresh Chandra Task Force on national security, set up by the then National Security Advisor, Shivshankar Menon in 2011. The committee proposed the establishment of three distinct commands, cyberspace, space, and special forces within the Indian military system. Consequently, the DCA was established after Prime Minister Narendra Modi approved the formation of these commands during the Combined Commanders' Conference held in Jodhpur in 2018. The agency was mandated to encounter any potential cyber threats from external aggressors with defensive and offensive options. The DCA was initially raised at the "agency" level but has since been upgraded to function at the "command" standard, as stated by the former Chief of Defence Staff General Bipin Rawat (Tribune, 2021). While the command functions under the IDS, it will be headed by a two-star general officer from any of the three services. Officials in the command are drawn from all the tri-services.[33] The headquarters of the cyber command would be based in New Delhi, but a few units of it would be stationed across the country. The command will function in association with NTRO, R&AW, the Defence Research and Development Organisation (DRDO), and National Security Council (NSC) to protect CIIs and enhance tools and skills in the domain (ANI, 2019).

Although the structure of the DCA remains undisclosed in open sources, it could operate with two key divisions: the Cyber Armed Division (CAD) and the Cyber Strategic Division (CSD). The CAD would primarily focus on military objectives, while the CSD would address broader national goals.

However, with support from the state security apparatus, the two divisions would be equipped to undertake full-spectrum military cyber operations and ensure national digital security.

1. *Cyber Armed Division.* The CAD would be responsible for planning, coordinating, integrating, synchronising and conduct of all cyber operations (Relia, 2015, pp. 231–235) by cooperating with the cyber units of the tri-services. To fulfil all these activities, three further units can be formed, the *defensive unit, offensive unit (cyber strike force), and intelligence unit.* While the defensive unit will be involved in securing the network, risk assessment, cyber forensics, and emergency response of military facilities, the offensive unit will be responsible for strikes or degrading the enemy's information system in a time of war and peace. Meanwhile, the intelligence unit will collect inputs that pose threats to the military's cyber ecosystem explicitly and to the nation's cyber security at large.
2. *Cyber Strategic Division.* The CSD will be involved in training, operational planning, protection of national CIIs, nuclear facilities, armed forces network, and issue threats and warnings. It will have three units including the *training unit, strategic assessment unit, and strategic operation unit* (offensive and defensive). The training unit will produce skillful human resources and train a pool of cyber talent to prepare for digital warfare. The assessment wing of the strategic cyber force will monitor strategic cyber weaponry systems including nuclear capabilities, big data, ledger technology, quantum computing, and advanced 5G technologies. In collaboration with the DRDO, it will conduct research, analysis, and development. The strategic operations unit will undertake activities to counter threats that impact not only the armed forces but also the broader national (civilian) interests.

Conclusion

Cyberwar is a non-physical conflict that can result in physical damage. Similar to other domains of warfare (land, sea, air, and space), cyberwarfare can also be considered a subset of traditional and modern warfare. While other forms of warfare are physical and conventional in nature, governed by international laws, cyberwarfare operates without such legal constraints, allowing for unrestricted operations. Subsequently, reports of frequent state-sponsored attacks aimed at achieving strategic objectives suggest that digital conflict is a continuous and ongoing phenomenon. While the objective of defeating or disrupting the enemy remains consistent in both conventional and cyberwarfare, the impact of both types of wars could be different, as conventional wars are designed for kinetic results, and cyber for non-kinetic. However, though an air strike can destroy an enemy's aircraft, a cyberattack could make two aircraft collide by controlling their air traffic system.

Dominion over traditional domains (sea, air, land) plays a critical role in winning a war, and similarly, control over the domain of cyberspace can provide a significant advantage in modern warfare. Just as states strive to become air or sea powers, they also face the challenge of establishing cyber power in the modern strategic landscape. Related to conventional warfare, concepts of militarisation, weaponisation, arms race, security dilemma, deterrence, and war doctrines are reasonably applicable to aspects of cyberwar. Though cyber weapons are based on standard codes or a combination of letters, numbers, and characters, their impacts are real. Some digital weapons have the potential to act as weapons of mass disruption (non-kinetic), if not destruction (kinetic). Consequently, regional or international conventions regulating strategic cyber weapons are likely to emerge in the future. Just as nuclear weapons transformed the dynamics of warfare in the international system, the development of cyber weapons is set to redefine the characteristics of modern warfare. However, with the rapid evolution of cyber technologies, the nature of warfare in the future will likely differ significantly. The establishment of a cyber command in countries like India signals their preparation for or involvement in cyberwarfare. This has been further reinforced by the recent development of a dedicated joint military cyberwar doctrine.

Notes

1 Though the book was written by a group of experts on the invitation of the NATO Cooperative Cyber Defence Centre of Excellence, the views in the book are not the responsibility by the organisation, only the authors (*Tallinn Manual 2.0*).
2 The "means" refers to computing-related devices, such as the physical layer or hardware, that serve as weapons to attack targets. However, "method" pertains to malware or viruses, representing the logical layer or software, employed to infiltrate and disrupt an adversary's digital infrastructure.
3 Cyberwar and cyberwarfare, though ontologically different, are used interchangeably based on the context of the explanation of digital engagement between two groups of state or non-state origin.
4 See Chapter XIV on That Which Concerns a Prince on the Subject of the Art of War, *The Prince*.
5 In 1830, two years before Clausewitz published his famous book, *On War* (1832), Jomini combined some of his early writings (essays and chapters on the military and warfare), and published them under the title, *Synoptic Analysis of the Art of War*. Another expanded volume of the same paper, with an amended title, *Summary of the Art of War*, was published in 1837/1838 after Jomini had read Clausewitz's famous book *On War*. This summary is today popularly known as Jomini's book on the *Art of War*.
6 The number of articles including citation and all others found by typing "Clausewitz" in Google Scholars is 121,000; "Jomini" is 17,100; and "Jomini Clausewitz" is 8,090. However, in JSTOR, while Clausewitz has 10,523 results in "all" search, Jomini has 1,620 results, and Jomini-Clausewitz has 654 records.
7 *Auftragstaktik* is "a mission tactic, a command method stressing decentralized initiative within an overall strategic design". In other words it is an action taken by a subordinate in the absence of orders from a higher authority to support the intent (objective) of the superior commanders. The method was popularly introduced by

158 *State, Security, and Cyberwar*

      Helmuth Von Moltke, who was the chief of general staff of the Prussian military service from 1857 to 1887 (Rothenberg, 1986, p. 296).
 8 This lack of distinction is evident in conflicts such as those involving Myanmar's Junta supported by Pyusawhti, Russia's Wagner Group, and Syria's National Defence Force.
 9 The rise of Taliban 2.0 in Afghanistan in 2021 and Hay'at Tahrir al-Sham in Syria in 2024 serve as classic examples of the "new war" paradigm of the 21st century. These developments highlight the blurred lines between state and non-state actors, as well as the growing importance of identity, religion, and regime change over traditional geopolitical conflicts.
10 IW is violent competition between state and non-state actors for legitimate control over the relevant population. While it is asymmetric and indirect in approach, there is no concrete definition of IW. It is a form of armed movement similar to low intensity conflict such as insurgency, terrorism, militancy, etc. The method of IW is employed at strategic, operational, and tactical level (Larson, 2008; DoD, 2007).
11 Liddell's idea is founded on anti-guerrillas, in contrast to the pro-guerrilla beliefs of Mao and Che.
12 A cyber kill chain is a step-by-step process to attack a cyber network system. Normally there are seven steps to a cyber kill chain system: reconnaissance, weaponisation, delivery, exploitation, installation, command and control, and actions on objectives (Jelle van Haaster, 2016, p. 46).
13 Harry Villegas was once a member of the Communist Party of Cuba and fought as a guerrilla alongside Che.
14 Harry Villegas has developed these tactical level, seven golden rules from Che's book, *Guerrilla Warfare*. This is not Harry's original idea, but an amended or modified idea from Che's writing. It should not be interpreted as "Harry's seven golden rules in guerrilla warfare" or so.
15 Another example could be, to win a war over Estonia in the cyber realm, Russia does not need to occupy Estonia's digital system or control the data of the country permanently, but a significant disruption to the cyber system is justified enough for Russia's victory of the cyber incursion as Russia could make the Estonian authority do what it desires. What Russia wants is to make Estonia suffer and seek help from others to fix the system.
16 Liddell explains that using nuclear weapons against the guerrilla would be using a hammer against a mosquito (Hart, 1954, 1967, p. 363).
17 Cyberwar should not be confused with cyber power. Power represents the application of war or the capabilities employed in it. Theories of land, sea, air, and space power are typically analysed in a military context, although they can also be studied commercially. Similarly, while cyber power can be understood in both military and commercial contexts, this study will focus exclusively on its military aspects. Here, cyber power is defined as a form of military power—a means to achieve victory in war and the ability to accomplish specific objectives.
18 Both the terms "heartland" and "land power" are used interchangeably in his book.
19 Mackinder, in his paper, divides the crescent into two, the *inner crescent* and *outer crescent*. Outside the pivot area is the great inner crescent, comprising countries such as Germany, Austria, Turkey, India, and China. The outer crescent includes Britain, South Africa, Australia, the United States, Canada, and Japan. Meanwhile, Eurasia, by Mackinder refers to Russia and the surrounding states.
20 In those days, the Air Force was a subordinate branch under the Army and Navy, rather than an independent and dedicated service within the military system as it functions today.

21 Reference to his notable books such as *Winged Defense* and *Skyway: A Book on Modern Aeronautics*.
22 One can also argue about the same thought for a space force as a separate service since it is also considered as a domain (if every force is to be raised for every domain).
23 The ultimate achievement of a war is always land based, for example an occupation of a territory, supported by sea and air powers in battle.
24 Article IV of the UN Open Space Treaty (1967) forbids all state parties from militarising space. No nuclear weapon or weapon of mass destruction is allowed to be stationed in orbit around the Earth, Moon, or other celestial bodies. Space should be used only for scientific research and non-military purposes. However, the use of military personnel for scientific research is not prohibited (UN, 2002, p. 4).
25 In 2006, the Institute for National Strategic Studies and Center for Technology and National Security Policy at the National Defense University, US, were assigned to develop theories of cyber power besides space power (Starr, 2009, p. 43).
26 The demonstration of this novel communication system was tested by the Space Applications Centre (SAC) and Physical Research Laboratory at Ahmedabad, Gujarat on 27 January 2022.
27 These laws include the law of nations, Geneva Convention (1949), United Nations Convention on the Law of the Sea (1982), Convention on International Civil Aviation or Chicago Convention (1944), Outer Space Treaty (1967), etc.
28 This was also the period when Pakistan began targeting Indian cyber facilities, as evidenced by the 1998 BARC attack, to which India responded accordingly.
29 The definition of the cyberwar doctrine has been constructed based on the definition of the Indian Army "doctrine" provided by the *Indian Army Doctrine-2004*. This interpretation would be best suited for the Indian military context.
30 While the *Cyber Doctrine* has not been formally revealed, the document was revealed as one of the bibliographies in the openly published *Indian Maritime Security Strategy-2015* (p. 181).
31 Operation Black Tornado was conducted by the National Security Guards (NSG) to challenge the terrorists. While NSG functions under the Indian Ministry of Home Affairs, its commandos are mostly drawn from the Indian Army. One army officer, a major attached to the NSG, lost his life in the encounter with the terrorists at the Taj Hotel in the incident.
32 While highlighting the value of cyberspace and its operational capabilities, the *Indian Maritime Security Strategy-2015* talks about cybersecurity technologies and the Indian Navy's plans to give "cyber security technologies and systems" top priority. However, the *Indian Maritime Doctrine-2009* does not address anything about cybersecurity or warfare.
33 DCA otherwise is a joint organisation with a similar structure to the Defence Intelligence Agency, a joint intelligence organisation of the tri-services that function under the IDS, created in the backdrop of the Kargil Conflict 1999.

References

Agency, A. C. (2023, February 9). StopRansomware: Ransomware attacks on critical infrastructure fund DPRK malicious cyber activities. Cybersecurity & Infrastructure Security Agency. Retrieved from https://www.cisa.gov/news-events/cybersecurity-advisories/aa23-040a

Alexander, B. B. (1986). Liddell Hart and De Gaulle: The doctrines of limited liability and mobile defense. In P. Paret (Ed.), Makers of modern strategy from Machiavelli to the nuclear age (pp. 598–623). Princeton, NJ: Princeton University.

ANI. (2019, April 30). India to have defence cyber agency in May; Rear Admiral Mohit to be its first chief. *India Today*. Retrieved from https://www.indiatoday.in/india/story/india-defence-cyber-agency-may-rear-admiral-mohit-1513381-2019-04-30

Armstrong, M. (2021, August 6). How many websites are there? *Statista*. Retrieved from https://www.statista.com/chart/19058/number-of-websites-online/

Army, I. (2018). *Land warfare doctrine*. New Delhi: Army Head Quarter.

Blomme, M. E. (2015). On theory: War and warfare reconsidered. Army War College Review, 1(3), 24–41.

Bommankanti, K. (2021, March 10). Chinese cyber escalation against India's electricity grid amidst the boundary crisis. *Observer Research Foundation*. Retrieved from https://www.orfonline.org/expert-speak/chinese-cyber-escalatio-india-electricity-grid-boundary-crisis/

Booth, K. (2007). *Theory of world security*. Cambridge: Cambridge University Press.

Booth, K., & Wheeler, N. J. (2008). The security dilemma: Fear, cooperation and trust in world politics. New York, NY: Palgrave Macmillan.

Borghard, E. D., & Schneider, J. (2019, May 9). Israel responded to a Hamas cyberattack with an airstrike. That's not such a big deal. The Washington Post. Retrieved from https://www.washingtonpost.com/politics/2019/05/09/israel-responded-hamas-cyberattack-with-an-airstrike-thats-big-deal/

Bull, H. (1961). The Control of the Arms Race: Disarmament and Arms Control in the Missile Age. London: Institute for Strategic Studies.

Buresh, D. L. (2021). Russian cyber-attacks on Estonia, Georgia, and Ukraine, including tactics, techniques, procedures, and effects. Journal of Advanced Forensic Sciences, 3(1), 15–26.

Buzan, B. (1987). An introduction to strategic studies: Military technology & international relations. London: Macmillan Press.

Christopher, N. M. (2003). *Art of war*. Chicago: University of Chicago Press.

CISA. (2024, September 5). *Russian* military cyber actors target US and global critical infrastructure. Retrieved from https://www.cisa.gov/news-events/cybersecurity-advisories/aa24-249a

Clausewitz, C. V. (1832, 2007). *On* war (M. Howard & P. Paret, Trans.). Oxford: Oxford University Press.

Colarik, A. M., & Janczewski, L. (2012). Establishing cyber warfare doctrine. Journal of Strategic Security, 5(1), 31–48.

Command, H. A. (2004). *Indian army doctrine*. Shimla: Headquarters Army Training Command.

Corps, U. M. (1989). *Mao tse-tung on guerrilla warfare*. Washington, DC: US Navy.

CRS. (2015, March 27). Cyberwarfare and cyberterrorism: In brief. Retrieved from https://crsreports.congress.gov/product/pdf/R/R43955

CSIS. (2022). Significant cyber incidents. Retrieved from https://www.csis.org/programs/strategic-technologies-program/significant-cyber-incidents

Cunningham, F. (2021, April 29). Was China behind last October's power outage in India? Here's what we know. The Washington Post. Retrieved from https://www.washingtonpost.com/politics/2021/04/29/was-china-behind-last-octobers-power-outage-india-heres-what-we-know/

DoD. (2007, September 11). Irregular warfare (IW) joint operating concept (JOC). Retrieved from https://www.jcs.mil/Portals/36/Documents/Doctrine/concepts/joc_iw_v1.pdf?ver=2017-12-28-162020-260

Douhet, G. (2019, 1921). The command of the air. Maxwell Air Force Base, AL: Air University Press.

Evera, S. V. (1998). Offense, defense, and the causes of war. International Security, 22(4), 5–43.

Ford, C. A. (2010). The trouble with cyber arms control. The New Atlantis, (29), 52–67.
Fortune Business Insights. (n.d.). Cyber weapons market size, share & industry analysis... Retrieved from https://www.fortunebusinessinsights.com/cyber-weapons-market-105535
Fredriksson, B. E. (2006). Globalness: Toward a space power theory. Maxwell Air Force Base, AL: Air University Press.
Garnett, J., & Baylis, J. (2019). The causes of war and the conditions of peace. In J. Baylis, J. Garnett, & P. Owens (Eds.), Strategy in the contemporary world (pp. 72–86). Oxford: Oxford University Press.
Gilbert, F. (1986). Machiavelli: The Renaissance of the art of war. In P. Paret (Ed.), Makers of modern strategy: From Machiavelli to the nuclear age (pp. 11–30). Princeton, NJ: Princeton University Press.
Giles, S. T. (2009). *Sun Tzu's The art of war*. Kansas City, Pax Librorium Publishing House.
Gomez, M. A. (2016). Arming cyberspace: The militarization of a virtual domain. Global Security and Intelligence Studies, 1(1), 42–65.
Gray, C. (1999). *Modern strategy*. New York: Oxford University Press.
Gray, C. S. (1971). The arms race phenomenon. World Politics, 24(1), 39–79.
Gray, C. S. (1996). The influence of space power upon history. Comparative Strategy, 15(4), 293–308.
Gray, C. S. (2013). Making strategic sense of cyber power: Why the sky is not falling. Carlisle, PA: U.S. Army War College Press.
Guevara, E. C. (2006). *Guerrilla warfare* (Authorized ed.). Melbourne: Ocean Press.
van Haaster, J., & Geers, R. (2016). Cyber guerilla. Cambridge: Elsevier.
Hammond, T. (2009). *The peloponnesian war*. New York: Oxford University Press.
Hart, B. L. (1954, 1967). *Strategy: Hudson street*. New York: Meridian, Penguin Group.
Hart, B. L. (1956). *The revolution in warfare*. London: Faber And Faber Ltd.
Hatch, B. B. (2018). Defining a class of cyber weapons as WMD: An examination of the merits. Journal of Strategic Security, 11(3), 43–61.
Herz, J. H. (1950). Idealist internationalism and the security dilemma. World Politics, 2(2), 157–180.
Huntington, S. P. (1958). The Soldier and the State: The Theory and Politics of Civil-Military Relations. Cambridge, MA: Belknap Press of Harvard University Press.
IDS. (2017). Joint doctrine Indian armed forces. New Delhi: Integrated Defence Staff.
Indian Air Force. (2012). Basic doctrine of the Indian Air Force. New Delhi: Air Head Quarter.
IndiaTV. (2020, November 19). Complete list of 267 Chinese apps banned in India: PUBG Mobile, TikTok, AliExpress and more. IndiaTVNews. Retrieved from https://www.indiatvnews.com/technology/news-list-of-all-chinese-apps-banned-in-india-2020-667131
ISRO. (2023). Quantum Key Distribution (QKD). https://www.isro.gov.in/Quantum%20Key%20Distribution%20(QKD).html
Jervis, R. (1979). Deterrence theory revisited. World Politics, 31(2), 289–324.
Jervis, R. (2011). Dilemmas about security dilemmas. Security Studies, 20(3), 416–23.
Jomini, B. A. (1830, 2008). The art of war (G. H. Mendell & W. P. Craighill, Trans.). Kingston, Canada: Legacy Books Press Classics.
Kaldor, M. (2012). New and old wars. Cambridge: Polity Press.
Kaldor, M. (2013). In defence of new wars. Stability, 2(1), 1–16.
Kautilya. (1915). Arthashastra (R. Shamasastry, Trans.). Mysore: Government Oriental Library.

Kennedy, P. (1988). The influence and the limitations of sea power. The International History Review, 10(1), 2–17.
Klein, J. J. (2021). Some lessons on spacepower from Colin Gray. Naval War College Review, 74(1), Article 7.
Kramer, F. D. (2009). Cyberpower and national security: Policy recommendations for a strategic framework. In F. D. Kramer, S. H. Starr, & L. K. Wentz (Eds.), Cyberpower and national security (pp. 2–23). Virginia: Potomac Books.
Kuehl, D. T. (2009). From cyberspace to cyberpower: Defining the problem. In F. D. Kramer, S. H. Starr, & L. K. Wentz (Eds.), Cyberpower and national security (pp. 24–42). Virginia: Potomac Books.
Lachow, I. (2009). Cyber terrorism: Menace or myth? In F. D. Kramer, S. H. Starr, & L. K. Wentz (Eds.), Cyberpower and national security (pp. 437–464). Virginia: Potomac Books.
Larson, E. V., & Eaglin, D. (2008). Assessing irregular warfare: A framework for intelligence analysis. Santa Monica, CA: RAND Corporation.
Libicki, M. C. (2007). Conquest in cyberspace: National security and information warfare. New York, NY: Cambridge University Press.
Libicki, M. C. (2009). Military cyberpower. In F. D. Kramer, S. H. Starr, & L. K. Wentz (Eds.), Cyberpower and national security (pp. 275–284). Virginia: Potomac Books.
Mackinder, H. J. (1904). The geographical pivot of history. The Geographical Journal, 23(4), 421–437.
Mackinder, H. J. (1919). Democratic ideals and reality: A study in the politics of reconstruction. New York, NY: Henry Holt and Company.
Mahan, A. (1987). The influence of sea power upon history, 1660–1783. New York, NY: Dover Publications Inc (First Publication, 1980, Little, Brown, and Company, Boston, in 1890.
Mansfield, N. M. (1998). The prince. Chicago, IL and London: University of Chicago Press.
McBurney, T. R. (2012). Cyber-weapons. The RUSI Journal, 157(1), 6–13.
Nation, R. C. (2008). Thucydides and contemporary strategy. In J. B. Bartholomees (Ed.), Theory of war and strategy (Vol. I, pp. 129–142). Carlisle, PA: Strategic Studies Institute, US Army War College.
NDTV. (2010, December 4). Hacked by 'Pakistan cyber army', CBI website still not restored. NDTV. Retrieved from https://www.ndtv.com/india-news/hacked-by-pakistan-cyber-army-cbi-website-still-not-restored-441100
NDTV. (2024, September 19). Unit 8200: Israel's secret intelligence arm linked to Hezbollah pager attacks. News Desk. Retrieved from https://www.ndtv.com/world-news/unit-8200-israels-secret-intelligence -arm-linked-to-hezbollah-pager-attacks-6599223
Nye, J. S. (2011). The future of power. New York, NY: Public Affairs.
Nye, J. S. (2017). Deterrence and dissuasion in cyberspace. International Security, 41(3), 44–71.
Paganini, P. (2012, May 05). The rise of cyber weapons and relative impact on cyberspace. Infosec Institute. Retrieved from https://resources.infosecinstitute.com/topic/the-rise-of-cyber-weapons-and-relative-impact-on-cyberspace /
Paret, P. (1986). Clausewitz. In P. Paret (Ed.), Makers of modern strategy: From Machiavelli to the nuclear age (pp. 186–213). Princeton, NJ: Princeton University Press.
Pilbeam, B. (2015). Reflecting on war and peace. In P. Hough, S. Malik, A. Moran, & B. Pilbeam (Eds.), International security studies: Theory and practice (pp. 3–11). London: Routledge.

PIB (2024, February 20). CDS Gen Anil Chauhan releases Joint Doctrine for Cyberspace Operations. Government of India. https://pib.gov.in/PressReleasePage.aspx?PRID=2026240

Posen, B. R. (1984). The sources of military doctrine: France, Britain, and Germany between the world wars. Ithaca, NY: Cornel University Press.

Relia, S. (2015). Cyber warfare: Its implication on national security. New Delhi: Vij Books India Pvt Ltd.

Rid, T., & McBurney, P. (2012). Cyber-weapons. The RUSI Journal, 157(1), 6–13.

Rosecrance, R. (1987). Explaining military doctrine. International Security, 11(3), 167–174.

Rothenberg, G. E. (1986). Moltke, Schlieffen, and the doctrine of strategic envelopment. In P. Paret (Ed.), Makers of modern strategy: From Machiavelli to the nuclear age (pp. 296–325). Princeton, NJ: Princeton University Press.

Samuel, C. (2021). *Leveraging cyber power: A study of the approaches and responses of the major powers*. New Delhi: MP-IDSA. Also, my interview with the author (telephonically) held on 29 June 2021.

Schelling, T. C. (2008, 1966). Arms and influence. New Haven, CT and London: Yale University.

Schmitt, M. N. (2017). Tallinn Manual 2.0 on the international law applicable to cyber operations. New York: Cambridge University Press.

Shaw, J. E. (1999). The influence of space power upon history 1944–1998. Air Power History, 46(4), 20–29.

Sheldon, J. B. (2016). The rise of cyberpower. In J. Baylis, J. J. Wirtz, & C. S. Gray (Eds.), Strategy in the contemporary world (pp. 291–307). Oxford: Oxford University Press.

Shy, J. (1986). Jomini. In P. Paret (Ed.), Makers of modern strategy: From Machiavelli to the nuclear age (pp. 143–185). Princeton, NJ: Princeton University Press.

Sloan, G. (2012). Military doctrine, command philosophy and the generation of fighting power: Genesis and theory. International Affairs, 88(2), 243–263.

Smith, T. C. (1980). Arms race instability and war. Journal of Conflict Resolution, 24(2), 253–284.

Spykman, N. J. (1942). America's strategy in world politics. New York: Harcourt, Brace and Company, Inc.

Starr, S. H. (2009). Toward a preliminary theory of cyberpower. In F. D. Kramer, S. H. Starr, & L. K. Wentz (Eds.), Cyberpower and national security (pp. 43–90). Virginia: Potomac Books, Inc.

Steiner, B. H. (1973). Arms Races, Diplomacy, and Recurring Behavior: Lessons from Two Cases. Beverly Hills, CA: Sage Publications.

Tribune. (2021, September). Talk by Chief of Defence Staff Gen. Bipin Rawat on "Towards Progressive Defence Reforms" at IIC. YouTube. Retrieved from https://www.youtube.com/watch?v=HRi4iHOhFPU

Tyagi, R. K. (2015). Understanding cyber warfare and its implications for Indian armed forces. New Delhi: Vij Books India Pvt Ltd.

United Nations. (2002). *United* Nations treaties and principles on outer space. New York: United Nations.

United Nations. (2013, June 24). Group of Governmental Experts on developments in the field of information and telecommunications in the context of international security. Retrieved from https://digitallibrary.un.org/record/753055?ln=en#record-files-collapse-header

UNICRI. (2023). Cyberwarfare. Retrieved from http://www.unicri.eu/special_topics/securing_cyberspace /cyber_threats/explanations/

UNIDIR. (2013). The cyber index: International security trends and realities. New York, NY: United Nations Institute for Disarmament Research.

UNRCPD. (2022). Weapons of mass destruction. Retrieved from https://unrcpd.org/wmd/

Waltz, K. (1981). The spread of nuclear weapons: More may be better (Adelphi Papers, No. 171). London: International Institute for Strategic Studies.

Waltz, K. (2001 (1959)). Man, the state and war. New York, NY: Colombia University Press.

Zagare, F. C. (2008). Game theory. In P. D. Williams (Ed.), Security studies: An introduction (pp. 44–58). London: Routledge.

5 Towards Cyber-Peace Initiatives

Introduction

Cyber technologies are undoubtedly a double-edged sword in modern society. While they are frequently recognised as instruments of warfare, used for cyberattacks, espionage, and disruption, they also have immense potential as tools for fostering peace, stability, and achieving the United Nations Sustainable Development Goals.[1] It is imperative for nation-states to collaborate and work together in order to preserve a peaceful global cyber order. This concluding chapter goes beyond the traditional approach of merely summarising the findings of the study or recapping the previous four chapters. Since each of the preceding chapters has its own conclusion, this chapter avoids repeating those ideas. Instead, as the final segment of the book, it centres on the factors that contribute to fostering peace in interstate cyber relations, aligning with the ultimate objectives of statecraft, security studies, and cyberwarfare analysis. It also discusses the possibility for in-depth study of emerging technologies in the future, which is outside the purview of this study. The first chapter evaluates the current situation of cyber affairs in the international system and explains why nations view cyberspace as a factor of strategic relevance. This is followed by the finding of the second chapter that the domain of cyberspace has a permanent connection to the state system and concerns such as population, geography, governance, sovereignty, and security. The third chapter features a succinct discussion regarding the study of national security and the framework for cyber defence in the global order. The fourth chapter looks at the theoretical perspective of interstate war in relation to cyberwarfare as well as the justification for states creating digital weapons.

Since ancient times, strategic thinkers and military scholars have upheld the adage, "If you wish for peace, prepare for war". In essence, this implies that a state's preparedness for war serves as a deterrent, ultimately reflecting its desire to maintain peace. Article 42 of the UN Charter even permits the Security Council to use military force to restore international peace and security (Carr, 2010, pp. xii, 49). The study of warfare itself is a means towards peace. Likewise, education of cyber warfare is a way to promote digital harmony. If cyberwar ever exists, peace should also follow. Referring

DOI: 10.4324/9781003630319-5

to the title of this book, the study of state's security and cyberwarfare would be incomplete without understanding cyber peace[2] initiatives. Cyberspace is a human construct and anarchic system where international laws are missing. Because of its lawless nature, states strive to safeguard their digital ecosystems through a combination of offensive and defensive measures—actions that carry the potential to escalate into conflicts. With the pervasive nature of cyber technologies and militarisation of the domain, it is difficult to delegitimise cyberwarfare or reverse the usage of cyberspace for hostile and "non-peaceful" purposes (Wegener, 2011, p. 77). Consequently, the progress of cyber-peace initiatives is impeded by the rapid proliferation of cyberweapons and their swift deployment for strategic objectives, all in the absence of effective oversight or regulatory mechanisms (Steinberg, 2022). Just like war and violence originate from the minds of humans, peace and tranquility can only come from humanity itself.

To study cyber peace, first it is imperative to identify what cyber peace means, as it is not so commonly defined or universally understood by the member states of the UN. In the book, *The Quest for Cyber Peace* published by the International Telecommunication Union (ITU), UN in 2011, the contributors try to explain its meaning. One of the cyber-peace contributors, Henning Wegener, quoting the UN *Declaration and Programme of Action on a Culture of Peace* of October 1999, argues that the definition of cyber peace should be kept open ended and not be watertight, though it should be intuitive and include defining elements. Peace is the complete state of tranquility and should be free from disorder, disturbance, and violence. It is not only the absence of direct violence or use of force, but indirect constraints as well. It is not simply the promotion of non-violence, but sharing a set of values, mode of behaviours, international law and order, positive impressions, active participation in the process, and respect of human rights (Wegener, 2011). Similarly, cyber peace is not just the absence of malware attacks in digital networks but to respecting norms and the sharing of positive values between states or waring actors. Temporary diplomatic cooperation may not work here, but a trustworthy, rule-based agreement should be adhered to permanently. For instance, in a historic development, the US–China Cyber Agreement was signed on 25 September 2015 to avoid cyber theft, hacking government networks, and cyber espionage (CRS, 2015), but it did not last long. A similar type of agreement was signed with India and other reliable countries such as Japan, Australia, France, etc., without anyone breaking the agreement so far. Such agreements are meaningful only when the corresponding actors enjoy good relations in the real world. The functioning of a cyberspace agreement is, in fact, directly proportional to geopolitical relationships.

There is no universal definition of cyber peace as cyberspace itself is a "pseudo-commons"[3]; no single meaning is shared by all (Shackelford, 2013, p. 1291). The Oxford English Dictionary defines "peace" as "freedom from disturbance (tranquility), and a state or period in which there is no war, or a war has ended". Similarly, cyber peace can be defined as freedom from disturbance in the digital platform, as well as the state, where there is no cyberwar, or it has ended. Marlin Bennett argues "cyber peace is sometimes understood as a social condition or quality, and sometimes as a set of practices, and sometimes as both". Its meaning is loosely used ranging from the safety of online platforms to offline war affairs. Meanwhile, cyber peace in the simplest term can be defined as "the practices to maintain the stability of the Internet and connected services" (Marlin-Bennett, 2022, pp. 4–7) though it is more than that. As per Heather Roff, cyber peace is closely associated with "cybersecurity" and both are considered as the two faces of the same coin. Cyber peace is the last goal or the endpoint of the cybersecurity process. It goes beyond merely the absence of cyberattacks, embodying a comprehensive and rigorous framework of conditions that ensure security and stability in cyberspace (Roff, 2016, pp. 10, 15).

If cybersecurity is attainable, cyber peace is ideally achievable, even if it may seem overly optimistic. Unfortunately, most of the frameworks on cyber peace have so far least not been converted into action because of their non-binding nature. Most transnational agreements or the frameworks of cyber peace, initiated by forums such as the Suzanne Mubarak Women's International Peace Movement (SMWIPM) (2007), World Federation of Scientists (WFS) (2009), ITU *Quest for Cyber Peace* (2011), and Paris Call (2018) are advisory and non-binding in principle. Subsequently, whatever efforts made by these bodies are based on "negative" peace (Johan Galtung framework of peace), which is more like controlling or managing the damage caused by cyberattacks instead of working for a sustainable long-term solution or an equitable status quo (Shackelford, 2022, p. xxi). However, in international cyber affairs, achieving even negative peace is good enough as a first step before attaining a more complex positive peace. After only achieving negative peace, shall positive peace eventually follow. To ascertain a permanent everlasting peace (positive peace), cyberwar has to stop or be controlled (negative peace) first. It would be better for cyber peace to exist as a negative peace (avoiding war) so that no country will initiate a war. When it becomes a "specific ideal system to achieve, then peace becomes something to strive for, even to the point of going to war" (Weber, 2022, p. 8).

Meanwhile, the non-physical and amorphous nature of cyber weapons contributes to the predicaments of the cyber-peace process. Cyber technologies are meant for dual purposes, both civil and military. Unless a clear distinction is made between civil and military cyber technologies (including cyberweapons), the concept of arms control as a peace initiative will remain challenging to implement in practice (Ford, 2010). Moreover, the legal and illegal weapons for digital warfare need to be classified. The dilemma of uncertainty in tracing (attribution or ownership) the origin of a cyberattack questions the credibility of the deterrence policy and reduces peace efforts. However, there is no cyberwar doctrine such as "no first use" or "no strike against the weaker states or non-cyber power" in cyber warfare. No liable punishment has been set for harbouring a cyberterrorist or criminals (Wegener, 2011). Nonetheless, global efforts have been made at the bi and multilateral levels to regulate and arrange cyber non-aggressions pacts. Nations can discourage private companies from producing sophisticated malware harmful to any cyber networks. National investment on research and developments for cyber-weapon programs (virus and malwares) should be stopped. The transfer of lethal cyber technologies should be avoided and monitored. While nations advance their digital military agendas by raising cyber commands, states should behave morally and support the peace initiatives.

Based on the above understanding, this chapter explores the possibility of developing theories of cyber peace by drawing comparisons with existing peace theories proposed by renowned thinkers such as Immanuel Kant, Johan Galtung, and Mahatma Gandhi. Meanwhile, it examines the concept of cyber peace along with the idea of conflict prevention, peacebuilding, peacemaking, peace enforcement, and peacekeeping commenced by the UN. These digital peace developments are analysed across various levels, including personal, local, state, national, regional, and international. Subsequently, the chapter highlights India's approaches to digital peace. In conclusion, it addresses the findings on cyber-peace initiatives within the international system, along with a forward-looking perspective aligned with the overarching theme of this book.

Towards the Theory of Cyber Peace

A theory is a set of thoughts and knowledge that are logically correlated to observe a phenomenon in a systematic way by empirically verifying the propositions. A theory becomes a scientific law when it is significantly verified and widely accepted. When it fails to do so, it develops a hypothesis. Theory, as a scientific law, explains and predicts phenomena by observation. As per M.V. Naidu, the "Theory of Peace" in general refers to the "presence of nonviolence", which is based on rational humanism and democratic distribution of the political economy. While rational humanism is based on ideological components such as free thought, conflict resolution, anti-racism, and anti-colonialism, democratic distribution is based on economic political democratisation such as de-monopolisation, reduction of consumerism and materialism, limits to industrialisation, maintaining ecological balance, and demilitarisation (Naidu, 1966). The following section examines the peace models proposed by renowned thinkers such as Kant, Galtung, and Gandhi, with the aim of adapting their ideas to the framework of creating a theory of cyber peace.

Kantian Thoughts and Cyber Peace

In his essay, *Toward Perpetual Peace: A Philosophical Sketch*, Immanuel Kant expressed the idea to promote liberal pacific union amongst nations. He advocated that real peace can only be achieved by the rule of just laws (positive peace) within and between states and this condition should be made global. Kant's concept of peace is founded on the principles of interdependence and close relationships between nations, transcending their military capabilities and technological advancements (Kleingeld, 2006, 1795, pp. xv, 201–204). Though he is not pessimistic enough to imagine perpetual peace is impossible to achieve, he is not optimist enough to believe that harmony can so easily be maintained through cooperation between nations. Though he understands that perpetual peace is as ideal as the fancy Utopian idea, it is difficult to achieve with the independent status of countries. Treaties are made between states and they remain binding until the signing parties are not interested and denounce them (Kant, 1903, 1795, p. 7). In the first section of his essay, Kant developed six basic principles or articles to build confidence between warring parties. First, any peace treaty will be valid only when it does not carry any hidden agenda to continue war. All countries should be trustworthy and every truce should not provide any scope for future conflict. Second, every state should respect each others' territorial integrity and independent countries (great or weak) are not subject to conquest, exchange, purchase, or donation. Third, the standing armies of states should be gradually reduced in size and ultimately abolished, as envisioned in the pursuit of lasting peace. Fourth, no nation must arrange or borrow money from others to accumulate their power or enhance war resources. Fifth, states should refrain from interfering in the constitution and administration of other states. Sixth, all waring states should not commit war crimes, use assassins or poisoners, which would destroy the scope for peace in the future and make it impossible (Doyle, 2006, p. 204; Kant, 1903, 1795, pp. 36–38).

Kant's idea of peace was formulated nearly two centuries before cyberspace became globally accessible, emerged as an agenda of security affairs, or evolved into a domain of warfare. His six articles of perpetual peace were designed to establish confidence-building measures between states during an era when wars were fought in physical form. Can these principles still be applied to contemporary cyber conflicts? Yes, they remain relevant, as long as states continue to be the primary actors behind cyberwars and peace formation is rooted in mutual interstate relationships (as Kant believes). Meanwhile, the reality of cyberwarfare has been recognised within the international system, leading to the subsequent pursuit of cyber peace, which is currently in its nascent stages. The following ideas on cyber peace are being developed based on Kant's six articles of perpetual peace.

1. No country while making a cyber truce should leave any scope for future war. Any treaty is invalid if it has a secret intent to conduct further cyber operation. The 2015 cyber truce between the US and China failed because of mistrust and undying intent to attack each other over the domain.
2. Every state must respect the jurisdictional integrity of cyberspace and must refrain from attacking, controlling, exchanging, or purchasing the

cyber networks or digital territories (property) of another state or its government.
3. To achieve cyber peace, the size of cyber commands and their affiliates within the military system must be gradually reduced and eventually abolished. However, in the realm of cyberwarfare, the absence of a formal cyber command does not preclude a state from engaging in strategic operations. States can still involve private technology companies or cyber mercenaries, as was evident in the 1990s, before the establishment of formal military digital commands.
4. No national debt should be incurred through excessive investment in digital technologies or weaponry to bolster cyber power. Instead, limited preparation and engagement should be maintained for cyberwarfare, ensuring resources are allocated responsibly and sustainably.
5. No independent state should interfere with the national digital peace policies of another state. Each independent nation should respect the cybersecurity strategy and frameworks of other.
6. States should never commit cyberwarcrimes by employing cyber mercenaries, hackers, or other entities that support offensive activities in the digital realm. Such practices must be prohibited, as they undermine the potential for peace settlements between cyber-warring states.

Galtung's Idea and Cyber Peace

According to Johan Galtung, the "theory of peace is intimately connected not only with conflict theory, but equally with development theory" (Galtung, 1969, p. 183). Ending violence could be a reason to seek peace and peace should be used as a social goal, which may be hard to achieve but possible to attain. He agrees that peace is a never-ending process and it is a combination of "direct peace, structural peace and cultural peace". Peace is what people achieve when conflicts are transformed (not resolved) non-violently in a creative manner (Galtung, 1996, p. 225). He distinguished violence into two categories, *personal* and *structural* violence. While personal violence refers to violence where actors are involved physically and is direct in nature, structural violence (also called social injustice) refers to the type of violence where such actors are not involved physically and it is indirect in nature. Structural violence is a "truncated violence" where it is not directly committed, but extremely important. A simple example of personal violence is if a son beats his elderly father but structural violence is if millions of sons ignore their fathers' need for shelter. Violence can further be divided into *physical*, which is somatic (killing or hurting an individual), and *psychological*, which is based on emotion and mental status (imprisoning a person). Violence is not solely defined by physical harm or destruction, it also encompasses psychological threats and harassment, which can cause significant emotional and mental distress. Hence, peace for Galtung is the absence of "personal and structural violence" in which the former and latter are based on negative peace and positive peace, respectively (Galtung, 1969, p. 183). Subsequently, peace has been popularly divided into two categories, *negative* and *positive* peace. While the former is achieved with the end of violence, the latter is attained with the absence of structural violence. While the recognition of negative and positive peace is attributed to Galtung, it was Martin Luther King Jr who introduced the terms when he wrote *Letter from Birmingham Jail* in 1963 that "negative peace which is the absence of tension" and "positive peace which is the presence of justice" (King, 1963). Interestingly, though missing the term "positive peace", "negative peace" was mentioned in the 23rd page of the book, *Newer Ideals of Peace* by Jane Addams, published in 1907.

Table 5.1 demonstrates that cyber violence can impact two fundamental layers: humans and machines (both software and hardware). The former encompasses somatic elements, including human beings, biological systems, and the surrounding environment. The latter, refers to the electronic domain, which includes computer networks, program codes, software applications, and algorithms. When protections fail at the machine layer, the resulting consequences inevitably affect the human layer. Based on Galtung's framework, cyber violence can be allocated into personal and structural violence with implications for cyberspace itself and beyond, which is the somatic (human body). *Personal violence* towards the "network environment" is the disruption of individuals' data and ICT systems, which is limited to the ambit of cyberspace and computer systems only. However, *personal violence* towards the "human environment" refers to harm or casualties inflicted through the use of cyber tools employed as weapons. Meanwhile, *structural violence* towards the "cyber environment" refers to a persistent campaign to extract information or spoil government (or non-government) infrastructures by a state (or non-state) actor for a political strategic objective (e.g., Moonlight Maze, Stuxnet, etc.). Subsequently, *structural violence towards a* "human environment" could be considered as continuous illegal activities that affect the rights of individuals carried out (by state or non-state actors) by means of cyber tools (e.g., Pegasus spyware incident in India, 2021).

While *physical violence towards* the "cyber environment" refers to the disruption and dysfunction of hardware or computer facilities caused by a digital attack, *physical violence* towards the "human environment" is using cyber technology and weapons to hurt or kill living beings. *Psychological violence* towards the "cyber environment" refers to assaults targeting the virtual (non-physical) components of cyberspace, such as software applications or algorithms and these attacks can disrupt system functioning and lead to widespread consequences. Similarly, *psychological violence* towards the "human environment" involves online harassment, trolling, and stalking, which cause stress and tension for individuals, with tangible effects in the real world. Both personal and structural violence, with their physical and psychological implications in cyberspace, highlight the urgent need to pursue and establish peace within the digital domain. While *negative peace* in the "cyber environment" can be achieved through the absence of violent digital conflicts,

Table 5.1 Impact of Violence and Peace on Network Facilities and Humans

Dimension of cyber violence

Sl No.	Types of violence	Cyber environment	Human environment
	Personal violence	Attack on users' computer network facilities	SCADA attack/failure leading to murder; collision of aircraft by hacking air traffic to kill a political leader; cause damage by hacking a life-saving device such as a pacemaker or neural brain implant
	Structural violence	Conduct of long-term cyberattack campaign by APT such as Lazarus Group/APT38, OilRig/APT 34, etc., involving state and non-state actors	Pegasus spyware planted in civilian smartphones; terrorist radicalisation through social media; communal campaign and trolling on social media
	Physical violence	Hardware damage, network outage	Human casualty caused by using cyber means as weapons
	Psychological violence	Non-hardware/physical component of a system; software is corrupted; computer program or algorithm is disturbed	Harassment of individuals by trolling, stalking, invading privacy, etc.

Dimension of cyber peace

	Positive peace	A just cyberworld: malware-free network system, virus-free digital environment, spyware-free cyber ecosystem	Data protection of individuals, no harassment or social injustice; accessible by every individual at an affordable price
	Negative peace	Absence of cyber violence; free from cyberattack, short-term agreement on ceasefire of cyberattack (US–China Cybersecurity Agreement, 2015)	UNGGE and UNOEWG efforts to encourage states to behave in cyberspace; bi/multilateral cooperation/agreement; and cybersecurity or digital peace conventions

Source: Author, by referring Galtung's ideas

in the "human environment", it can be attained through bilateral or multilateral agreements and the establishment of cyber conventions. However, *positive peace* in the "cyber environment" can be achieved through the absence of structural violence and it can be obtained in the "human environment" by respecting the digital rights of the individual. Consequently, negative cyber peace pertains to physical (direct) violence within digital networks and its broader impacts on the real (somatic) world, whereas positive cyber peace addresses the "psychological" (indirect) dimensions of the cyber realm and its impact on the social spheres (biological).

Liberal (Democratic) Peace and Cyber Peace

Although they may have distinct literal definitions, the terms "liberal peace", "democratic peace", and "liberal democratic peace" are often used interchangeably in peace studies, as they complement and reinforce one another (Doyle, 2005; Rosato, 2005). They do not oppose one another nor compete against each other, instead, they coexist and mutually support their principles. While liberal peace is based on citizens participating in the decision-making process of a war, democratic peace is state centric, based on the proposition that democracies do not wage war against each other. Liberal democratic peace could be considered a combination of both (citizens and state working together). The theory of liberal peace can be understood as the achievement of harmony in the national and international system when people in society have a larger control over political and economic decisions. Individuals are normally peace loving and always self-interested in non-violence as they are able to attain wealth and wellbeing only during the time of peace (Herge, 2021). Meanwhile, John Owen argues that liberal ideas foster democratic peace, preventing war between liberal states. However, these same ideas often drive liberal states to engage in conflict with "non-liberal" states. Like Kant's articles, Owen proposed six hypotheses related to liberal peace. First, liberals are inherently pacific and trust only other liberals, not non-liberal states. Second, liberals expect pacific relations with other liberals once other liberals meet the first liberal's standards. Third, liberals share their achievements for the welfare of the citizens and in the interest of the public, which non-liberals do not. Fourth, in times of dispute between two liberals, neither party will not change their impression that both are still liberals. Fifth, liberal populations tend to protest against war with another liberal state but are less likely to oppose conflict with an non-liberal state, especially if the war aligns with their interests. Sixth, liberal statespeople will stick to their liberal principles and find ways to diffuse disputes with another liberal (Owen, 1994).

Referring to Kant and the role of the republic in fostering peace, Michael Doyle argues that democratic nations predominantly maintain peace because they are inherently cautious and share common values of mutual respect.

This shared commitment encourages the promotion of peace and reduces the likelihood of conflict between them. He developed three pillars or hypotheses of liberal peace. The first pillar expresses that democratic governments maintain accountable close relationships with the voting public (voters) who oppose going to war. The second pillar states that liberals share converging interests, democratic principles, and norms and rights of individuals, leading them to respect each other. The third pillar refers to the liberal economy, that the "spirit of commerce" between democracies will support building peace and averting conflicts (Doyle, 2005). Although Sebastian Rosato agreed with Doyle's claim that "liberals are careful and respect each other to prevent conflict and sustain peace", he criticised the notion that democratic standards and democratic governments are the foundation of the peace that democracies experience. In addition, critics such as David E. Spiro have challenged the empirical validity of the democratic peace theory, arguing that the small number of conflicts between liberal democracies over the past two centuries is too limited to be statistically significant (Spiro, 1994, p. 51).

Because cyberwars are conducted covertly in an invisible realm, it is inherently challenging to evaluate how well each peace plan will work. As a result, difficulties will arise when comparing the physical world and the cyber world in terms of peace theory. However, liberal cyber peace can be understood as the harmony achieved in national and international digital affairs when internet users or cyber firms actively participate in and influence the decision-making processes of state-led cyberwarfare. Major corporations like Apple or Microsoft, which have substantial business operations in China, may not favor a U.S. war against China, as such a conflict could result in significant financial losses for them. However, the concept of democratic cyber peace suggests that "democracies would not engage in cyberwarfare against one another". However, this principle is unlikely to manifest as consistently in cyberspace as it does in traditional geopolitical conflicts. Nonetheless, with the growing number of bilateral and multilateral agreements on cybersecurity issues, a form of "conditional" cyber peace is still achievable. Democracies or liberal democracies will refrain from cyberwarfare primarily due to the shared respect, values, morals, and trust among them. Besides, they would avoid war by calculating the costs and benefits of the attack. However, leveraging the covert and largely unregulated nature of cyberspace, democracies may not hesitate in violating another nation's digital sovereignty to advance their strategic interests, as evidenced by the WikiLeaks revelations on NSA spying against its allies. While such actions may not escalate into a full-scale cyberwar, the aggrieved nation is likely to seek retribution in the future.

Gandhi's Satyagraha *and Cyber Pacifism*

Efforts to establish peace in the international system are older than the oldest peace societies[4] established in the early part of the 18th century. Hundreds of such peace groups were formed before World War I commenced (Buckam,

1996, p. 88). Though pacifism is used in a divergent sense, the best approach to define pacifism is as a "doctrine or a combination of doctrines" (Narveson, 1965) that teaches that murdering living things, especially people, is unacceptable in all circumstances. While it is a doctrine that promotes peace, it condemns war (Stevenson, 1934, p. 437). Bertrand Russell suggested that this doctrine was followed by Tolstoy and Gandhi, and in certain circumstances it is the most applicable practical policy to promote peace. While such belief is reflected in religious holy books such as the Bible (Christian), Quran (Muslim), or Geeta (Hindu), in practice, the doctrine was widely adopted in India during a struggle for freedom. Pacifism can be seen from two aspects, *absolute pacifism* and *relative pacifism*. While absolute pacifism is based on complete non-violence (church/temple/mosque and Gandhian approach), relative pacifism acknowledges that war is necessary in certain circumstances. Pacifism can further be divided into *individual* and *political* pacifism based on personal and institutional ideas. While the individual pacifist commits that he would not be involved in war no matter what his government commands, a political pacifist will protect his government from going to war (Russell, 1943–1944, pp. 7–8).

John Buckham offered three fundamental ideas to define pacifism by, interestingly, defining what it is not. Buckham's first idea is that pacifism is not a novel phenomenon and it is not limit to one place (America) only. His second idea is that pacifism is not a passive philosophy but rather an active, optimistic, and far-reaching pursuit of peace rather than its preservation. His third idea is that pacifism is not the type of peace that is attained by comfortably isolating oneself from another's problems, or by adopting a *laissez faire* mentality. Pacifism does not ignore the noble virtue and achievements associated with war, along with the noble fight with lives sacrificed. Meanwhile, from a positive side, Buckham introduced four more concepts on pacifism. The first one is that pacifism is a set of principles or a doctrine, not a sentiment based on the "rational concept of human society and its permanent forces". The second concept is that pacifism is not only a principle but a policy that promotes cooperation and friendship, which would provide equal space and rights in the international system. His third concept is that war is a criminal exercise whose continuation leads to obscurantism and folly. His fourth concept asserts that the way to peace is only by choosing the path of peace, not war, because "one cannot expect silver ore in a tin mine" (Gandhi, 1933). Lastly, he suggested that these concepts are the means to bring welfare for both humanity and society. And "if they are not reliable enough, then pacifism itself is erroneous; and if they are, then it is the utmost knowledge to enforce them" (Buckham, 1996).

Gandhi's philosophy of pacifism and *satyagraha*, a doctrine of non-violent political resistance, has been extensively cited in peace and conflict studies by scholars and activists, including several Nobel Peace Prize laureates (Weber, 2001). However, for some, he speaks more on "non-violence" than peace and the necessity to abolish injustice from society (GWU, 2022). Though *satyagraha* is often interpreted as "passive resistance" and linked to pacifism, Gandhi distinguished it from the latter, which he associated with movements like the suffragettes. While passive resistance is regarded as a "weapon of the weak", it can use arms when they are strong enough, or as the situation demands. However, *satyagraha* is rooted in the concept of using truth as a force ("truth-force"), and since truth is synonymous with the soul or spirit, it is also referred to as "soul-force". Gandhi distinguishes between soul-force and body-force, with the latter involving the use of violence by an individual to oppose a government (the adversary) in an attempt to enact a desired legislation. However, if an individual chooses to make a sacrifice and willingly bears the cost of refusing to resort to violence, he is exercising soul-force (Gandhi, 1933). So, *Satyagraha* in more appropriate terms is "non-violent resistance" not passive resistance (Gandhi, 2001, 1961, p. 19). Though *satyagraha* is used as a means or movement to achieve political objectives against opponents, it is not purely a doctrine of war like deterrence or balance of power, which rely on the logic of coercion and peace through strength. The aim of Gandhi's policy is to use persuasion as a non-violent form of coercion to challenge foreign invaders. However, scholars such as Horsburgh suggest that this policy may not be applicable in declared conventional warfare when enemies are prepared to use the utmost force. No passive resistance can protect a country physically when it is invaded by a ruthless power (Pittock, 1968, p. 189).

Cyber pacifism is a doctrine or a set of pacific policies that harming or hurting someone by using cyberspace as a tool is immoral in any circumstance. It is a doctrine that encourages cyber cooperation and avoid conflict in the domain. Cyber pacifism can be divided into two categories, *absolute digital pacifism* and *relative digital pacifism*. While the former focuses on the total refrain from violence in cyberspace (no use of cyber weapons or cyber disarmament), the latter emphasises partial pacifism that gives permission to protect the cyber ecosystem with an impact on the aggressor (e.g., a firewall that has the capability to automatically affect an aggressor's tools when it attempts to intrude on a target or system). Cyber pacifism can be further categorised into *individual* and *political digital pacifism*. The first aspect pertains to cyber operatives, including military cyber command personnel, who take an oath to abstain from engaging in cyberwarfare, even when directed by the state. Meanwhile, the second aspect refers to a firm stance adopted by cyber political pacifists and elite groups to prevent their government from engaging in digital warfare. Based on Buckham's idea, cyber peace should be an active process seeking digital harmony in the international system. Even states that are not directly involved in digital conflicts should actively support peace initiatives rather than adopting a passive "let-them-fight" attitude. While cyber violence is a criminal activity, the platform should be used to cooperate or communicate, instead it should bridge the digital gap between "North and South" (digitally poor and rich countries).

Interestingly, based on Gandhi's doctrine, the concept of *cyber satyagraha*, which is based on cyber soul-force (CSF), embodies truth and morality but stands distinct from cyber passive-resistance (CPR). CPR is a weapon of the weak, but as it gains strength, it may eventually resort to cyber arms to counter the aggressor. In contrast, CSF entirely rejects the possibility of cyberwarfare. Even if an aggressor launches an attack, the prospective victim will not retaliate in kind but would instead seek resolution through political dialogue, fostering the possibility of future reconciliation and friendship. For instance, if the US were to attack or spy on Germany's network infrastructure, Germany, instead of retaliating, would seek a peaceful resolution through diplomatic negotiations and bilateral agreements to prevent future acts of cyber aggression (BBC, 2021). CSF nations will not take up cyber arms or manufacture digital weapons if they are capable of doing so to challenge the enemy.

UN Peace Instruments and Cyber-Peace Applications

UN peace instruments such as "conflict prevention, peacemaking, peacekeeping, peace enforcement, and peacebuilding" serve as collective mechanisms for maintaining peace in the international system. However, their respective roles increasingly overlap in practice. There is no singular approach that defines peace operations, as they encompass a range of strategies tailored to specific conflicts and contexts. Despite the significant expansion of peace initiatives, they often fail to achieve their objectives due to disagreements among the *Big Five* and the absence of essential organisational mechanisms such as "advance planning, early warning systems, and an ad-hoc administrative framework" (Risse-Kappen, 2002, 1997, p. 271). Meanwhile, the role of the UN remains limited in the domain of international cyber-peace policies, as states have not reached a unanimous agreement on global cyber standards. However, some cybersecurity initiatives have been undertaken through the UN Group of Government Experts (UNGGE) and the Open Ended Working Group (UNOEWG) to address "State behavior in cyberspace in the context of international security". This initiative represents the first of its kind, focusing on advancing the agenda of digital peace in the international system. Based on the range of peace and security operations implemented by the UN, cyber peace may be classified into five peace applications, "cyber conflict prevention, cyber peacemaking, cyber peacekeeping, cyber peace-enforcement, and cyber peacebuilding" (UN, 2008, p. 17).

Cyber Conflict Prevention

Since the end of the Second World War, the United Nations has been actively engaged in preventing conflict between states through diplomatic efforts, peacekeeping missions, and conflict resolution initiatives. Though the Cold War has ended, the emergence of the Balkan Wars and Rwandan Genocide among others led the international community to concentrate on internal conflicts (new war). Consequently, political leaders and international bodies began to seek reliable mechanisms to proactively resolve crises before they escalate into violence, leading to the introduction of the concept of conflict prevention. The study of conflict prevention was extensively discussed in the *Carnegie Commission on the Prevention of Deadly Conflict* (1999). It defines conflict prevention as a mechanism, action, or a set of policies aimed at preventing a situation from escalating into violence, while simultaneously identifying means to resolve potential tensions. It also embraced the strategy of restraining an ongoing conflict and stopping its spread with a mechanism to deter the re-emergence of violence (UN, 2004). It is also a strategic instrument that relies on diplomatic and structural measures to prevent intrastate and interstate tensions or disputes from escalating into violent conflict. It operates through early warning mechanisms, data collection, and situational analysis of activities that could potentially trigger a conflict (UN, 2008). It can be approached through two ways, *operational prevention* and *structural prevention*. While the former focuses on direct prevention through immediate actions, such as deploying diplomatic missions, imposing economic sanctions, and implementing weapons collection programs (negative peace), the latter addresses the root causes of conflict, such as poverty, political differences, and unequal resource distribution which, if left unaddressed, could escalate into violence (positive peace). Conflict prevention operates at two critical points: A) when a conflict has already begun, efforts are made to prevent its escalation; B) When a dispute has recently ended, but peace remains fragile, and the risk of conflict resurgence persists. However, many argue that proactive early warning measures to prevent violence before it begins or taking action before a conflict erupts, remain ineffective and highly challenging (UN, 2004).

Cyber conflict prevention can be understood as a mechanism designed to prevent the escalation of digital warfare between states or non-state actors through operational and structural preventive measures. Cyber conflicts can be prevented by assessing the enduring situations of disputes, issuing early warnings, and analysing the underlying factors that contribute to digital warfare. Cyber operation prevention involves implementing appropriate measures to avert the escalation of cyber violence through the direct involvement of international communities and institutional (state) stakeholders. For instance, organisations such as the UN or peace missions may intervene to halt cyber conflicts between nations like Iran and the US or Russia and Ukraine, aiming to prevent escalation and maintain stability in the cyber domain. Meanwhile, cyber structural prevention focuses on identifying and addressing the underlying causes of cyber discrepancies including digital divides, online radicalisation, and political differences that have the potential to incite digital violence. For example, North Korea's cyberattack on Sony, driven by political grievances, demonstrates how such disputes can escalate into broader cyber conflicts between states. Similar to the physical world, conflict prevention in cyberspace operates under two key hypotheses: preventing the escalation of an ongoing digital war and avoiding the re-emergence of cyber conflict after a fragile peace. However, in cyberspace, conflict prevention can also take place even before an actual cyber war begins. For instance, after the US and Israel were identified as the perpetrators of the Stuxnet attack on Iran's nuclear facilities, stakeholders and international communities voiced their concerns and exerted diplomatic influence to halt such actions, thereby preventing further escalation or recurrence of similar cyberattacks.

Cyber Peacemaking

Peacemaking in the physical world refers to actions performed by peacemakers using diplomatic measures to bring the warring parties of a continuing conflict into a negotiated agreement. The role of the peacemaker can be "envoys, governments, groups of states, regional organisations or the UN, non-official or non-governmental organisations, prominent personality working independently, etc." The office of the UN Secretary General can provide its goodwill assistance to resolve conflicts (UN, 2022). The role of the peacemaker or negotiator is crucial in the peace-making process, as the durability of the agreements reached during negotiations determines whether the conflict will be resolved sustainably or risk resurfacing and escalating in the future. The agreement should be strong enough to end the war and began a new era of peace by practising reliable mechanisms such as "demilitarized zones, confidence-building measures, and careful monitoring", which could also improve trust between the parties (Werner, 2005, p. 261). One of the classic examples of peacemaking in international affairs is the involvement of US President Jimmy Carter in the 1978 Camp David Accords between Israel and Egypt. Another example is *Naga Hoho's*[5] participation in peace negotiations and its influence in ending hostilities between Naga rebel groups and the Indian government.

Because cyberwarfare is covert and takes place in virtual battlegrounds, the damage it causes is often not visible and can be ignored or intentionally hidden.[6] Since peacemaking can only be conducted while a dispute is actively ongoing, the cyber-peacemaking approach can also be employed when a "cyberwar is unfolding". Cyber conflict, involving state and non-state actors, is an ongoing reality. This is evident in the increasing frequency of digital attacks, carried out for both criminal and strategic purposes, on a daily basis. Consequently, states engaged in cyberwarfare should at any time be prepared for peacemaking. However, effective mediation becomes challenging not only when identifying the two warring groups but also when warring countries, such as Ukraine and Russia, are openly engaged in cyber conflict. The lack of international law (International Humanitarian Law) in cyberspace (or cyberwar) and the non-binding nature of the UNGGE and OEWG guidelines pose a serious challenge to mediating the cyber conflict. Meanwhile, the OEWG Report released on 10 March 2021 suggests that cyber conflict and disputes should be settled by states with "peaceful means such as negotiation, enquiry, *mediation*, conciliation, arbitration, judicial settlement, and resort to regional agencies or arrangements, or other peaceful means of their own choice" (UN-OEWG, 2021). If mediation is ever used to resolve a digital conflict, the cyber mediator should be a state, institution, group, or individual, preferably with some scientific knowledge of cyberspace, though not necessarily a technology expert. It is also interesting to note that "cyber mediation" is increasingly viewed as a means to resolve conventional conflicts (disputes arising in the physical world) through the use of ICT, particularly blockchain applications and artificial intelligence, both of which were widely utilised during the COVID-19 pandemic (DiPLO, 2018).

Cyber-Peace Enforcement

Peace enforcement is one of the means to maintain peace in an ongoing conflict by using coercive measures or military force. The UN Security Council takes sole responsibility to carefully authorise the use of forces even without the consent of the conflicting parties or countries. The council sensibly examines the circumstances of the incident before making a decision to take action based on a "threat to the peace, breach of the peace, or act of aggression". The purpose of taking this action is to restore peace and security in the world order. The council, under the provision of the UN Charter, can exercise its authority wherever it is right with the help of regional organisations and agencies to take enforcement activities (UN, 2022). Generally, peace enforcement is carried out at a transition phase between conflict and peace by using both the components of war fighting and peacekeeping (Tubbs, 1997, p. 5). However, critics such as Leland Goodrich convey that though it is a first intergovernmental effort that plays an important role in preventing conflict, *peace enforcement* is an ambiguous and possibly misleading term (Goodrich, 1969, p. 657). Supporting the idea, quoting N.D. White and Robert Oakley, Mohammed A. Osman agrees that the terminology is confusing with other terms such as "peacekeeping, peacemaking, preventive deployment, collective self-defence and humanitarian intervention". Different countries interpret the term in different ways; the US refers to it as "peace enforcement", while the UK uses the term "peacemaking" (Osman, 2018, p. 19). In the meanwhile, Harri Holkeri, a former Finnish Prime Minister and UN General Assembly president, stated that "peace enforcement is a much more difficult kind of operation than peacekeeping". In fact, both peace enforcement and peacekeeping are military-based approaches that use tactics or influence to prevent conflict and restore peace. While peace enforcement operates without the consent of the main parties, peacekeeping requires their consent to take action (UN, 2022).

Cyber peace enforcement can be defined as the measures taken to achieve peace in cyber realm by using digital military forces. However, raising a cyber force or digital command in the UN military setup would be a contentious matter when the organisation is against the militarisation and weaponisation of cyberspace or seeking a secured cyber ecosystem in international affairs. The primary duty of UN cyber troops, often known as "cyber blue helmets", is to restore peace in situations involving digital conflict or cyberwarfare. Research and ideas have been emerging to develop concepts of cyber enforcement (or cyber peacekeeping), with contributions from scholars such as Cahill, Robinson, and Nabeel, among others (Robinson, 2018; Nabeel, 2019). Deploying cyber peace enforcement in any situation would not be an easy task unless a cyber conflict is explicitly identified. However, because cyberwarfare itself is ambiguous and imprecise, with challenges such as unclear cyber borders, lawlessness, and difficulties in attribution, these issues should not prevent the establishment of the UN's cyber enforcement mechanisms (Nabeel, 2019, p. 21). If such a force were developed in the future under the explicit authority of the UN Security Council, then a cyber-enforcement unit would have the right to conduct operations against warring parties with the objective of restoring digital peace. Even though cyberwar principles may be developed in the future, UN impartiality is likely to remain, just as it does in the physical world. The UN's impartial or neutral approach to the cyber peace-enforcement mechanism in conflict resolution may face several challenges, including difficulties in attribution, varying national interests, lack of consensus on cyber norms, and the rapidly evolving nature of cyber threats.

Cyber Peacekeeping

As mentioned above, peacekeeping is synonymously used with peace enforcement by different countries (UK, US, etc.). However, peacekeeping is more favourably discussed than peace enforcement or other peace activities. Peacekeeping is a means to navigate the rough path from conflict to peace. It has a unique strength of "legitimacy, burden sharing, ability to deploy and sustain troops/police around the globe, and integration of these peacekeepers with civil participants". The UN peacekeepers' mandate is to provide assistance for security, political, and peacebuilding mechanisms to encourage nation-states to transform from conflict to peace (UN, 2022). Peacekeeping functions through three basic principles. First, the peacekeepers carry out their activities only with the consent of the parties involved. Second, peacekeeping is based on impartiality, as any failure in maintaining neutrality could undermine the legitimacy and credibility of the mission. Third, the use of force should be limited to self-defence and actions mandated by the UN defence system. Peacekeeping operatives are not principally seen as enforcement forces. However, with authorisation from the UN Security Council and the consent of the host nation, offensive actions may be permitted at the tactical level under the peacekeeping principle of "self-defense and defense of the mandate". Peacekeeping operatives are authorised to use offensive actions by using all necessary means to prevent threats affecting the political stability and civil populace, and support states authorities in maintaining law and order (UN, 2022).

Cyber peacekeeping can be defined as defensive or offensive actions taken in cyberspace to preserve peace, ensuring that a digital conflict has ended while supporting and reinforcing agreements facilitated by cyber peacemakers (Robinson, 2018, p. 4). The UN used cyberspace as a means to support "digital peacekeeping" operations at both tactical and non-tactical levels. For instance, the Department of Peace Operations and Department of Operational Support (DOS) have undertaken various initiatives for "digital transformation of peacekeeping". These departments have leveraged cyberspace or ICT as an enabler to enhance peacekeeping analysis, improve conflict situational awareness, strengthen the safety and security of personnel, and ensure more effective and responsive mandate implementation (UN, 2021). An expert panel on technology and innovation in UN Peacekeeping was established in 2014 to improve the implementation of cyber technologies in peacekeeping operations (Best, n.d.). The DPO/DOS created the "Partnership for Technology in Peacekeeping" in the same year to expand the role of peacekeeping through ICT approaches and enhance global operations (UN, 2022). Digital peacekeeping functions in passive (non-offensive) areas such as scientific studies, ICT design and evaluation, research, seminars, workshop, policy papers, and academic activities (Best, n.d.). However, with the growing recognition of cyberwarfare in the international system and the increasing frequency of such activities among states, the role of peacekeeping can be expanded with both offensive and defensive options. Under the Department of Peace Operations, a "Cyber Peacekeeping Unit" (CPU) was established to function, with or without the consent of the third party, under the authority of the UN Security Council. Peacekeepers should be permitted to operate at both tactical and strategic levels against interstate cyber conflicts, which would otherwise be restricted for member states under Article 2(4) of the UN Charter (prohibiting the threat or use of force in international relations by member nations). Cyber peacekeepers can monitor and respond to cyber threats based on four principles, considering the capabilities and resources of the cyber mission, respect for human rights and following those principles in operation, a robust mandate should be adopted for the mission, and the response should be proportionate to the level of the cyber threat (Nabeel, 2019, p. 23). Though challenging, the increasing prevalence of cyber threats involving both state and non-state actors compels the UN to establish a dedicated cyber peacekeeping unit within its peace operations system.

Cyber Peacebuilding

While peacebuilding is interpreted differently across various departments[7] (Barnett, 2007, p. 37), it is generally defined as a set of measures aimed at reducing the risk of conflict recurrence or relapse. This involves mechanisms such as strengthening national institutions and enhancing their functionality to achieve sustainable peace and development (UN, 2022). It can also be considered as an activity in which external interventions are involved during the transition phase from conflict to peace of a country by implementing holistic programs and policies. Former UN Secretary-General Boutros Boutros-Ghali originally defined peacebuilding as the "action to identify and support structures which will tend to strengthen and solidify peace in order to avoid relapse into conflict". The goal of peacebuilding according to him is to develop a "structure for the institutionalization of peace". Meanwhile, Michael Barnett and colleagues (2007), by quoting Charles Call, explain that peacebuilding is more than the removal of armed conflict, but achieving stability by balance or threat of force (using peace operatives). Peacebuilding is normally based on post-conflict scenarios to rehabilitate and stabilise the affected states back to sustainable functioning. The core elements of peacebuilding comprise the proper exercise of the state institute (good governance), legitimacy, capacity building, and social/human security. Earl Conteh-Morgan placed significant emphasis on human security as a fundamental pillar of sustainable peace within the framework of peacebuilding. He argues that human security at personal, institutional, and structural levels would play an important role in peacebuilding. The individual source of human insecurity refers to banditry, looting, rioting, and crimes and institutional sources are based on oppression, corruption, torture, brutality (by state's force), and tyranny. The social structural sources of human insecurity are poverty, hunger, inequality, and unemployment. The elimination of such insecurities encourages the peacebuilding process in a post-conflict state's system (Conteh-Morgan, 2005).

Although the UN recognised the importance of ICT (cyberspace) in promoting peace, it also reminded member states that maintaining neutrality in international relations would serve to lower the danger of conflict and tensions related to geopolitical cyber issues. Cyber peacebuilding may be defined as the reduction of risk and dangers that might fuel a cyberwar or relapse into a digital conflict, and it aims to bring about long-term peace and growth in the domain. It can also be seen as a process that involves external interventions (or supports) during the transition period of a cyber conflict into a threat-free digital ecosystem by implementing policies and programs. These initiatives include the development of good cyber governance, cyber laws, digital cooperation, cyber economy, and digital rights. Without a formal declaration, states are experiencing cyberattacks and that is the reason why the UN advises maintaining neutrality in cyberspace to prevent such crimes. Practising neutrality in digital networks leads to stability and security that are the key elements of economic, social, and political prosperity. On this agenda, the Center for Security Studies, ETH Zurich, and the UN Institute for Disarmament Research conducted a session on *Neutrality and Peacebuilding in Cyberspace* on 3 November 2020 (UNIDIR, 2020). Digital peace has become an important agenda for the Geneva Peace Week (GPW) and the forum has introduced the "Digital Series" as one of its core focus areas (GPW, 2022). Amongst the themes discussed in the GPW 2022 held from 31 October to 4 November 2022, "Digital peace: The power and limits of innovation in peacebuilding" was one of the core agendas (GPW, 2022). While it is undeniable that establishing peace in a cyber environment is more difficult than in the physical world, member states' collaboration, transparency, and neutrality will go a long way towards reducing the likelihood of cyberwarfare and the recurrence of cyber conflict.

Level of Cyber Peace

Peace can be cultivated at multiple levels, ranging from an individual's inner soul to the broader concept of global peace. According to the Chinese philosopher Lao Tzu, founder of *Taoism* and author of the *Tao Te Ching* (fourth century BCE), although he did not explicitly refer to "peace", he conveyed a holistic vision of transforming the world into a harmonious and peaceful place, akin to "heaven". Chapter 54 of his volume discusses peace for oneself, followed by home, village (town), realm (cities/states), world, and the universe. The exact translated verse is as follows.

> Cultivate the way *yourself*, and your virtue will be genuine. Cultivate it in the *home*, and its virtue will overflow. Cultivate it in the *village*, and it will endure. Cultivate it in the *realm*, and the realm will flourish. Cultivate it in the *world*, and the virtue will be universal.
> (Tzu, 1983, 1955, p. 107; Tse, 2008, 1981, p. 98)

In the same context, peace theologians and scholars have interpreted it slightly differently: to achieve peace in the world, there must first be peace within nations. For a nation to sustain peace, its cities must be harmonious, for cities to maintain harmony, neighbourhoods must be free from threats, for neighbourhoods to remain calm, families must be peaceful, and for homes to be in harmony, individuals must cultivate inner peace[8] (Ludden, 2010, p. 175). According to the World Council of Curriculum and Instruction, (WCCI) peace has been classified into nine segments: intrapersonal (non-conflict in one's mind), interpersonal (conflict between two or more individuals), intragroup peace (peace within groups), intergroup peace (no conflict between two or more groups), intraracial peace (peace within a race), interracial peace (non-conflict between races), intranational peace (peace within nations), international peace (no war between nations), and world peace or universal peace (Concept of Peace, n.d., p. 28). Referring to Lao Tzu's philosophy and the WCCI's classification on peace, cyber peace may be analysed in six hierarchical levels: individual, local, subnational, national, regional, and global.

Individuals and the Local Level

"The root of all evil is man, and thus he himself is the root of the specific evil, war" (Waltz, 2001, 1954, 1959, p. 3). Individuals are the primary agents of threat in cyberspace, as every cyberattack or network disruption (excluding routine technical glitches) is ultimately driven by human intent and action. The first malware attack in the history of the internet was carried out by an individual,[9] not a group, institute, or company. Threats posed by individuals span from high-ranking officials who plan and direct operations (or illicit activities) to the operatives who execute these actions. In the same context, no machines, but humans alone, are the origin of peace in cyberspace. Therefore, both state and non-state actors should avoid engaging in interpersonal strategic or non-strategic (criminal) cyberattacks against one another. As Clausewitz states, "war is nothing but a duel on a larger scale" and a *cyber duel* between individuals can escalate into a full-scale cyberwar between nations. For example, conflict or animosity between two leaders, such as those of the US and Iran, would not only result in harming each other's computers but also draw their respective state militaries into confrontation. Individuals from diverse fields can play crucial roles in promoting cyber peace. Politicians can design cyber-peace policies, while military personnel can offer insights on cyber-peace strategies and doctrines. Diplomats can facilitate cyber-peace agreements, and legal experts can create laws that support cyber peace. Cyber scholars can contribute by researching and advocating for a threat-free cyberspace, while digital activists can lead campaigns to reduce cyber vulnerabilities. In addition to various other measures, the Ministry of Home Affairs in India launched the *Cyber Crime Volunteer Program* as a significant step toward promoting cyber peace. This initiative allows citizens to actively participate in identifying and reporting cybercrime, helping to create a safer digital environment and contributing to the larger goal of reducing cyber threats and vulnerabilities.

Cyber peace at the local level refers to the creation and maintenance of a safe and secure digital ecosystem by and for local communities. These communities can consist of individuals, local governments, clubs, neighbourhoods, institutions, companies, and more. By fostering a culture of cyber awareness and responsibility, these local entities can play a crucial role in promoting cyber peace. They can avoid becoming involved in cyberconflicts by adhering to best practices, educating others on cyber hygiene, and collectively working to minimise risks, thereby contributing to a more secure and harmonious digital environment. With the support of youth, schools, institutions, and governments, community cyber peacebuilding can be achieved through the implementation of initiatives, strategies, and techniques that promote peace and foster development in cyberspace (Alliance, n.d.). According to the UN Development Programme, local governance is the "subnational institutes, systems, and process, which provide services for citizens' interest, rights, settling differences, etc." (Tschudin, 2018). In India, at the local level, *Panchayats* (village council), municipal councils, and municipal committees along with non-government organisations are involved in providing education and awareness programs on computer skills under national schemes such as *Pradhan Mantri Kaushal Vikas Yojana* (Prime Minister's

Skill Development Scheme) and *Rashtriya Gram Swaraj Abhiyan* (National Village Swaraj Campaign). Although rural India does not have a specific cyber-peace program, it has the opportunity to engage with metropolitan areas and gain awareness about online activities. Meanwhile, "non-cyber" local bodies can play a significant role in controlling illegal or violent activities on social media. For example, in Manipur, a northeastern state of India, different ethnic communities, the Meitei, Naga, and Kuki, have been engaging in online trolling against each other. In addition to local law enforcement agencies monitoring and addressing the situation, civil society groups from these communities, such as *Meira Paibis* (a women's organisation of the Meitei community), *Kuki Inpi* (an umbrella organisation of the Kuki tribe), and the United Naga Council (a civil society representing the Naga tribe), can contribute to curbing hate campaigns on social media.

Subnational and National Level

Subnational institutions and groups play a crucial role in cyber peacebuilding. Cyber peace at the subnational level can be defined as a state of tranquility within a country's districts, divisions, or states, characterised by the absence of cyber conflicts. For instance, the Karnataka and Tamil Nadu in India have longstanding disputes over water sharing, as rivers originating in Karnataka flow through Tamil Nadu before reaching the Bay of Bengal (ET, 2018). In a scenario where Karnataka refuses to release water, Tamil Nadu could potentially resort to cyberattacks on Karnataka's Supervisory Control and Data Acquisition system controlling dam operations to force the discharge of water. The 2013 Bowman Dam cyberattack in New York, carried out by Iranian hackers, serves as a relevant example of a cyber assault on critical infrastructure. Although it was an international incident, it highlights the potential risks of cyberattacks on dams. Despite the infiltration, the attack did not cause significant damage to the dam (Berger, 2016).

In the intranational conflict between Assam and Mizoram over a border dispute in July 2021, five Assamese policemen were killed by their Mizoram counterparts (Karmakar, 2021). Such internal conflicts can escalate through the use of cyber platforms to spread hate news and misinformation. Additionally, rival groups may exploit cyber means to target network infrastructure. Therefore, rather than merely settling territorial disputes, the respective states should establish institutional mechanisms to prevent offensive activities in cyberspace and promote cyber peace. While not always explicitly a cyber-peace initiative, states undertake various initiatives to secure cyberspace and combat digital crimes, following directives from the government of India (GoI). Based on the GoI's directives, cybercrime cells have been established within state police forces to monitor and prevent cyber offences, fostering a more cyber-secure and peaceful environment. Additionally, states make independent efforts to control cybercrime within their jurisdictions. For example, Gujarat installed 75,000 closed-circuit televisions at key locations across 34 districts, establishing 34 command centres, all managed under a single centralised command system (Indian Express, 2020). Meanwhile, cooperation between states and resource sharing to promote cyber peace should not be overlooked. The establishment of IT parks in every state, guided by the central government, serves as a platform for collaboration and mutual support in advancing IT initiatives and cybersecurity efforts.

Cyber peace at the national level can be defined as the absence of cyber violence and the establishment of a secure, threat-free digital environment within a country. In both national and international cyber affairs, the nation serves as the primary actor in establishing and maintaining cyber peace. A nation is not only responsible for maintaining a peaceful cyber ecosystem within its borders but also for deciding whether to engage in or avoid hostilities with other countries in the cyber domain. At the domestic level, the government issues national guidelines for all its units to follow cybersecurity policies, ensuring the safety and stability of cyberspace. It also utilises law enforcement agencies to prevent and control cyber violence when necessary. India fosters cyber peace and ensures the security of its digital domain through a two-layered system. The first layer operates through federal government ministries, while the second functions via state government departments. The Indian government has dedicated institutions, including the Ministry of Electronics and Information Technology (MeitY), alongside other key ministries such as home affairs, science and technology, finance, and defence, to uphold peace and tranquility for digital networks in the country. Meanwhile, each state, through its IT department and law enforcement agencies, functions autonomously, by adhering to central government guidelines and support, to formulate and implement policies within its jurisdiction, manage cybercrimes, and promote cyber peace. While the union ministries made national laws and norms on cyberspace such as the *IT Act 2000* or *National Cyber Security Policy 2013*, state departments also contribute to maintaining the digital ecosystem by introducing state-level cybersecurity policies (BSCB, 2021). In addition to government functionaries, Indian private organisations such as the *Cyberpeace Foundation*, *eProtect Foundation*, and *Cyber Safe India* actively work to address cybersecurity challenges and combat cybercrime, contributing to a safer and more resilient cyber environment in the country.

Regional and Global Level

Cyber peace at the regional level refers to a state of digital harmony among a group of countries within the same region or continent, characterised by the absence of cyber conflicts and a shared commitment to common goals in cyberspace. According to Brandon Valeriano and Ryan Maness, 93 per cent of cyber rivalries within a region stem from territorial disputes, while 75 per cent of global cyber conflicts are driven by regional rivalries (Maness, 2015, p. 99). This highlights the strong connection between geopolitical tensions and cyber hostilities, emphasising how territorial and regional issues often spill over into the digital domain. Regional associations such as the European Union (EU) and Association for Southeast Asian Nations (ASEAN) can play an important role in cyber peacebuilding at their provincial level. While the EU does not have a specialised department focused on "cyber peace", it established the EU Agency for Cybersecurity (ENISA) in 2004 with a mandate to foster a secure and resilient cyber ecosystem across Europe. Working with the broader community, the agency focuses on strengthening trust in the digital economy and infrastructure among the member states (ENISA, 2022). To promote peace in cyberspace and de-escalate digital conflicts, the EU advocates for "cyber diplomacy", an approach that contrasts with cyber defence. While cyber defence focuses on protecting against digital threats, cyber diplomacy emphasises dialogue, cooperation, and trust-building among nations to prevent or resolve digital conflict. About 30 members of the EU are assigned as cyber foreign commissioners or ambassadors to support confidence-building measures in cyber affairs (Bendiek, 2018).

The ASEAN approach to cyber peace is inclusive and development-focused, differing from the more security-centric strategies of advanced European nations. The ten ASEAN member states prioritise expanding internet access and digital inclusion in rural and remote areas. In 2020, ASEAN launched the *Go Digital ASEAN* initiative, led by The Asia Foundation, aiming to empower two million individuals from rural and underserved communities by enhancing their participation in the digital economy, business, and enterprise development (The Asia Foundation, 2022). ASEAN established dialogue partnership with friendly nations including India to create mutual benefits on digital cooperation and development. To promote the aspect of cyber peace and prosperity in other areas, ASEAN, along with India, published the report, *Plan of Action to Implement the ASEAN-India Partnership for Peace, Progress, and Shared Prosperity (2021–2025)* in September 2020 (ASEAN, 2021). Subsequently, the report on *Cybersecurity Cooperation Strategy (2021–2025)* was released during the second ASEAN Digital Minister Meeting held on 27 and 28 January 2022. One of the objectives of the report is to establish a rule-based cyberspace with "open, secure, stable, accessible, interoperable and peaceful" mandates (ASEAN, 2022, p. 7). Meanwhile, the *Digital Master Plan 2025*, released in 2021, looks forward to making ASEAN a prosperous community in digital economies and services with a safe and secure cyber ecosystem (ASEAN, 2021). In West Asia, Bahrain hosted the *Arab International Cybersecurity Conference and Exhibition* from 6 to 8 December 2022, aiming to enhance international collaboration on cyber peace and security. This is the largest summit in the West Asia region for public-private sector professionals, focusing on cyber strategies and IT systems (Welcome Message, 2022).

Since states are the first unit of the international system, they play a crucial role in fostering peace and stability in global cyber affairs. Through the UN and other international forums, states have collectively undertaken initiatives to protect cyberspace. Russia was the first to submit a draft resolution titled, *Developments in the Field of Information and Telecommunications in the Context of International Security* (A/C.1/53/L.17/Rev.1) on 2 November 1998, recognising potential cyber threats and urging the international community to collaborate on securing cyberspace. Unfortunately, the draft does not explicitly address the use of ICT for "peaceful means" or the maintenance of peace in cyberspace. However, UN bodies such as the UNGGE and the OEWG, established after Russia's initiative, incorporated the concept of cyber peace by advocating for the application of international norms and promoting responsible state behaviour in cyberspace. The groups frequently reference the terms "peace" and "peaceful" across various sections of their reports. They emphasise the importance of preventing conflicts and interstate violence in cyberspace, while also promoting social and economic development through the implementation of established norms and frameworks (UNGGA, 2021; UNOEWG, 2021). Meanwhile, the International Telecommunication Union (ITU) published the book, *The Quest for Cyber Peace*,[10] on January 2011 marking a significant step toward fostering international collaboration in cyberspace. The publication addresses critical issues such as cyber threats and the establishment of peaceful frameworks in the digital domain (Toure, 2011). Hamadoun Touré, former ITU secretary-general and author of the book urged all states, in several international meetings held in 2009 and 2010, to commit to a no-first-strike policy in cyberspace. He also called on all member states to sign a cyber-peace treaty to promote stability and security in the digital domain (Gjelten, 2010). In other developments, the leaders of 56 Commonwealth countries signed the *Commonwealth Cyber Declaration-2018* "to support cyberspace that promote economic and social development, and rights online" (Commonwealth Cyber Declaration Programme, 2022).

Other international associations including the World Federation of Scientists (WFS) and Suzanne Mubarak Women's International Peace Movement (SMWIPM), actively participated in global cyber-peace initiatives. The WFS established its Permanent Monitoring Panel on Information Security in 2001 and submitted the report, *Toward a Universal Order of Cyberspace: Managing Threats from Cybercrime to Cyberwar*, to the first United Nations' World Summit on the Information Society held in Geneva in 2003. Thereafter, the *Erice Declaration on Principles of Cyber Stability and Cyber Peace* was drafted and circulated among the member states of the UN in 2009 for governments and scientists to cooperate and defend cyberspace (Shackelford, 2022, p. xxi). This draft is a crucial document for scientific communities, as they play a technical role in both developing advanced cyber technologies (weapons) and protective measures against them. The SMWIPM conducted a cyber-peace initiative in 2007 aimed at empowering youth with ICT resources and promoting the safety of digital environments across nations (Toure, 2011, p. 78). Other international forums such as the Paris Peace Forum led the *Paris Call for Trust and Security in Cyberspace* on 11 December 2018. In this initiative,

81 countries, along with private sector entities and civil society organisations, endorsed a non-binding declaration advocating for "an open, secure, stable, accessible, and peaceful cyberspace". While the US and EU joined the forum in 2021, countries such as China, India, and Russia are yet to participate (Call, 2018). Other non-governmental organisations such as Access Now, the Association for Progressive Communications, the Media Foundation for West Africa, the Women's International League for Peace and Freedom, the Centre for Internet and Global Politics (Cardiff University), the Centre for Internet and Society, the Cyberpeace Institute, the DiploFoundation, the Global Forum on Cyber Expertise, Global Partners Digital, the ICT4Peace Foundation, Internet Society, and Cybersecurity Tech Accord, directly or indirectly support the development of cyber peace by contributing their ideas and suggestions to the OEWG (2022). Initiated by the regional organisation, the European Council, the *Budapest Convention*, also known as the *Convention on Cybercrime* (2001) is open to global participation and aims to combat crime and violence involving computers. The draft *Convention on Cybercrime* (ETS 185) focuses on two key areas: the abolition of "racism and xenophobia" (an aspect of positive cyber peace) in cyberspace and promoting international cooperation to achieve this objective (CoE, 2022).

India's Approach to Cyber Peace

India is a land of Buddha and Gandhi, and has been revered as the sanctum of peace for centuries. However, considering the traditional security dynamics and dilemmas in the domestic (militancy/terrorism) and regional sphere (Pakistan/China factor), India follows both the cooperative and non-cooperative security policies. While the former is based on soft power (non-coercive), the latter comprises the elements of hard power (coercive force). With the advancement of new technologies, cyberspace has become a critical domain for managing security affairs across all levels, ranging from individual and community to substate, state, regional, and international spheres. To counter the rising digital threats and the involvement of state and non-state actors over the past two decades, India's traditional peace policy, such as *satyagraha* (or the possibility of practising *cyber satyagraha*), may be challenging to implement. As cyberspace grows increasingly vulnerable, the need to safeguard the domain has led to the introduction of various cyber agencies and policies in India. Consequently, in pursuit of peace at both domestic and international levels, India adopted a range of state and national policies. Against this backdrop, this section explores India's approach to cyber peace at both external and internal levels, analysing it through the lens of negative and positive peace, with support from government and private entities, as indicated in Table 5.2.

External Dimension of Cyber Peace

India's external approach to digital peace affairs can broadly be discussed through the dual perspectives of negative peace and positive peace. While

Table 5.2 India's Approach to Cyber Peace

Sl No	Dimension of cyber peace	Types of cyber peace	Peace activity	Peace actors
1	External cyber peace	Negative	Free from interstate cyber conflict, incursion, spying, network security, etc.	Government, NGOs, private firms, industries, etc.
		Positive	Threat-free cyberworld, Internet accessible by everyone, reduce gap between cyber haves and have-nots, respect digital sovereignty, interstate cyber cooperation	MEA, MeitY, civil societies, companies
2	Internal cyber peace	Negative	Free from domestic cybercrime including financial fraud, sextortion, child pornography, black marketing, intrastate digital conflict; cyber terrorism, etc.	Ministry of Home Affairs, state police departments, cyber volunteers, cyber peace NGOs (Infosis, Tata Consultancy Services, etc)
		Positive	Digital outreach to villages, internet available at affordable prices, data protection, respect of individual digital rights	MeitY and other national agencies, state IT departments, human rights activists, cyber volunteers

Source: Author

the concept of India's *negative external peace* focuses on its contribution to reducing cyber conflict and minimising digital threats within the international system, *positive external peace* aims to create a sustained, threat-free cyber world that eliminates digital injustice and bridges the digital divide. Notably, Indian NGOs have played a commendable role in advancing international cyber-peace initiatives, fostering international collaboration, establishing norms for responsible state behaviour, and promoting trust-building measures to create a stable and cooperative cyberspace.

Negative External Cyber Peace

India actively engages in cyber-peace initiatives led by international organisations and contributes to the development of a rules-based cyber framework in global affairs. It has entered into bilateral and multilateral agreements with other nations to prevent cyber violence. Subsequently, NGOs in India support maintaining a peaceful global cyberspace. Since the inception of the UNGGE, India has been actively advocating for the application of international law to cyberspace, including amendments to the UN Charter, to uphold peace and stability in the domain.[11] India offers suggestions to amend the OEWG *Zero Draft* by adding terms such as "peace and security" and "peace and stability" in several appropriate places (India's remarks on the OEWG *Zero Draft Report*, 2021). Meanwhile, Indian NGOs and institutes such as the Centre for Communication Governance (CCG) (National Law University, Delhi), Observer Research Foundation (ORF), America Chapter (Indian based think tank), and the Cyberpeace Foundation, among others, are involved in developing a sustainable cyber-peace system. While the CCG raises concerns about the militarisation of cyberspace, it also emphasises the need for states to enhance research and development in the field for peaceful purposes. The CCG submits its opinions to the OEWG report, highlighting the role of individuals in supporting states to promote "peace and stability" in cyberspace (CCG, 2021, p. 2). The ORF, as a civil society institute, provides its comments on the *Zero Draft* report to encourage trust among countries, develop sustainable peace and rule-based international order, and enhance capacity building over the domain of cyberspace (ORF, 2021). By conducting regular *global conferences on cyberspace* and providing cyber-peace advocacy, along with conducting research in digital peace affairs, the Cyberpeace Foundation plays an important role in global cyber-peace affairs with support from the Indian government and UN (Cyberpeace Foundation, 2021). Meanwhile, the role of the Ministry of Defence in conducting joint cyber exercises with friendly nations (HT, 2021), along with the Ministry of External Affairs and MeitY in engaging in bilateral (EU, US, UK, Russia, Japan) and multilateral (G20, BRICS, SCO, World Bank, WTO, ASEAN, etc.) dialogues on cyber-peace programs, remains crucial (MeitY, 2022).

Positive External Cyber Peace

India not only advocates for negative cyber peace by preventing cyber conflicts but also actively promotes positive cyber peace by fostering cooperation, stability, and development in the global cyber order. In addition to eliminating systemic digital violence, India has a constructive cyber-peace strategy that includes promoting a sustainable digital economy or improving socioeconomic situations in global society. It assists especially underdeveloped countries in capacity building, network development, improving digital infrastructure and networks, e-governance, research and education, guidance for policy and planning, providing training for stakeholders, and acquiring a sustainable peaceful cyber ecosystem. Stakeholders of positive cyber peace include both government and non-government or private organisations. India's MeitY has a dedicated division, the *International Cooperation Division* (ICD) to promote transnational cooperation and engage with bilateral, multilateral, and regional frameworks on ICT-related areas. It supports underprivileged global societies and tries to bridge the divide between digital haves and have nots (MetY, 2022). On 18 April 2017, when the Prime Minister of Bangladesh visited India, a Memorandum of Understanding (MoU) was signed between India and Bangladesh on areas including "e-governance, m-Governance, e-Public Services Delivery, cyber security, software technology parks, start-ups, etc." Subsequently, leaders of the ICT ministry of the two countries met on 26 April 2022 and discussed improvements of the above-mentioned areas. When the Indian Prime Minister visited Bhutan on 15 and 16 June 2014, India assured Bhutan it would assist in establishing e-library facilities for school and colleges, a central repository, and other e-library centres for the education ministry (ToI, 2014). On the non-governmental front, the Cyberpeace Foundation, a globally recognised Indian NGO, plays a vital role in promoting positive cyber peace by focusing on capacity building, educating individuals on online law, and advocating for sustainable digital practices. By providing counseling, technical support, and collaborating with law enforcement agencies, it also aids victims of unethical digital activities in their pursuit of justice (CPF, 2021). It contributes significantly to the maintenance of digital peace by delivering awareness campaigns to the public and crafting high-level policy recommendations for national and international stakeholders.

Internal Dimension of Cyber Peace

India's internal approach to cyber peace can be analysed through the lens of both positive and negative peace theories. *Negative internal cyber peace* pertains to the activities carried out by the government and non-government organisations to control or avoid violence, crime, and illegal activities among state actors (intrastate) or non-state actors, or between the two within a nation, by using hard power (defensive-offensive mechanisms, installation of malware, etc.). *Positive internal cyber peace* refers to the programs or initiatives designed to bridge digital gaps and the efforts made by various stakeholders to establish a sustainable and secure cyber ecosystem within a nation. Unlike negative cyber peace, which is a temporary solution, positive cyber peace is built on a long-term foundation.

Negative Internal Cyber Peace

At the domestic level, the Indian government, along with NGOs and private firms, has actively engaged in efforts to control violence in cyberspace. The Indian government neither has a dedicated Ministry or Department of cyber peace nor explicitly prioritises its promotion as a distinct policy focus.[12] However, for a safe and secure cyber ecosystem, it has multiple central ministries and respective state departments that are working directly or indirectly towards the objectives of cyber peace. While the MeitY plays an important role in providing national cyber policies and guidelines, state IT departments take the responsibility to issue rules and regulations for the "peaceful" usage of cyberspace at the state level. The *IT Act of 2000* (amended in 2008) and the *National Cyber Security Policy of 2013*, under the MeitY, serve as the fundamental pillars for maintaining a secure and peaceful cyber ecosystem in India.

Additionally, various state-level policies, such as the *Information Technology Policy for Manipur State-2022* (DIT, 2022), and similar frameworks of other states, ensure the safety and security of digital spaces. Meanwhile, the Ministry of Home Affairs, through its dedicated Cyber and Information Security Division, periodically issues guidelines for state security agencies to monitor and prevent violent activities in cyberspace. State police forces have reinforced this effort by establishing district-level cyber cells within their respective departments to investigate, apprehend, and prosecute cybercriminals. The contributions of NGOs and private companies, such as Infosys and Tata Consultancy Services, in developing software and hardware solutions (like anti-virus programs) are integral to safeguarding the cyber realm and fostering a culture of cyber peace.

Positive Internal Cyber Peace

Along with the agenda to protect cyberspace from digital violence and conflict, the Indian government took several initiatives to achieve sustainable cyber peace by promoting digital rights, and eliminating the digital divide between rural and urban areas. These efforts have also been supported by NGOs and private companies by providing better services (training, education, other facilities) to the public sphere. The Indian government has taken a holistic approach to e-service for its citizens. In other words, the country does not have any discrimination in providing online facilities to customers of different origin, be it urban or rural, caste or religion, poor or rich. Under the *Digital India* program (2015) and *State Wide Area Network* scheme, all states and Union Territories are connected to deliver services to the state governments, citizens, and business. To bridge the "digital divide", India connects rural areas by laying fibre-optic cables to 1.54 lakh *Gram Panchayats* (village council) covering 519,000 kilometres (MeitY, 2020). Meanwhile, 365,000 Common Services Centres were established providing more than 350 e-services to rural areas. providing jobs and employments to more than 12,000 people (MeitY, 2022). To combat cybercrime, particularly those targeting children and women, the *National Cybercrime Portal* was launched to facilitate complaint registration. Supported by law enforcement agencies, victims can report incidents either through the portal or by calling the dedicated helpline number (National Cyber Crime Reporting Portal, 2022). Since 2011, the Infosys Foundation, an initiative of Infosys Limited, has launched *eVidyaloka*, a program aimed at providing education to underprivileged children in remote rural areas of India. The initiative offers digital classroom facilities and is supported by expert educators from across the globe (eVidyaloka, 2018). Indian NGOs such as the *Cyber Crime Awareness Society* provide technical training and legal support to cybercrime victims. *Cyber Safe India* spreads awareness on emerging technological crimes and fraud by providing nationwide seminars, workshops, and training. The *Cyberveer Foundation* and *Akancha Against Harassment* work on areas pertaining to a cybercrime-free country and empowering a cybersafe environment, respectively. While these government and NGOs aim to protect people from cybercrime and violence by providing reliable digital services, their efforts directly or indirectly contribute to positive cyber peace.

Conclusion

The commitment of states to uphold peace in cyberspace is both genuine and increasingly apparent. However, the lack of comprehensive frameworks, coupled with the rapidly evolving nature of digital technology, has made this a challenging endeavour. The majority of nations and international communities prefer the term "cybersecurity" over "cyber peace", even though the two concepts are related but not entirely equal. Cyber peace cannot be replaced by cybersecurity, as merely securing online networks does not equate to achieving true peace in cyberspace. What truly matters, however, is how security and peace are defined and understood in the context of cyberspace. More than maintaining peace in the domain, international efforts are primarily directed toward establishing laws, regulations, and norms that define the conditions under which states can employ offensive cyber operations in alignment with legal war principles. The non-physical and lawless nature of digital space create ambiguities in practising the rational theories of peace and security in cyberspace. Security concepts such as (cyber) deterrence, balance of (cyber) power, (cyber) disarmament, (cyber) weapon control, and (digital) armistice that are successfully practised to avoid violence or achieve peace in the physical world face challenges in the virtual cyber platform. The increasing establishment of military cyber commands across nations, coupled with the rapid evolution of cyber technologies, further intensifies this challenge.

The UN peace initiatives on conflict prevention, peacebuilding, peacemaking, peace enforcement, and peacekeeping will remain difficult to implement unless cyber conflicts are universally recognised and governed by international laws. However, both formal and informal efforts can still be undertaken to promote cyber peace at various levels: individual, local, state, national, regional, and global. Among these actors, states, as the primary stakeholders, play a crucial role in preserving peace and security in cyberspace, supported by the active involvement of NGOs and other private entities. Disengagement and noninterference in cyber activities against each nation could preserve a peaceful cyber ecosystem at the international level. States are the sovereign actor for international cooperation and have the authority to disarm any stockpile of cyber-weaponry systems (malware, spyware, worms, etc.). Also, cooperation at the bi and multilateral level amongst countries with common agendas should be encouraged to promote both negative and positive cyber peace in the digital system. In the Indian context, there is no clear distinction between government agencies working for cyber peace and those operating for cyber "non-peace", as their roles often overlap in addressing both security and peace-building in cyberspace. While peace is an inherent aspect of cybersecurity efforts, government measures are primarily focused on the protection of digital threat or security (digital-war or crime -free state). NGOs operating in India function voluntarily, adopting a humanistic and social approach in the digital realm, focusing on issues such as justice, equality, and inclusivity in cyberspace. In fact, the government's approach primarily aligns with *negative cyber peace*, focusing on threat mitigation and enforcement, while non-governmental efforts lean towards *positive cyber peace*, emphasising inclusivity, justice, and long-term digital harmony.

Research/Book Findings

Since each chapter includes its own conclusion, a combined summary has been omitted to avoid redundancy. Instead, the research findings, which serve as the primary premise of this book, are highlighted here. This study demonstrates that the state, security, cyberwar, and cyber peace are deeply interconnected, collectively influencing and defining the dynamics of modern cyberspace. No state can function effectively without ensuring its security and this security remains incomplete without cyber safety. Cyberspace is truly safe only when it is free from cyberwar or digital threats. Moreover, cyber peace cannot be achieved in the presence of cyberwarfare, as the two are fundamentally incompatible. While the state defends its own cyberspace, it attacks others to achieve strategic goals. Based on their strategic interests, the selfish behaviour of states in cyberspace is unlikely to change. The expansion of cybersecurity policies and the introduction of cyber commands in state military systems indicates cyberspace is a component of strategic affairs. Similarly, in the virtual world, data, algorithms, digital networks, and cyber power (decision-making capability) serve as fundamental components, just as people, territory, government, and sovereignty define a state in the physical world. Cyber peace is a state construct and the role of humans behind the machine is essential in shaping and sustaining it. The misuse of cyber technologies by both state and non-state actors has contributed to cyber insecurities, posing significant risks and harm to society. Countries of all power levels, great, middle, and small, with technological capabilities can play influential and disruptive roles in cyber affairs. The absence of comprehensive international laws on cyber governance remains a primary driver of cyber warfare.

Cybersecurity is a non-static symbol and its agenda will continue to evolve in response to technological advancements. Most digital threats revolve around cybercrime, cyberterrorism, cyber espionage, and cyberwarfare, which necessitate a multi-tiered security approach, requiring active participation at all levels, from individuals and local institutions to subnational,

national, regional, and global frameworks. The growing number of cybersecurity policies and agencies within state security frameworks underscores cyberspace as an essential and integral element of national security. In addition, the militarisation and weaponisation of digital technologies have solidified cyberspace as a critical component of modern warfare. The debates on the theory and practice of cyberwarfare will continue until a universal norm on cyberspace is established. Cyberspace has been used as a force multiplier in physical kinetic conflicts, while in covert or undeclared conflicts, states have leveraged it to advance their strategic objectives.

Cyber peace is unlikely to be achieved without common international cyber laws. Given the self-interested behaviour of states and the anarchic nature of the digital domain, establishing digital peace remains a significant challenge. States should strategically plan for cyber peace even as they prepare for cyberwar, ensuring a balanced approach to both security and stability in the digital realm. Any cyberwar should be followed by efforts to establish digital peace to prevent the recurrence of conflict. States must prioritise not only cybersecurity but also promote cyber peace to ensure long-term stability in the digital domain. While most governments prioritise defending against cyberattacks and network incursions (negative cyber peace), the use of cyberspace for cooperation and development (positive cyber peace) is seldom considered. Yet, greater international collaboration is necessary to establish common regulations for a more significant objective to preserve peace in the domain.

India, as an emerging global power and the second-largest internet user in the world, is not only focused on enhancing its domestic digital landscape but also seeks to expand its influence and actively shape global cyber affairs. Like other competing countries, its approach to cyberspace is both civil and military centric concerning domestic and foreign affairs. On the security front of the domain, to protect its internal digital affairs, IT laws and cyber policies are implemented with timely amendment along with support from enforcement agencies (C&IS Division, India). Subsequently, to protect external cyber aggression, it established a cyber command (DCA) under the state military systems. Various other government institutes are also functioning at the national ministerial and state departmental levels, with the assistance of NGOs at different levels. Regarding cyberwarfare, it perceived threats from neighbouring nations such as Pakistan or China, which are still in a state of competition or war (proxy or asymmetric). However, attention is drawn towards China rather than Pakistan, as the former is technologically strong in the domain. On the aspect of cyber peace, India believes in national development by means of cyber technology (positive cyber peace) and protecting the domain by focusing on digital threats and security (negative cyber peace).

Way Forward

In this globalised society, the interconnection between the state, security, and cyberspace is inseparable and will continue to define the future. Their interaction will get more difficult as developing technologies (5G, internet of things, big data, AI, blockchain, quantum computing, etc.) advance. The emergence of new technologies and inefficiency in their regulations will pose a significant threat to national security. Due to lack of international laws and interstate cooperation, these vulnerabilities will keep increasing in the days to come. Unless cyberspace is fully safeguarded against conflicts and other threats, the international system cannot achieve complete security. Digital technology will continue to remain a strategic component of national and international security agendas. Every nation, great or small, will continue to take advantage of unregulated cyberspace and will put them in a digital security dilemma. This phenomenon will cause a competition or race for cyberpower as states strive to secure their strategic objectives. Meanwhile the changing nature of cyber technology makes every digital policy ineffective over a period. No cyber policy implemented today will be suitable enough to address the upcoming digital threats brought by emerging technologies.

The debate on the theory and concept of cybersecurity will continue to evolve as new technological advancement always introduces new risks. Cybersecurity, as a subset of non-traditional security studies, encompasses a "widening" and "deepening" agenda. It remains intrinsically connected to state politics, national economy, and military strategies. Any cyber risk will inevitably affect the state system, either directly or indirectly. Such insecurities in cyberspace will lead to additional digital laws, policies, structures, frameworks, and cooperation in the upcoming decades. The effectiveness of cybersecurity depends on the preventative policies implemented by the state. Cybersecurity policy will continue to operate on two levels: safeguarding network security in the virtual realm and addressing cyber-enabled violence in the physical world. This dual nature of cyberspace makes the concept of a future digital security system increasingly complex. Without a shared understanding of cyber operations, defining a violent attack as a "cyberwar" will remain a significant challenge.

Concerning states' strategic interest, cyberwarfare will persist, and its impact will extend far beyond the digital domain, with significant physical consequences. Just as land, sea, air, and space powers hold significant influence in the international system, cyber power will also play a pivotal role in shaping global power dynamics. Cyber technology will serve as a force multiplier, enhancing traditional military capabilities, or act as a complementary tool in conventional warfare. Consequently, the continued militarisation and weaponisation of digital technology, coupled with the absence of an international convention, will amplify the risks of digital wars. Although challenging to achieve, peace initiatives and cooperation in cyberspace are likely to emerge in interstate relations, driven by mutual interests and common benefits. Forging peace agreements in cyberspace will remain difficult without comprehensive international legislation. Nevertheless, individual nations will continue to uphold both negative and positive cyber peace. While states will primarily focus on preventing violent cyber conflicts (negative cyber peace), they will also seek cooperation, development, and digital inclusivity to bridge technological gaps and foster positive cyber peace.

Although India's public engagement in cyberspace began in the 1990s, the *IT Act 2000* marked the formal regulation of the domain, aimed at safeguarding against threats and the misuse of computer technology. However, as new technologies proliferate and the user population expands, India will experience more insecurities from both internal and external agencies. To address these emerging challenges, India must amend and update its existing IT laws and policies to align with the rapid evolution of cyberspace. It also requires active participation in the global cyber-power competition to establish itself a leading cyber power in the international system. India should continue its multi-pronged cybersecurity approach focusing on both the domestic and foreign dimensions with support from dedicated organisations including C&IS, DCA, and the New and Emerging Strategic Technologies division of the Ministry of External Affairs (amongst others). Every new sophisticated attack exposes weaknesses in the security system, therefore, the nation must stay several steps ahead of cyber adversaries to ensure resilience and preparedness. Instead of having several cybersecurity organisations, India might try out a single framework that deals with all cyber threats. While India's establishment of a cyber military command is commendable, the 2024 *Joint Doctrine for Cyberspace Operations* of the armed forces will further enhance the capabilities and structure of its digital warfare units. India should continue to advance cyber-peace initiatives by addressing cybersecurity and cyber violence (negative cyber peace), strengthening alliances with other nations, and promoting social growth, prosperity, and digital rights (positive cyber peace).

Notes

1 While writing the preface of the book, *Information and Communication Technology for Peace: The Role of ICT in Preventing, Responding to and Recovering from Conflict*, published by the United Nations Information and Communication Technologies Task Force in New York in 2005, Kofi Annan expressed that "the role of ICTs (cyberspace) in efforts to achieve the Millennium Development Goals is the contributions they make in our work to promote peace and help the victims of humanitarian emergencies".
2 Cyber peace is used interchangeably with digital peace.
3 Cyberspace is often described as an "imperfect commons" due to its shared ownership and the lack of clearly defined rules. Scott J. Shackelford refers to this concept as a "pseudo-commons", highlighting its hybrid nature and the complexities of its governance.
4 Pacifist groups such as the London Peace Society, earlier recognised as the Society for the Promotion of Permanent and Universal Peace, was established in 1816. Similarly, the American Peace Society was founded in 1828 (Kirchwey, 1917) followed by a series of foundations including the Universal Peace Union (1866), the France Peace Society (1889) and the German Peace Society (1892).
5 "*Naga Hoho* is a cultural and social body to bring under one umbrella Nagas of Assam, Manipur and Arunachal Pradesh" (Singh, 2022).

6 States and businesses frequently conceal the damage caused by cyberattacks in order to protect their reputation or out of fear of losing their customers.
7 The UK and US defence departments define peacebuilding in terms of stabilisation and its connection to security missions. Meanwhile, some other agencies in both countries view it more as post-conflict recovery and reconstruction rather than traditional peacebuilding. Canada's foreign affairs department considers post-conflict work as conflict prevention and its government describes it as action to support peace operations and economic development. Japan's foreign affairs ministry used it in the context of conflict prevention, and its defence agency as reconstruction assistance. France and Germany prefer to call it crisis management and conflict prevention (Barnett, 2007, p. 43).
8 This is exact text,

> If there is to be peace in the world, there must be peace in the nations. If there is to be peace in the nations, there must be peace in the cities. If there is to be peace in the cities, there must be peace between neighbours. If there is to be peace between neighbors, there must be peace in the home. If there is to be peace in the home, there must be peace in the heart.

9 Robert Tappan Morris is widely known as the first hacker or cyberattacker whose hack affected approximately 60,000 computers in colleges and public and private research institutes on 2 November 1988. He was convicted in 1989 under the USA *Computer Fraud and Abuse Act-1986* (FBI, 2018).
10 Hamadoun Toure was an electrical engineer from Mali and had trained in the Soviet Union. He was said to be backed by Russia in the ITU secretary general election for him to get the position. As a return gift, he supported Russia's 1998 approach to UN for the regulation of ICT for international safety and security, which was a sort of initiative for "cyber arms control or disarmament" in the international system (Gjelten, 2010).
11 However, this initiative primarily focuses on establishing regulations and laws for cyberwarfare, aligning with the framework of negative cyber peace, rather than promoting positive cyber peace.
12 Cyber peace is not popularly debated as "cybersecurity". Institutes functioning in India or globally are paying more attention to cybersecurity than cyber peace. Though both are related, peace can never be substituted by security, or in other words, being secure is not the same as being at peace.

References

About Cyber Peace Foundation. (2021). *Cyber peace foundation*. Retrieved from https://www.cyber peace.org

About eVidyaloka. (2018). *eVidyaloka*. Retrieved from https://www.evidyaloka.org/about/

Alliance, P. (n.d.). *Community peacebuilding: Overview*. The Peace Alliance. Retrieved from https://peacealliance.org/community-peacebuilding/#collapse_0_strategies

ASEAN. (2022, January). *ASEAN cybersecurity cooperation strategy*. Association of South East Asian Nations. Retrieved from https://asean.org/wp-content/uploads/2022/02/01-ASEAN-Cybersecurity-Cooperation-Paper-2021-2025_final-23-0122.pdf

ASEAN. (2021). *ASEAN digital masterplan 2025*. Association of South East Asian Nation. Retrieved from https://asean.org/wp-content/uploads/2021/08/ASEAN-Digital-Masterplan-2025.pdf

ASEAN. (2021, March 11). *Plan of action to implement the ASEAN-India partnership for peace, progress, and shared prosperity (2921–2025)*. ASEAN. Retrieved from https://asean.org/asean2020/wp-content/uploads/2021/03/11.-ASEAN-India-POA-2021-2025-Final.pdf

BBC. (2021, May 21). NSA spying row: Denmark accused of helping US spy on European officials. *BBC News*. Retrieved from https://www.bbc.com/news/world-europe-57302806

Bendiek, A. (2018, April 19). *The EU as a force for peace in international cyber diplomacy*. German Institute for International and Security Affairs. Retrieved from https://www.swp-berlin.org/publications/products/comments/2018C19_bdk.pdf

Berger, J. (2016, March 25). A dam, small and unsung, is caught up in an Iranian hacking case. *The New York Times*. Retrieved from https://www.nytimes.com/2016/03/26/nyregion/rye-brook-dam-caught-in-computer-hacking-case.html

BSCB. (2021). *Cyber security policy for the state co-operative bank Ltd*. The Manipur State Co-operative Bank Limited. Retrieved from http://mscbmanipur.in/wp-content/uploads/2021/10/CYBER-SECURITY-POLICY-FOR-MSCB-LTD.pdf

Buckham, J. W. (1916). The principles of pacifism (pp. 88–90). The Biblical World, 48(2), 88–90. -.

Call, P. (2018, December 11). *Home*. Paris Call for Trust and Security in Cyberspace. Retrieved from https://pariscall.international/en/

Carr, J. (2010). *Inside cyber warfare*. Sebastopol, CA: O'Reilly Media.

CCG. (2021). *Comments to the initial pre-draft of the report of the OEWG on developments in the field of information and telecommunications in the context of international security*. Office of Disarmament Affairs. Retrieved from https://front.un-arm.org/wp-content/uploads/2020/04/ccg-nlu-comments-to-the-pre-draft-of-oewg-on-ict.pdf

CoE. (2022). *First additional protocol to the convention on cybercrime, concerning the criminalisation of acts of a racist and xenophobic nature committed through computer systems* (ETS No. 189). Council of Europe Portal. Retrieved from https://www.coe.int/en/web/cybercrime/first-additional-protocol

Commonwealth Cyber Declaration Programme. (2022). *The commonwealth*. Retrieved from https://thecommonwealth.org/our-work/commonwealth-cyber-declaration-programme

Concept of Peace. (n.d.). *University of Peshawar, Pakistan*. Retrieved from http://www.uop.edu.pk/ocontents/concept%20of%20peace.pdf

CPF. (2021). *Our initiatives*. Cyber Peace Foundation. Retrieved from https://www.cyberpeace.org/our-initiatives/

CRS. (2015, October 7). *Chinese president Xi's September 2015 state visit*. Congressional Research Service. Retrieved from https://crsreports.congress.gov/product/pdf/IF/IF10291

DiPLO. (2018, October 12). Cybermediation: What role for blockchain and artificial intelligence? Diplo Foundation. https://www.diplomacy.edu/blog/cybermediation-what-role-blockchain-and-artificial-intelligence

DIT. (2022). Information technology policy for Manipur State – 2022. Government of Manipur. http://www.ditmanipur.gov.in/wp-content/uploads/2015/06/ditmanipur.gov.in_2022-05-17_09-14-28.pdf

Doyle, M. W. (2005). Three pillars of the liberal peace. American Political Science Review, 99(3), 463–466.

Doyle, M. W. (2006, 1795). Kant and liberal internationalism. In I. Kant (Ed.), Toward perpetual peace and other writings on politics, peace, and history (pp. 201–242). London: Yale University Press.

Draft Substantive Report [Zero Draft]. (2021). *Office for disarmament affairs*. Retrieved from https://front.un-arm.org/wp-content/uploads/2021/02/India-Latest-Edits-to-OEWG-Zero-draft.pdf

ENISA. (2022). About ENISA – The European union agency for cybersecurity. European Union Agency for Cybersecurity. Retrieved from https://www.enisa.europa.eu/about-enisa

ET. (2018, April 10). A brief history of the Cauvery dispute. *The Economic Times*. Retrieved from https://economictimes.indiatimes.com/news/politics-and-nation/a-brief-history-of-the-cauvery-dispute/tale-of-two-states /slideshow/63698683.cms

FBI. (2018, November 2). The Morris Worm: 30 years since first major attack on the internet. FBI. Retrieved from https://www.fbi.gov/news/stories/morris-worm-30-years-since-first-major-attack-on-internet-110218

Ford, C. A. (2010). The trouble with cyber arms control. The New Atlantis, 29, 52–67.

Galtung, J. (1969). Violence, peace and peace research. Journal of Peace Research, 6(3), 167–191.

Galtung, J. (1996). Peace by peaceful means: Peace and conflict, development, and civilization. London: Sage Publication.

Gandhi, M. (2001, 1961). Non-violent resistance (Satyagraha). New York, NY: Dover Publications.

Gandhi, M. K. (1933). Hind Swaraj or Indian home rule. Ahmedabad: Navajivan Publishing House.

Gjelten, T. (2010). Shadow wars: Debating cyber 'disarmament'. World Affairs Journal, 172(2), 33–42.

Goodrich, L. M. (1969). Peace enforcement in perspective. International Journal, 24(4), 657–672.

GPW. (2022). *Geneva peace week*. Digital Series. Retrieved from https://eu.eventscloud.com/website/3030/digital-series-gpw22/

GWU. (2022, November 9). Theories of peace. George Washington University Peace Studies Program. Retrieved from https://blogs.gwu.edu/ccas-panamericanos/about/

Herge, H. (2021). The limits of the liberal peace [PhD thesis]. Peace Research Institute Oslo. Retrieved from https://www.prio.org/publications/3179

HT. (2021, June 30). *Hindustan Times*. Retrieved from https://www.hindustantimes.com/india-news/india-military -personnel-to-train-in-us-on-cybersecurity -command-in-the-offing-101625025032655.html

India's remarks/comments on the OEWG Zero draft. (2021, February 18-22). Office for Disarmament Affairs. Retrieved from https://front.un-arm.org/wp-content/uploads/2021/02/India-comments-OEWG-Feb-2021.pdf

Kant, I. (1903, 1795). Perpetual peace: A philosophical essay (M. Campbell Smith, Trans.). London: George Allen & Unwin Ltd.

Kant, I. (1903, 1795). Preface. In R. Latta (Ed.), Perpetual peace: A philosophical essay (M. Campbell Smith, Trans.). London: George Allen & Unwin Ltd.

Karmakar, R. (2021, July 26). 5 Assam policemen killed in border clash with Mizoram. The Hindu. Retrieved from https://www.thehindu.com/news/national/other-states /assam-police-personnel-dead-many-injured-as-violence-at-border-with-mizoram-intensifies/article61436896.ece

King, M. L. (1963, April 16). Letter from Birmingham jail. The Martin Luther King, Jr. Research and Education Institute, Stanford University. Retrieved from https://kinginstitute.stanford.edu/sites/mlk/files/letterfrombirmingham_wwcw_0.pdf

Kirchwey, G. W., & Davis, A. (1917). The American Peace Society: Founded 1828. The Advocate of Peace (1894–1920), 79(7), 168–180.

Kleingeld, P. (2006, 1795). In I. Kant, Toward perpetual peace and other writings on politics, peace, and history (D. L. Colclasure, Trans.). London: Yale University Press.

Ludden, K. (2010). *Mystic apprenticeship volume 2: Intuitive skills.* Morrisville, NC: Lulu.

Maness, B. V. (2015). Cyber war versus cyber realities: Cyber conflict in the international system. New York: Oxford University Press.

Marlin-Bennett, R. (2022). Cyber peace: Is that a thing? In F. D. Kramer, S. J. Shackelford, & M. Ben-Israel (Eds.), Cyber peace: Charting a path toward a sustainable, stable, and secure cyberspace (pp. 3–21). Cambridge: Cambridge University Press.

MeitY. (2020). Digital India programme. National e-Governance Division. Retrieved from https://negd.gov.in/sites/default/files/Digital%20India%20PPT_2021.pdf

MeitY. (2022). Annual report 2021–22. New Delhi: Ministry of Electronics & Information Technology, Government of India.

MetY. (2022, November 23). ICD objectives & activities. Ministry of Electronics and Information Technology. Retrieved from https://www.meity.gov.in/content/icd-objectives

MeitY. (2022, November 23). International co-operation. Ministry of Electronics & Information Technology. Retrieved from https://www.meity.gov.in/international-co-operation

Michael, B., & Kim, H. (2007). Peacebuilding: What is in a name? Global Governance, 13(1), 35–58.

Michael, L. B., & Diamond, M. (n.d.). Digital peacekeeping. Institute on Computing and Society, United Nations University. Retrieved from https://i.unu.edu/media/cs.unu.edu/attachment/4030/Peacekeeping_web.pdf

Michael, R., Jones, K., & Janicke, H. (2018). An introduction to cyber peacekeeping. Journal of Network and Computer Applications, 114, 70–87.

Morgan, E. C. (2005). Perspective, peacebuilding and human security: A constructivist. International Journal of Peace Studies, 10(1), 69–86.

Nabeel, F. (2019). Establishment of UN cyber peacekeeping force: Prospects and challenges. NUST Journal of International Peace & Stability, 2(1), 17–31.

Naidu, M. (1966). A proposal for a general peace theory. Peace Research, 1(1), 1–22.

Narveson, J. (1965). Pacifism: A philosophical analysis. Ethics, 75(4), 259–271.

National Cyber Crime Reporting Portal. (2022). Filing a complaint on National Cyber Crime Reporting Portal. National Cyber Crime Reporting Portal. Retrieved from https://www.cybercrime.gov.in

ORF. (2021, March 3). Comments from the cyberspace cooperation initiative at the observer research foundation America on the Zero Draft Report of the UN Open-ended Working Group on developments in the field of information and telecommunications in the context of international security. Office for Disarmament Affairs. Retrieved from https://front.un-arm.org/wp-content/uploads/2021/03/ORF-America-Submission-for-OEWG-Zero-Draft-Report_3-March-2021.pdf

Osman, M. A. (2018). The United Nations and peace enforcement: Wars, terrorism and democracy. Excerpt from the United Nations and Peace Enforcement: Wars, Terrorism and Democracy Mohamed Awad Osman. London: Routledge. Retrieved from https://itunes.apple.com/WebObjects/MZStore.woa/wa/viewBook?id=0. London: Routledge.

Owen, J. M. (1994). How liberalism produces democratic peace. International Security, 19(2), 87–125.

Pittock, M. (1968). Gandhi's pacifism. The Cambridge Quarterly, 3(3), 287–94.

Risse-Kappen, T. (2002, 1997). Between a new world order and none: Explaining the reemergence of the United Nations in world politics. In K. Krause & M. C. Williams (Eds.), Critical security studies: Concepts and cases (pp. 255–298). London: UCL Press.

Roff, H. M. (2016, March). Cyber peace: Cybersecurity through the lens of positive peace. *New America*. Retrieved from https://static.newamerica.org/attachments/12554-cyber-peace/FOR%20PRINTING-Cyber_Peace_Roff.2fbbb0b16b69482e8b6312937607ad66.pdf.

Rosato, S. (2005). Explaining the democratic peace. The American Political Science Review, 99(3), 467–472.

Russell, B. (1943–1944). The future of pacifism. The American Scholar, 13(1), 7–13.

Scott, J. Shackelford, & Kramer, F. D. (2022). Introduction. In F. D. Kramer, S. J. Shackelford, & M. Ben-Israel (Eds.), Cyber peace: Charting a path toward a sustainable, stable, and secure cyberspace (pp. xix–xxxi). New York: Cambridge University Press.

Service, I. E. (2020, January 12). Gujarat Police initiative: Union Home Minister flags off projects for safety of citizens and cyber security. Indian Express. Retrieved from https://indianexpress.com/article/india/gujarat-police-initiative-amit-shah-flags-off-projects-for-safety-of-citizens-and-cyber-security-6212070/

Shackelford, S. J. (2013). Toward cyber peace: Managing cyberattacks through polycentric governance. American University Law Review, 62(5), 1273–1364.

Singh, B. (2022, June 16). Pan Naga Hoho does not undermine any democratic political institution, says NSCN-IM. Economic Times. Retrieved from https://economictimes.indiatimes.com/news/india/pan-naga-hoho-does-not-undermine-any-democratic-political-institution-says-nscn-im/articleshow/92259732.cms

Spiro, D. E. (1994). The insignificance of the liberal peace. International Security, 19(2), 50–86.

Steinberg, J., & Enright, C. (2022). Domestic digital repression and cyber peace. In S. J. Shackelford & F. D. Kramer (Eds.), Cyber peace: Charting a path toward a sustainable, stable, and secure cyberspace (pp. 22–38). Cambridge: Cambridge University Press.

Stevenson, R. C. (1934). The evolution of pacifism. International Journal of Ethics, 44(4), 437–451.

The Asia Foundation. (2022, June 26). *Go digital ASEAN: Regional impact summary*. Retrieved from https://asiafoundation.org/publication/go-digital-asean-regional-impact-summary/

ToI. (2014, June 16). India to set up digital library in Bhutan. Retrieved from Times of India: https://timesofindia.indiatimes.com/india/india-to-set-up-digital-library-in-bhutan/articleshow/36635448.cms

Toure, H. I. (2011). The quest for cyber peace. New York: International Telecommunication Union.

Tschudin, A. (2018). The role of local governance in sustaining peace. New York: International Peace Institute.

Tse, L. (2008, 1981). Tao Te Ching (or the Tao and its characteristics). Auckland: The Floating Press.

Tubbs, J. O. (1997). Beyond gunboat diplomacy. Maxwell Air Force Base, AL: Air University Press.

TV Nannaya News. (2019, January 18). AP wrestling championship 2019 [Video]. YouTube. Retrieved November 2022, from https://www.youtube.com/watch?v=0kVpw1tI5P8

Tzu, L. (1983, 1955). The way of life: A new translation of Tao Te Ching. Ontario, Canada: Penguin.

UN. (2004). Conflict prevention, resolution and reconstruction. United Nation Peace Maker. Retrieved from https://peacemaker.un.org/sites/peacemaker.un.org/files/ToolkitWomenandConflictPreventionandResolution_InternationalAlert2004.pdf

UN. (2008). United Nations peacekeeping operations: Principles and guidelines. United Nation Peace Keeping. Retrieved from https://peacekeeping.un.org/sites/default/files/capstone_eng_0.pdf

UN. (2021). Strategy for the digital transformation of UN peacekeeping. New York: United Nations Peacekeeping.

UN. (2022). Open-ended Working Group. United Nations. Retrieved from https://www.un.org/disarmament/open-ended-working-group/

UN. (2022). Partnership for technology in peacekeeping. Department of Operational Support. Retrieved from https://operationalsupport.un.org/en/partnership-technology-peacekeeping

UN. (2022). Principles of peacekeeping. United Nations Peacekeeping. Retrieved from https://peacekeeping.un.org/en/principles-of-peacekeeping

UN. (2022). Terminology, peacebuilding. United Nations Peacekeeping. Retrieved from https://peacekeeping.un.org/en/terminology

UN. (2022). United Nations peacekeeping. United Nations Peacekeeping. Retrieved from https://peacekeeping.un.org/en/terminology

UN. (2022). What is peacekeeping. United Nations Peacekeeping. Retrieved from https://peacekeeping.un.org/en/what-is-peacekeeping

UN-OEWG. (2021). Final substantive report: Open-ended working group on developments in the field of information and telecommunications in the context of international security. New York: United Nations.

UNGGA. (2021, July 14). Group of governmental experts on advancing responsible state behaviour in cyberspace in the context of international security. United Nations General Assembly. Retrieved from https://front.un-arm.org/wp-content/uploads/2021/08/A_76_135-2104030E-1.pdf

UNIDIR. (2020, November 03). Neutrality and peacebuilding in cyberspace. UN Institute for Disarmament Research. Retrieved from https://unidir.org/events/neutrality-and-peacebuilding-cyberspace

UNOEWG. (2021, March 10). Open-ended working group on developments in the field of information and telecommunications in the context of international security. United Nations General Assembly. Retrieved from https://front.un-arm.org/wp-content/uploads/2021/03/Final-report-A-AC.290-2021-CRP.2.pdf

Waltz, K. N. (2001, 1954, 1959). Man, the state and war: A theoretical analysis. New York: Colombia University Press.

Weber, D. P. (2022). Peace and conflict studies (5th ed.). London: Sage Publishers.

Weber, T. (2001). Gandhian philosophy, conflict resolution theory and practical approaches to negotiation. Journal of Peace Research, 38(4), 493–513.

Wegener, H. (2011). A concept of cyber peace. In H. I. Touré (Ed.), The quest for cyber peace (pp. 77–85). Geneva: International Telecommunication Union.

Welcome Message. (2022, December 6-8). The arab international cybersecurity conference & exhibition. Retrieved from https://www.arab-cybersecurity.com/welcome/welcome-message

Werner, S., & Yuen, A. (2005). Making and keeping peace. International Organization, 59(2), 261–292.

Index

2G 136
3G 23
4G 23
5G 3, 25, 94, 152, 198

abacus 18
Abdul Kalam 54
absolute pacifism 175
academic 10, 11, 50, 55, 64, 69, 83, 92, 98, 182
academic activities 182
Ad Hoc Committee 12, 46, 66
Advanced Persistent Threats 114
aerial battle(s) 130
aerial bombings 130
Afghanistan 27, 28, 52, 88, 139
Africa 30, 38, 46, 76, 190
African Union 67
AI 2, 3, 19, 20, 27, 36, 38, 46, 68, 81, 91, 96, 97, 132, 137, 149, 198
air 2, 3, 6, 9, 21, 39, 43, 45, 70, 110, 113, 126–128, 130–132, 135, 137–138, 144–146, 156, 198
air strike 156
airpower 129–132
airspace 23, 130
Alfred Thayer Mahan 113
algorithm(s) 18–20, 24, 25, 46, 171, 196
AliExpress 86, 152
Amadey Spyware 116
ambiguous 51
analysis 6, 21, 59, 67, 68, 75, 113, 120, 132, 156, 165, 178, 182
Anantnag District 88
anarchic system 4, 12, 110
ancient 17, 52, 113–114, 165
Annan, Kofi 54
anti-racism 168
antivirus 19, 25, 80, 82, 142, 145, 146

Apple 31
Arab Spring 5, 9, 42, 122–123
Arab World 76
Argentina 34
Aristotle 17, 20
arm of future 148
arm race 136, 140–142
armed attack 63, 137
armed conflict 63, 110, 183
Armed Forces Special Power's Act-1958 52
Armenia 38
armistice 55, 195
armoured vehicles 2
arms 60, 89, 113, 115, 117, 135, 140–142, 148–149, 176, 177
arms control 55, 139, 167, 188
arms race 10, 110, 115, 140–142
Arnold Wolfers 53, 57, 142
Art of War 114–115, 117–118, 157
Arthashastra 117
Article 51, 138
artificial neural networks 27
Arunachal Pradesh 86, 199
ASEAN 58, 67, 69, 188, 192
ASEAN Digital Minister Meeting 188
Asia 1, 30, 34, 41, 59, 70, 76, 162, 188
Assam 186, 199
atom/atomic bomb 54, 129, 148, 149
atomic explosive weapons 148
attribution 123
audio(s) 20, 21
Auftragstaktik 120
Augustine 6
Australia 30, 34–35, 37, 39, 73–74, 77, 166
aviation 129

Bajpai, Kanti 60
balance of power 55, 135, 176

ballistic missile 40, 136
bandwidth 23
Bangalore 87
Bangladesh 77, 84, 87, 123, 193
Bangladesh Grey Hat Hackers 123
banking 8, 40, 62, 140; systems 8
Barlow 6, 13, 18, 21, 23, 25
barriers 22
Barry Buzan 10, 59–60
Basic Act of Cybersecurity 74
Basic Doctrine of the Indian Air Force
  8, 43, 63, 91, 153–154
battleground 37, 111, 127, 137, 151
BD 3, 19
Bhabha Atomic Research Center 86, 152
Bhutan 193
Bible 175
big data 3, 91, 97, 155, 198
Big Five 177
bilateral agreements 73, 177
binary 21; digits 26
biological 9; weapons 144, 148
Bipin Rawat 155
bipolar/bipolarity 10, 139
Bitcoin 88
blackout in Mumbai 128
blockchain 81, 91, 93, 136, 198, 200; system 136
body-force 176
Boeing 149
bombing civilians 130
Booth, Ken 5, 53, 54, 57, 60, 139
border 11, 23, 86, 152, 186
boundary 22–23, 27
Boutros Boutros-Ghali 183
Bowman Dam cyberattack 186
Branch 255 2
Brazil 34, 46
Britain 144
British 25, 56, 125, 130
Brodie, Bernard 142
Brussels Summit 70
BSNL 81
Budapest Convention 35–37, 74, 77, 190
Buddha 190
Bull, Hedley 5
bulletproof 2
Bureau of Police Research and Development 92
bureaucrat 7, 8
Burhan Wani 87

Buzan, B. 2, 5, 7, 10, 16, 53, 56–60, 67, 98, 136, 142

C++ 25
Cabinet Committee on Security 92
calculator 18
California 31
camouflage war 125
Camp David Accords 179
Canada 1, 28–30, 34–36, 46, 47, 72, 75
Canada Armed Forces 35
Canada Security Intelligence Service 35
Canadian Centre for Cyber Security 75
capacities building 92
Carr, E. H. 53
catastrophic 148
Cavelty 11
CBI 44, 86, 152
CCDCOE 70
CCTNS 98
Central Bureau of Investigation 44, 86, 152
Central Monitoring System 92
Central University of Gujarat 81
Chandra, Naresh 155
chapter 7, 11, 16, 28, 34, 36, 50, 60, 62, 64, 72, 75, 88, 91, 113, 117, 119, 129, 133, 146, 165, 168, 196
Che Guevara 113, 122, 124
chemical 9
  weapons 147
Chennai 87
Chief Information Security Officer 78
Chief of Defence Staff 64, 153, 155
child pornography 82, 89
China 1, 7–11, 20, 22, 28–33, 35, 37, 39–42, 44–46, 48, 58, 66, 70–74, 83, 86, 87, 129, 139–140, 144–145, 150–151, 158, 166, 169, 174, 190, 197
China's White Paper 32
Chinese Red Hacker Alliance 123
Chinese telecom 86, 152
chips 18, 21
CIIs 75, 84, 86, 92, 95, 124, 155–156
Cisco Systems 149
CISO 78–81, 93
civil armed volunteers 121
civil war 2, 121
civilians 62
Clausewitz 9, 62, 113, 115, 120–121, 123, 128, 137, 157, 185
cloud computing 3, 19, 81, 91

Index   209

coercion 6, 17, 25, 27, 176
Cold War 1, 9, 10, 16, 51–59, 61, 97, 115, 121, 136, 139, 142–143, 177
Colin Gray 113, 127, 131–132, 137, 141
combat 20, 35, 81, 114, 117, 121, 124, 130, 132, 136, 141, 149, 151, 186, 187, 190, 194
combat zones 117
combatant 123
command 2, 8, 10, 31–33, 35–36, 43, 45, 83, 91, 98, 113, 118, 124, 130, 146, 150, 151, 155, 157, 170, 175, 179, 187, 196, 199
command, control, communication 36
Common Service Centres 43
communication 1, 2, 7–8, 10–12, 18, 21, 23–26, 34, 36, 44, 50, 52, 61, 63, 65, 66, 78–80, 88, 91, 93, 94, 96, 97, 122, 126, 130, 131, 136, 137, 146, 151
   networks 136
   systems 2, 136
   technology 12, 42, 67
Communist Party of China 73
computer 2, 3, 6, 9, 17, 19, 25, 26, 33, 35, 36, 39, 63–66, 74, 79–82, 86, 91, 93, 96, 116, 123, 133, 135, 137, 147, 152, 171, 172, 185, 199, 200
   program 25
   technology 199
Computer Misuse Act 74, 1990 35
Computers Law 39
confidence-building measures 179
conflict 2, 3, 5, 9, 10, 22–24, 27, 33, 37, 41, 52–54, 58–60, 63, 65, 83, 110, 114–115, 117, 120–123, 126–127, 135, 137, 139–140, 145, 148, 151–154, 156, 166, 168–171, 173–186, 188–189, 191–192, 194–195, 197–198
conquest 112, 169
constructivism 5
control systems 151
Convention on Cybercrime 77, 190
Conventional Cyberwar 112
conventional wars 156
Converted cyber-spies 116
Cooperative Cyber Defence Centre of Excellence 70, 110, 115
Copenhagen School 5, 7, 50, 56
counter insurgency 121
Counter Terrorism Centre 64

COVID 12, 180
crime 40, 56, 60, 63, 66, 73, 78, 83, 84, 87, 89, 91, 97, 137, 185, 189, 193, 194
Criminal Code 35
critical element 110
Critical Information Infrastructure 45, 73, 92, 106, 124
critical infrastructure 86
critical security study 54
Critical theorists 5
critical theory 5
cryptocurrency 77, 88
Cuban Missile Crisis 55
Cyber and Information Security 112
cyber arm race 140–142
Cyber Armed Division 155, 156
cyber armies 117
cyber armistice 12
cyber arms 4, 7, 109, 135, 141, 148–149, 177
cyber attacks 69
cyber blue helmets 181
cyber command(s) 8, 110, 118, 140, 146, 150, 168, 170, 195, 196
cyber conflict prevention 177
Cyber conflicts 177
Cyber Crime Awareness Society 194
Cyber Crime Volunteer Program 185
Cyber Defence Command 38
Cyber Defence Group 37, 75
Cyber Defence Unit 37, 75
Cyber Defense Command 115
Cyber defensive doctrine 145
cyber deterrence 11, 143, 145
Cyber deterrent doctrines 145
cyber diplomacy 28, 31, 33, 34, 36, 37, 42, 95, 98, 188
Cyber Diplomacy Division 45
cyber duel 185
cyber economy 41, 183
cyber ecosystem 2, 3, 12, 24, 29, 36–37, 41, 44, 50, 67, 71, 73–74, 76, 79, 83, 87, 92, 110, 136, 151, 156, 172, 176, 181, 186–187, 192–193, 195
cyber espionage 4, 9, 62, 66, 115, 118, 166, 196
Cyber Eurasia 128
cyber force 45, 131–132, 156, 180
cyber guerrilla 122, 123; warfare 123
cyber intelligence 115
cyber kill chain system 158
cyber law(s) 1, 19, 20, 149, 183

cyber nationalism 140
Cyber offensive doctrines 145
cyber operations 3, 76, 110, 138, 195
Cyber pacifism 174
cyber peacebuilding 177, 183, 186, 188
cyber peace-enforcement 177
cyber peacekeeping 177, 181, 182
Cyber Peacekeeping Unit 182
cyber peacemaking 177, 179
Cyber Police 38
Cyber policies 30
cyber politics 1
cyber power 1, 16, 30, 42, 45, 46, 64, 73, 76, 127, 132, 154, 155, 167, 198
Cyber Power Index 30
Cyber Safe India 187
Cyber Satyagraha 176, 190
Cyber Security Association of China 73
Cyber Strategic Division 155, 156
cyber technolog(ies) 135, 165, 197
cyber terrorism 4, 9, 65, 71, 191
cyber terrorist 65, 168
cyber theft 166
cyber theorist 21
cyber threat(s) 11, 36, 37, 39, 43, 45, 56, 66, 70, 72, 74, 75, 82, 83, 91, 95, 148, 155, 181, 185, 189, 199
cyber tools 18
cyber violence 171, 172, 176, 178, 187, 191
cyber volunteer 82
cyber warfare 9, 40, 63, 111, 123, 126, 137, 140, 144, 145, 151, 153, 155, 164, 166
cyber weapons 9, 37, 40, 132, 143, 144, 146–150, 156, 167
Cyber Westphalia 11
cyberattack(s) 9, 40, 62, 63, 72, 84, 87, 112, 115, 117, 121, 138, 147, 165, 167, 178, 183, 185
CYBERCOM 31
Cybercrime Cell(s) 79, 92
cybercrime(s) 3, 4, 7, 9, 12, 15, 35, 44, 46, 50, 62, 65, 66, 68, 71, 74, 75, 78, 79, 82–84, 89, 90, 92, 96, 98, 106, 111, 139, 185, 194, 195
cybercriminal 4, 98
cyberpeace 12, 63, 190
CyberPeace Foundation 12, 187, 192, 193
CyberPeace Institute 190
cyberpower 1, 10, 91, 127, 133, 135, 198

cybersecurity 1, 4, 8, 11, 13, 16, 23, 32, 35–37, 39, 43, 45–46, 50–51, 62–63, 66–84, 89–98, 136, 140, 142, 145, 151, 153, 158, 167, 170, 172, 174, 177, 187, 195–199
Cybersecurity Index 39
Cybersecurity Law 32
Cybersecurity Strategy Headquarters 74
cyber-soul-force 177
cyberspace 1–12, 16–28, 30–47, 50, 52, 58, 61–62, 64–65, 69–78, 82–84, 86–89, 91–98, 110–114, 117, 120–123, 125–129, 131–134, 138, 139, 143, 145–147, 149–151, 153–156, 169, 171–172, 174–179, 181–182, 185–199
Cyberspace Administration of China 32
Cyberspace Security Strategy 32
cyberterrorism 3, 62, 137, 196
cyberwar 3–4, 8–11, 37, 39, 62–63, 67, 70–71, 90–91, 98, 110–113, 116–125, 128, 131, 135, 137–140, 145–146, 149, 151–153, 155–156, 165–167, 174, 179, 181, 183, 185, 196–198
cyberwar doctrine 112, 119, 144
cyberwarfare 4, 9, 11–12, 38, 50, 62–63, 91, 110–111, 117–119, 122–123, 129, 135, 137–138, 146, 153, 156, 166, 170–171, 174, 179, 181, 184, 196–198

dam (s) 128, 148, 186
darknet 87–89
data 3, 6, 12, 17–21, 23, 28–29, 31, 33, 35, 38, 44, 46–47, 55, 64, 66, 68, 73, 79, 81, 86, 91–97, 116, 125, 128, 132–133, 136, 140, 149–150, 171, 178, 191, 196
data governance 93
data protection 93
data science 96
data.gov.in 96
DCA 8, 43
DDoS 76
de Wilde, Jaap 7
death 65
decentralised 121, 123
decisive battle 123
Declared Cyberwar 112
deepeners 59
defence 2, 8, 11, 24, 30, 37–38, 45, 47, 56, 58, 70, 74, 77, 83, 90–91, 117,

Index   211

120, 124–125, 136, 137, 141, 143, 146, 154, 158, 165, 179, 182, 187
Defence Cyber Agency 8, 43, 63, 83, 91, 112
Defence Information Assurance Agency 154
defensive 7, 45
definition 66
demilitarization 168, 179
democratic peace 173
denial-of-service 9
Department of Cyber peace 193
Department of Defence 31, 72
Department of Homeland Security 72
Department of Justice 64
Department of Science and Technology 96
Department of Telecommunication 93
Departments of Homeland Security 30
destroy 9, 63, 122–123, 132, 137, 144, 152, 156, 169
détente 55
deterrence 11–12, 39, 45–46, 55, 58, 64, 113, 133–136, 142–145, 157, 167, 176, 195
Deterrence by Denial 143
Deterrence by Punishment 143
deterrence theory 142
digital conflict 110, 156, 180, 182
digital cooperation 183, 188
digital diplomacy 1, 31, 92, 117
digital economy 2, 31, 42, 188, 192
Digital Economy Report 28
digital engineering 81
digital gap 176
digital harmony 164
Digital India 43, 194
digital infrastructure 50
digital media 96
digital network 18, 36, 67, 71, 74–76, 86, 196
digital operation 117, 118
digital pacifism 176
digital payment 95
digital peace 11, 168, 177, 181, 192, 197
digital policy 198
digital power 1, 29
digital rights 173, 183, 191, 194, 199
digital rules 140
digital security 50, 75, 83, 90, 93, 98, 156, 198
digital security dilemma 198

Digital Series 183
digital space 9, 131
digital tactics 137
digital war 117–119, 138, 140
digital warfare 11, 13, 63, 129, 176, 178
digital weapons 141
digital world 137
dilemma 6, 110, 113, 115, 136, 139, 140, 157, 167
diplomacy 24, 45, 56, 95, 188
Directorate for Signals Intelligence 37
Directorate of Information 79
disarm 120, 144, 145, 195
disarmament 11, 136, 139, 176, 183, 195
discrimination 6, 53, 61, 194
disk 19
disruption 8, 9, 62, 123–124, 130, 132, 138, 145–147, 152, 157, 165, 171, 185
Dissuasion by Norms 143
disturb 42
doctrine 2, 35, 37, 43, 45–46, 58, 62, 63, 91, 112–113, 119, 125, 136, 144–146, 153–155, 157, 175, 176, 185
domain 3–12, 16, 18–19, 21–22, 27, 30, 33–37, 39–41, 43, 46, 50, 56, 61–62, 67, 70, 73, 76, 81–82, 90–91, 96–97, 110, 111, 113–114, 120, 124, 126–128, 130–132, 137–138, 140, 143, 146–147, 149, 151, 154–156, 165, 169, 171, 176–178, 183, 187–189, 192
Domain Name System (DNS) 23
Doomed cyber-spies 116
Douhet, Giulio 113, 130
Doyle, Michael 173
DPRK 28, 41, 77
drones 27, 65, 149
drug trafficking 59, 65, 66, 87, 88

E-commerce 42
economic 1–2, 5, 9–10, 16, 20, 27, 30, 34, 41–42, 54–57, 59–61, 64, 66, 70, 76–77, 79, 84, 87, 95, 97, 110, 117, 125–126, 129, 139–140, 151, 168, 173, 178, 183, 189
economic growth 2, 41, 54, 76, 95, 97
ecosystem 8, 10, 25, 46, 61, 67, 79, 80, 84, 90, 92, 142, 181, 185, 186, 192, 193

212 Index

education 24, 60–61, 133, 165, 185, 192, 193
e-governance 78, 192
electricity 2
Electronic Communications Act 2000 74
Electronic Media Monitoring Centre 96
electronic network 21
electronic system 1, 137
electronic technology 2
Emancipation 61
emerging technologies 3, 97, 98, 165, 198
energy 8, 10, 31, 57, 60, 62, 96, 131
enforcement 25, 27, 44, 66–67, 71, 79, 83–84, 88–92, 119, 168, 177, 180–181, 186–187, 193–194, 197
entanglement 143
environment 7
eProtect Foundation 187
espionage 4, 19, 40, 62, 76, 77, 115, 118, 137, 152, 165
Estonia 9, 46, 115, 128, 148, 158
Ethiopia 52
ethnicity 121
Eurasia 127
Europe 1, 30, 34, 69, 76, 128, 188
European Union 67, 69, 188, 190, 192
European Union Agency for Cybersecurity (ENISA) 188
evolution 17
evolution of technology 147
explosives 130

Fabrizio Colonna 118
Facebook 23, 32, 42, 88, 96
facsimile 94
fake news 96, 134
fear 5, 52–53, 114–115, 130, 141–143, 150
Fearon, James 5
feminism 5
feminist 5
fifth domain 43, 110
financial attacks 140
Financial Intelligence Network 95
Financial Intelligence Unit 95
financial networks 121
financial sectors 62
firepower 2, 136
firewall(s) 6, 19, 25, 80, 125–126, 142, 145, 176
first industrial revolution 2

first layer 3, 187
floppy 19
footprint 110, 119
foreign policy 22, 42, 54, 56, 128
France 33–35, 37, 46, 73–74, 87, 119, 144, 166
Frankfurt School 5
Franklin, Benjamin 140
future military 154

G7 69
Galtung, Johan 11, 167, 168, 170
Gandhi 11, 168, 174–176, 190
Garner, J. W. 24
GCHQ 34, 35, 74
Geeta 175
General Anil Chauhan 64, 153
General Bipin Rawat 155
General Kofi Annan 54
Geneva Peace Week 183
geography 20, 128
geopolitical 1, 39, 41, 45, 84, 121, 128–129, 151, 153, 155, 166, 174, 183, 187
geopolitical structure 1
Georgia 9, 63, 115, 128, 148
German/Germany 17, 34, 39, 46, 77, 87, 150, 177, 199
G-Force Pakistan 86
Gibson, William 22
global cybersecurity 95, 98
Global Cybersecurity Index 29, 34, 40, 69
global politics 50, 190
global security 51, 56
Go Digital ASEAN 188
Golden Crescent 88
Golden Shield Project 32
Golden Triangle 88
Google 31, 87
governance 4–5, 16–19, 25–26, 28–31, 33, 38–40, 42–43, 45, 68, 73, 78–80, 83, 93, 95, 97, 117, 120, 131, 133, 165, 183, 185, 192, 196
government 7–8, 12, 16–17, 19–20, 24, 26, 30, 33, 35–36, 38–40, 42, 47, 50, 53, 55, 58, 62, 64, 66, 68, 70, 74–77, 83, 89, 92–94, 106, 110, 114, 116, 121, 124, 125, 129–130, 133, 146, 152, 166, 170–171, 174–175, 179, 185, 186, 189–193, 195–196
Government Communications Headquarters (GCHQ) 74

Index

Great Firewall of China 32
great power 1, 10, 28, 37, 52, 111, 114, 143
Group of Government Experts 12, 16, 110, 177
Guerrilla Cyberwar 112
guerrilla war 124
guerrilla warfare 124, 158
Gujarat 68, 78, 80–81, 92, 186
Gujarat Police 79
Gulf region 24
gun running 65

Habermas, Jurgen 5
hacker(s) 25, 77, 86, 87, 111, 123–124, 128, 152, 170, 186
hactivism 63
Hamas 2, 115, 119, 121, 138, 140
harassment 171, 195
hardware 3, 54, 136, 149
hate mail 87
Headley, David Coleman 87
health 24
heartland 127, 128
Hezbollah 2, 116, 118, 119
Hiroshima and Nagasaki 148
hit-and-run 123
Hizbul Mujahideen 88, 140
Hobbs 53
Homeland Security 30
hostilities 137
HTS 52
Huawei 86, 94, 152
human rights 61
human security 53, 56, 57, 60, 183
humanitarian laws 136
hunger 183
hybrid war 121
hypersonic missiles 2

I3.0, 2, 3
ICANN 23, 31
ICT 16
identity 121
ideologies 7
illicit trade 121
Imphal 65
Independence of Cyberspace 6, 21, 47
India 1, 6–8, 10, 12, 16, 20, 22–24, 30, 32–37, 41–47, 50, 52, 54, 58, 61, 65–69, 71–73, 75, 78, 80, 83–84, 86–97, 111–112, 119, 129, 136, 139, 140, 146, 150–153, 157–159, 166, 171, 175, 185–188, 190–193, 195–197, 199–200
Indian Armed Forces 45
Indian Army Doctrine 8, 43, 63, 91, 152, 153, 159
Indian Cyber Crime Coordination Centre 83
Indian Cyber Force 123
Indian Maritime Doctrine 154
Indian Maritime Security Strategy 154
Indian Mujahideen 87
industrial revolution 2, 6
Industry 2, 4.0 (I4.0) 1
inequalities 183
infiltration 186
information 2–3, 8–12, 20–21, 33–34, 36–37, 39–40, 42, 63–65, 67, 69, 71–72, 74, 76–79, 81–82, 84, 88, 92–93, 95–97, 116, 121–124, 128–129, 132–134, 136–137, 140, 143–144, 147–148, 150, 152, 154–156, 171
Information and Communications Technology 37
Information Technology 37, 78, 93, 97
Information Technology Act-2000 16
Information Warfare 63
Infosys 194
injury 65
Instagram 42
insurgency 151
Integrated Defence Staff 154
integrity 42
intellectual property 66
intelligence 2, 19, 30, 35, 36, 38–40, 73, 75, 77, 91, 93, 96–97, 116, 118, 124, 132, 134, 136, 137, 156
intelligence gathering 2, 91
intermediaries 83, 97
international 1–3, 5, 9–13, 16, 19–20, 22, 28, 30–35, 37–41, 45–46, 50–53, 55–58, 60–61, 63, 66–68, 70–71, 73–74, 79, 84, 95, 97–98, 110–111, 114, 116, 118, 120–121, 125, 134–138, 140–142, 146–149, 155, 164–168, 172–178, 180–183, 185–190, 192, 194–197, 200
international collaboration 197
international cyber laws 147, 149, 197
international forum(s) 32, 62, 188
international law 32, 63, 110, 137, 192
international organizations 14
International Relations 5, 13, 183

international security 11, 12, 50, 55, 61, 69, 74, 198
international system 1–2, 5, 10–11, 16, 19, 23, 45–46, 50–52, 55, 57–58, 60, 63, 67, 71, 97, 110, 115, 117, 119, 135–136, 139, 141, 143, 150, 157, 165, 168–169, 173–177, 182, 188, 191, 198
International Telecommunication Union 2, 28, 67, 189
internet 2–3, 10–11, 13, 19–20, 22–23, 28–36, 38–40, 42–44, 61–62, 64–66, 73, 76–78, 80–81, 88–89, 93–94, 96–97, 129, 134, 151, 167, 174, 185, 188, 190–191, 197
Internet connectivity 42
Internet of Things(IoT) 3, 19, 27, 36, 65, 75, 94, 96, 97
Internet Protocol 23
Internet user 31
Interstate Cyberwar 112
Intranet 81
Intrastate Cyberwar 112
Inward cyber spies 116
IP address 126
Iran 1, 4, 7, 9, 28–29, 34, 37–38, 63, 72, 76, 84, 87–88, 114–115, 120–121, 126, 143–144, 149–150, 178, 185
Iranian Cyber Army 76, 123
Iranian Government 76
Iraq 9, 27, 32, 87, 139
irregular migration 59
irregular warfare 122
ISIS 88
Islamic 7, 38, 69, 87, 140, 151
Israel 1–2, 28–29, 37, 39, 63, 72, 76–77, 115–116, 118–119, 121, 144, 179
Israel Defence Forces (IDF) 39
ISRO 137
IT Act 26
IT (Amendment) Act 2008 42, 65, 66, 93
IT industry 42
IT laws 98, 197, 199
IT Rule 2000 42
IT sector 42
its anarchic system 147
ITU 2, 28–30, 34, 39–40, 47, 67–68, 166–167, 189

Jammu Airport 65
Jammu and Kashmir 23, 84, 151

Japan 1, 28–29, 33–37, 46, 52, 72–74, 77, 166, 192
Japanese Government 37
Java 25
Joint Doctrine for Cyberspace Operations 8, 43, 45, 91, 112, 120, 146, 153, 199
Joint Doctrine: Indian Armed Forces 8
Joint Secretary 80
Joint Training Doctrine Indian Armed Forces 45
Jomini 53, 113, 119, 120
Jus ad bellum 111, 138, 155
jus in bello 111, 138

Kaldor 10
Kant, Immanuel 11, 168
Kargil conflict 152
Kaspersky Lab 149
Kathmandu 71
Kautilya 53, 113, 117
Kenneth Waltz 6, 53, 55, 150
Keohane, Robert 5, 55
Kerala 67, 78
Kerala Police 78
Kim Jong un 40
kinetic attack 138
kinetic force 63, 135, 137, 138
Kochi 78
Kosovo 32
Kuki 65, 186
Kuki militants 65
Kwangmyon 77
Kwangmyong 40

Lab 110 40
laissez faire 175
land 2–3, 6, 9, 21–23, 43, 70, 82, 110, 113, 121, 126–129, 132–133, 135, 137, 144, 146–147, 153, 155, 190, 198
land power 127, 132
Land Warfare Doctrine 8, 43, 63, 91, 153–155
Lao Tzu 184
Laos 88
law and order 91, 181
law enforcement agencies 44, 66, 71, 79, 83, 88, 119, 186–187, 193, 194
lawless 24, 76, 150, 166, 195
lawless society 24
lawlessness 4, 147, 181
laws 74

Index

Lazarus Group 172
Left Wing Extremism 84, 151
legal jurisdictions 137
legitimacy 6, 16, 181, 183
Letter from Birmingham Jail 171
liberal democracies 174
liberal democratic peace 173
liberal peace 173, 174
liberal states 173
liberalism 5
Libicki 62
Liddell Hart 113
Limited Cyberwar 112
LinkedIn 24, 42
lobbyists 7, 8
Local Area Network 81
Local cyber-spies 116
Locke, John 5
Lockheed Martin 146, 149
logic bombs 147
logical layer 3, 19–20, 23, 25, 27, 116
London Peace Society 199

Machiavelli 53, 113, 118
machines 21
Mackinder, Halford 113
Maharashtra 86
Mahatma Gandhi 168
Mahbub ul Haq 56, 57, 60
major powers 1
malware 2, 40, 65, 76, 87, 116, 119, 122, 125–126, 128, 134, 142–143, 146–147, 149, 152, 166, 172, 185, 195
Manipur 65, 67, 186, 194, 199
Mao Zedong 113, 122
Martin Luther King 171
Mary Kaldor 111, 113, 121
Mass Media 33
massive attack 123
mathematical theory 25
McAfee 145, 149
McNamara, Robert 54
Mearsheimer, John 5, 10, 53
mechanised army 125
Meitei 65, 186
MeitY 44–46, 68, 80, 82, 84, 89–90, 93, 95, 97, 187, 191–192
mercenaries 111
mercenary groups 121
Mexico 34
Microsoft 31
Microsoft Word 25

Middle East 30
middle powers 1, 28, 34, 72
militancy 84, 87, 88, 151, 190
militarisation 131, 146, 157, 166, 180, 192, 197
militarisation of cyberspace 147
militarisation of space 131
military 1–2, 6–8, 10, 16, 20, 22, 27, 30, 32–46, 52, 54–59, 61–64, 69–70, 72, 75, 79–80, 83–84, 86, 91–92, 98, 110–114, 117–121, 124–127, 129–133, 135–147, 149–157, 165, 167–170, 176, 180, 185, 195–199
military affair 91
military command 8, 63
military digital commands 170
military network 131
military operations 132, 136, 144, 146, 149
military policy 119
military tactics 137
military threats 56
military weapon 151
militias 122
Minister 35
Ministry of Communication 44, 84, 93
Ministry of Defence 8, 33, 35, 45, 56, 74, 75, 91, 112
Ministry of Electronics and Information Technology 93
Ministry of External Affairs 45, 56, 80, 95
Ministry of Finance 45, 84, 94
Ministry of Home Affairs 44, 65, 91, 112, 185
Ministry of Information and Broadcasting 84
Ministry of Law and Justice 84
Ministry of Science and Technology 45
missile attack 132
Mitchell 127
Mizoram 52, 186
modern warfare 121, 129, 155
Modi, Narendra 155
Mohammed Ayoob 56, 57, 59, 60
monetary 111
money fraud(s) 94
money laundering 88
Monitoring Unit 91
Moonlight Maze 7, 171
Moore's law 18
Morgenthau 53
Morris Worm 114

Moscow 33
MS&T 45
multilateral agreements 31, 32, 173, 174, 191
multilateral collaborations 117
multilateral cooperation(s) 12
multilateral relations 74, 76
multipolar 1, 3, 110, 140
multipolarity 10
Mumbai power grid 152
Myanmar 28, 88

Naga 179, 186
Napoleon 119
Narcotics Control Bureau (NCB) 88
National Critical Information Infrastructure Protection Centre 45
National Cyber Bureau 39, 76
National Cyber Crime Reporting Portal 66
National Cyber Crime Unit 74
National Cyber Force 34
National Cyber Power Index 30
National Cyber Security Policy-2013 8, 16, 26, 41–42, 67
National Cybersecurity Coordinator 45, 92, 94
national laws 90, 187
national politics 120
national security 6, 8, 50, 53–56, 76, 92, 136, 151, 165, 197, 198
National Security Agency (NSA) 31, 72, 76
National Security Council (NSC) 45
National Security Council Secretariat (NSCS) 84, 92, 94
National Technical Research Organisation 45
National Telecom Policy 94
nation-state 9
NATO 13, 28, 36, 62, 68–70, 110, 115, 118, 129
naval 39
NCIIPC 45, 92
NCRB report 89
negative peace 167, 170, 171, 190, 193
negotiations 121, 177, 179, 180
Neo liberals 5
Netherlands 150
network attacks 37, 117
network security 73, 198
network system 19, 23, 25, 112, 123, 126, 131, 158

New Delhi 153
New Emerging and Strategic Technologies 45
New Media Wing 96
new war/s 121, 122
New York 12, 66, 77, 78, 186, 199
New York Police Department 78
New Zealand 30
Nigeria 52
Nirmala Sitharaman 88
Non Alignment Movement 58
non-military 57
non-offensive 182
nonphysical 22
non-state actors 5, 9–10, 36, 50, 83–84, 87, 89, 95, 98, 111, 119, 121–123, 125–126, 134–136, 139, 140, 146, 147, 152, 171–172, 178, 182, 185, 190, 193, 196
non-strategic 44, 45, 111, 185
non-traditional 3, 50, 53, 56–59, 97, 198
nonviolence 168
norms 5
North East India 86
North Korea 1, 4, 7, 9, 28–29, 37, 40, 72, 77, 84, 87, 114, 120, 121, 129, 139, 143, 150, 178
NSA 31, 45, 92, 174
NTRO 151, 155
nuclear 1, 7, 10, 40, 55–57, 59, 63, 115, 118, 120, 125–126, 136, 138, 142–144, 146–148, 150, 156, 179
nuclear attack 10
nuclear capabilities 1, 156
nuclear weapons 55, 125, 146, 150, 157
Nye, Joseph 5, 55, 60, 127, 132–133, 142–143
NYPD 78

obscene 67, 83
OEWG 179, 180, 189, 190, 192
offensive 7, 31, 33–40, 43, 45, 58, 63, 64, 72, 76–77, 82, 89–91, 110, 117, 119–120, 130, 132, 134, 139, 141–142, 144–147, 150–151, 153–156, 166, 170, 181–182, 186, 193, 195
offensive capabilities 31, 35, 36, 91, 154
Office 98 40
Office of Drugs and Crime 66
old war 121
On Guerrilla Warfare 122

On War 9, 113, 117, 119, 120, 157
Onuf, Nicholas 5
Open Ended Working Group 12, 43, 110, 138, 177
Operation Desert Storm 132
operatives 120
Oreshnik 2
organisations 62
origin of cyberspace 18

pacific relations 173
pacifism 174–176
pager attack 118
paid militia 118
Pakistan 7–8, 10, 22, 41, 45–46, 58, 70–71, 83, 84, 86–88, 111, 116, 119, 123, 129, 140, 150–152, 190, 197
Pakistan Cyber Army 86, 119
Panchayats 43, 185, 194
password 142
peace 5, 11–12, 27, 70–71, 73, 91–92, 123, 125, 126, 129–130, 132, 135, 138, 149, 153, 155, 156, 165–200
peace enforcement 180, 181
Peace operatives 183
peacebuilding 11, 168, 177, 181–183, 195, 200
peacekeepers/peacekeeping 168, 177, 180–182, 195
peacemaker/peacemaking 168, 177, 179, 180
Pegasus 116, 171, 172
Peloponnesian War 115, 139
People Liberation Army 73
People's War 123
perpetual peace 168
Personal violence 170, 171
Petya 84, 87, 126, 128
physical layer 20, 116, 147
physical space 10
physical violence 171
physical world 1
pictures 21
pivot areas 128
Plato 17, 20
poison gas 130
policies 55
policy papers 182
policymakers 59, 83, 133
political leaders 7, 8, 178
population 2, 10, 16–25, 28–30, 32, 34–36, 38, 42–44, 46, 50, 52–53, 94, 123–124, 129–130, 165, 199

pornography 87, 89, 135, 191
Posen, B.R. 144
positive peace 167, 169, 171–173, 178, 190
poverty 56, 60–61, 63, 97, 178, 183
power 1, 4–7, 9–10, 16–21, 23–38, 40–41, 43, 45–46, 53, 56, 58, 61, 63, 76, 83, 86, 90–91, 111, 113, 115, 117, 119, 124, 126–136, 138–141, 145, 147, 150, 152, 159, 169, 176, 184, 190, 193, 195–198
power grid 86, 128, 138
power plant 128
power politics 10
PRISM 31
privacy 67
private industries 5
programming 19
propaganda 9, 121, 149
prosecution 67
protests 23, 121
proxy 197
Psychological violence 171
PUBG Mobile 86, 152
public sphere 5, 74, 77, 194
punishment 25
Punishment for Cyber Terrorism 65
Punjab police 89

quantum communication 136
quantum computing 3, 36, 91, 96, 97, 156
quantum technologies 2
Quran 175

radicalisation 172, 175
radiological materials 148
RAND 55
ransomware 65, 126, 142, 147
rationalism 5
Rationalists 5
realism 5
Rebel Radio 124
reconnaissance 36, 123, 124, 126, 130, 132
reconnaissance aircraft 130
Reconnaissance General Bureau (RGB) 40, 77
referent object 7
Regional Anti-Terrorist Structure (RATS) 71
relative pacifism 175
research and development 31

research papers 96
Reserve Bank Information Technology Pvt. Ltd. (ReBIT) 95, 98
Reserve Bank of India (RBI) 94, 95
revolution in military affairs 136
revolutionary groups 62
RGB *see* Reconnaissance General Bureau
Rimland 127, 128
Royal Air Force (RAF) 129
rural 22
Russell, Bertrand 175
Russia 1–2, 7–8, 10–11, 28–33, 38, 40, 46, 67, 71–72, 87, 115–116, 118–119, 139, 149, 150, 178–179, 189–190, 192
Rwanda 58

SAARC 28, 46, 58, 67–71
SAARC Submit 71
sacrifice 53
safety 51
satellite communications 137
Satyagraha 174, 175, 190
SCADA 128, 134, 137, 172
science fiction 22
scientists 96
SCO 68, 69, 71, 73, 192
sea 2–3, 6, 9, 21–22, 43, 70, 110, 113, 126–129, 132–133, 135, 137–138, 144, 146–147, 156, 198
sea power 127–129, 132
second layer 3
security 1–5, 7–8, 11–12, 16, 23, 25, 27–28, 32–34, 36–37, 40–42, 46, 50–56, 58–67, 69–76, 79–84, 86, 89–97, 110, 112, 115, 131–133, 136–137, 139–140, 142, 145, 150–152, 154–157, 167, 169, 177, 180–183, 187–200
Security Council 31, 33, 54, 58, 64, 73, 74, 84, 92, 94, 155, 180–182
security debate 8
security dilemma 115, 136
security studies 55
Self Defence Forces 75
seminars 96
sensitive data 110
sextortion 66, 191
sexual exploitation 67
Shivshankar Menon 155
Sikkim 86
Silicon Valley 77
Singapore 37

small powers 16, 30, 72, 84
smaller nation 1
smuggling 59
snooping 19
social layer 19, 22, 24–27
social media 9, 42, 44, 78, 83, 86–88, 91–92, 97–98, 116, 122, 131, 135, 140, 172, 186
soft power 133–135
software 1, 3, 18, 25–26, 41, 77, 80, 83, 88, 116–117, 136, 142, 146–147, 149, 171–172, 193–194
Somalia 28, 58
Sony attack 140, 150
Sony Pictures Entertainment 77
soul-force 176
South Africa 33
South Korea 37, 46, 73, 96, 150
Southeast Asia 30
sovereign power 32
sovereignty 6–7, 11, 16–19, 21, 23, 27–29, 37–39, 42–43, 46, 50, 65, 73, 83, 95, 110, 138, 140, 174, 191, 196
space 3, 6, 10, 12, 21–23, 28, 43, 46, 51, 73, 76, 78, 88, 90, 92, 96, 110, 113, 126–128, 131–133, 135, 137–138, 146–147, 150, 152–153, 155–156, 175, 195, 198
space power 127, 131, 132
spacecraft 25
speeds 24
Spinoza 6
spying 86, 114–115, 174, 191
Spykman 22, 127–129
spyware 142
stalking 66, 171, 172
states 1, 3–7, 9–10, 12, 16–20, 22–24, 27–29, 32–34, 37–43, 45–47, 52–53, 56–59, 61–63, 65–73, 78–79, 82–84, 87, 89, 91, 95, 97, 110–111, 114, 117, 119, 122, 126–130, 135, 137–140, 144–146, 148–150, 157, 165–167, 169–170, 172–174, 176–179, 181–186, 188–189, 192, 194–198
states-of-concerns 28
steam engine 127
strategic affairs 50
strategic interest/s 30, 37, 198
strategic objective/s 9, 87, 118, 123, 129, 139, 146, 153, 171, 197
strategic operations 46, 151, 156, 170
Strategic Support Force 73
strategic technologies 95

strategic thinkers 113
strategic weapon 126
strategy 2, 5, 8–11, 31–34, 36–37, 39, 43, 45–46, 50, 55–56, 62, 67–68, 70–76, 83, 92, 95, 98, 114, 117, 119–120, 122–127, 130–132, 134, 136–137, 142–146, 151, 153–154, 159, 170, 177–178, 185, 188, 192, 196
Strong, C.F. 24
structural violence 170–173
Stuxnet 9, 38
submarine 30, 132
Subrahmanyam K 54
Subsystems 58
Sun Tzu 53, 113–115, 117, 137
surprise attacks 119
surveillance 19, 31–33, 36, 86, 92, 97, 116, 118, 132, 134, 140
survival 51
surviving spies 115, 116
sustainable peace 183, 192
Switzerland 119
Syrian 2, 52, 123
Syrian Electronic Army 2, 123

tactic/s 114, 119–120, 124–125, 144
Tallin Manual 2.0 3, 19, 70, 110, 138, 147
tanks 121
Taoism 184
Tata Consultancy Services (TCS) 81, 194
technological advancements 196
technology 1–2, 8, 16, 19, 22, 24, 25, 27, 32–34, 37–38, 40, 44, 46, 68, 75, 77–81, 84, 88–89, 91, 93, 95–97, 119, 132, 135–136, 139–140, 142, 144–145, 148, 151, 156, 159, 167, 170, 182, 187, 189–190, 193–196, 198–199
Telecom Regulatory Authority of India 44
telegram 18, 26, 42, 88
telegraphs 91, 136
telegraphy 94
telephone 18, 22, 26, 91, 94
territory 6, 16–20, 22–23, 27–28, 43, 45–46, 50, 52–53, 56–57, 59, 125, 129, 131, 135, 196
terrorism 4, 56, 63–66, 77, 84, 151, 153, 190
terrorists 5, 35, 62, 64, 111, 121, 126
Thailand 33, 38, 73, 88

The Art of War 114
The Command of the Air 130
The Peloponnesian War 115
The Prince 118
third industrial revolution 2
third layer 3
Thomas Schelling 141
Threats 52, 61–62, 83, 84, 87, 115, 116, 143, 185, 189
Thucydides 53, 113, 115, 139
TikTok 86
Tolstoy 175
Total Cyberwar 112
total war 128
traditional 6, 7, 10, 19, 50–51, 53–54, 56, 58–59, 65, 97, 110–111, 113–115, 120–121, 124–125, 127–128, 131, 156, 174, 190, 198
traffic system 128
TRAI 44
tranquility 166
transistor 18, 19, 21
transparency 149, 184
Transparent Tribe 86, 123
Transport 31
Trenchard 127
tribal 30
Tripura 52
trojans 142
truncated violence 170
trusted sources 94
truth-force 176
typewriters 24

Uganda 38
UK *see* United Kingdom
Ukraine 2, 7, 33, 84, 87, 115–116, 118, 126, 178–179
Ullman, Richard 53
UN Charter 138, 180, 182, 192
UN Group of Government Experts (UNGGE) 12, 16, 27, 32–33, 35–37, 43, 45, 69, 73–74, 95, 110, 138, 172, 179, 189, 192
UN Office on Drugs and Crime (UNODC) 66, 68
UN Open Ended Working Group (UNOEWG) 12, 46, 117, 189
unemployment 183
unilateral power 139
Union Bank of India 87
unipolarity 10
Unit 91 40; 180 40; 8200 118; 29155 118

United Kingdom (UK) 1, 28–29, 34–36, 46, 52, 72–74, 87, 112, 149, 180–181, 192
United Nations 1, 11, 28, 63, 67–69, 177, 189
United Nations Conference on Trade and Commerce (UNCTAD) 28
United Nations Office for Disarmament Affairs 69
unrest 23
urban 22
US 1, 7–10, 19, 23, 27–33, 35–36, 38–39, 42, 46, 52, 55, 61, 63–64, 66, 68, 72–77, 87, 97, 112, 114–116, 118, 120–121, 129–132, 135, 139–140, 143–144, 149–150, 159, 166, 169, 172, 178–181, 185, 190, 192, 200
US Department of Defense 30
U.S. Mariner-1 25
US Space Force 132
USSR 52, 55
Utopian idea 169

video 3, 20–21, 44, 96
Vietnam 37, 46, 55, 144
Vietnam War 55
virtual wars 121
virtual world 1, 19–20, 23, 25, 116, 122, 138, 196
virus/es 6, 9, 86, 122, 142, 148, 168, 172, 194

Waever, Ole 53, 56, 59
Walt, Stephen 54, 57, 58
Walter Lippmann 53, 57, 60, 61
WannaCry 77, 139
war 2, 5, 9–12, 17, 19, 24, 41, 45, 52–56, 58, 62–63, 82, 91–92, 110–115, 117–121, 123–127, 129–132, 135–141, 144, 151–153, 155–156, 165–167, 169, 173–176, 179–180, 184, 195–197
war and peace 91, 126, 129, 156
war crimes 169
war fighting 121, 180
warfare 2–3, 6, 9–10, 12, 21, 39, 41, 43, 55, 63–64, 66, 71, 73, 86–88, 110–115, 117–132, 135, 137–139, 144–146, 149, 151, 153–156, 167, 169, 176, 178, 196, 198–199

warlords 121
Weapon of Mass Destruction 125, 147, 149
weapon of mass destruction WMD 147, 148
weaponisation 122, 132, 146–147, 157, 180, 198
weaponised software 149
weaponry 2, 6, 10, 89, 135, 139, 141, 142, 146, 149, 156, 170, 195
weapons 117
WeChat 86, 152
Weibo 86, 152
Wendt, Alexander 51
Wendth, Alexander 5
West Asia 39, 188
Western societies 7
Westphalian system 52
Whatsapp 24, 32, 42, 89, 96
white paper 37, 86
wideners 59, 60
Wi-Fi 81
WikiLeaks 174
wireless 91, 94
wires 21
Working Group on Internet Governance 11
Working Group on Internet Governance (WGIG) 11
World Federation of Scientists 167
world order 4, 6, 10–11, 16, 34, 45, 50, 72, 83, 110, 129, 136, 140, 146, 180
World Summit on the Information Society (WSIS) 11, 40, 69, 189
World War I 144
World Wide Web (WWW) 61
worms 195
WSIS *see* World Summit on the Information Society

YouTube 24, 32, 42, 88
Yugoslavia 58

Zero Draft 192
Zero Draft Report 192
zero-day 114
ZTE 86, 94, 152

Printed in the United States
by Baker & Taylor Publisher Services